Universality, Selectivity, and Effectiveness in Social Policy

Studies in Social Policy and Welfare
Edited by R. A. Pinker

In the same series

Universality, Selectivity, and Effectiveness in Social Policy

Bleddyn Davies
in association with
Michael Reddin

HEINEMANN
LONDON

Heinemann Educational Books Ltd
LONDON EDINBURGH MELBOURNE AUCKLAND TORONTO
HONG KONG SINGAPORE KUALA LUMPUR NEW DELHI
NAIROBI JOHANNESBURG LUSAKA IBADAN
KINGSTON

ISBN 0 435 82266 7

Published by Heinemann Educational Books Ltd,
48 Charles Street, London W1X 8AH

Filmset in Great Britain by
Northumberland Press Ltd, Gateshead, Tyne and Wear
and printed and bound in Great Britain by
Richard Clay (The Chaucer Press) Ltd, Bungay, Suffolk

Contents

Preface

The origins of this book lie in the distant world of the late 1960s. The Department of Education and Science commissioned Mike Reddin and myself to undertake research into the reasons for the non-uptake of school meals. These were duly completed and a straightforward descriptive report based on the results of the surveys was submitted to the Department.

In the years that followed, other obligations made it necessary to concentrate my research efforts elsewhere—in particular, the second and third books of the territorial justice trilogy[1] were being written, and I was about to be seconded for two years to direct the project that led to *University Costs and Outputs*,[2] and I was heavily involved in the prototype analyses and papers on which was based the writing of *Gambling Work and Leisure*.[3] Two years later, although my period of secondment had come to an end, the work on higher education costs continued, and *Policy and Politics* had become a major consumer of my time. However, in 1972/3, I was able to write the papers on which Chapters 4–8 and the more elaborate parts of Chapter 2 are based. The work was almost completed by the end of 1973/4. However, it had again to be put away when I set up the Personal Social Services Research Unit. It was not until 1975 that I was able to up-date the argument and weld the various drafts into a book.

Mike Reddin shared in the direction of the project leading to the report to the Department of Education and Science. In particular, he made major contributions to the design of the questionnaire, its pre-testing, and the extensive preparation of interviewers. He also undertook much work on sub-projects associated with the survey of mothers

---

[1] *Social Needs and Resources in Local Services*, Michael Joseph, London, 1968; *Variations in Services for the Aged*, Bell, London, 1971; and *Variations in Children's Services amongst British Urban Authorities*, Bell, London, 1972.

[2] Elsevier, Amsterdam, 1975.

[3] Routledge & Kegan Paul, London, 1976.

that are not drawn on extensively in this book. I have used freely the ideas we discussed with one another in designing the research, though Mike should not be held responsible for the ways in which I have developed them. He has given me every encouragement and much help with the subsequent analysis. Susan Thorne was Research Assistant to the project in the eighteen months during which it was funded by the Department of Education and Science. Without Susan's exceptional diligence, capacity for organization, and intelligence, the report to the Department could not have been completed so quickly. The L.S.E. computer service ran the remaining analyses for the book, notably those summarized in the diagrams in Chapter 2 and Chapters 5 and 6. For this, I am particularly indebted to John Wakeford and Richard O'Reilly. Andrew Barton wrote the program that derived income variables by applying to our survey data the means test for school meals. The drafts on which the manuscript was ultimately based were patiently typed by Bridget Atkinson, and the final edited version was typed by Marie Wetherill, who also read the proofs. In the last stages, my determination to revise the manuscript for publication has been immeasurably strengthened by the encouragement and helpful criticisms of Della Nevitt, Robert Pinker, and colleagues on the Boards of Studies of Economics, Politics, Quantitative Social Science and Social Policy and Social Work at the University of Kent.

It is with some diffidence that I present the book that draws on data collected in 1968. Undoubtedly some of the relationships that then existed will now have changed. I have three excuses for using these data. The first is that even old evidence is a better basis for theoretical and policy argument than none; and it is unlikely that the relationships will have changed so much as to make its conclusions substantially invalid. Secondly, much of the interest of the book is that it is the first attempt to discuss policies for means-testing and charging, using survey evidence interpreted in the light of some mainstream theoretical areas of economics and sociology. Thirdly, not to discuss the evidence would deny to readers the chance to react to the general *modus operandi*. If we are to be able to conduct this style of policy analysis quickly, it is as necessary to develop such *modus operandi* as it is to explicate our theoretical and policy arguments. My hope is that the book will help to structure issues for those who can collect new and better evidence to undertake analyses of alternative policies for fixing and remitting charges in social services.

1 The Policy Issues and the Research

Commitment to universalist and selectivist arguments most clearly differentiates the approaches to social expenditure policy of the right and left in British politics. The arguments reflect differences in attitudes to the most fundamental of issues; issues like the role of the State and the nature of the relationships between individuals and groups within it. The application of the arguments in one policy context after another has generated a large literature, much heat, and not a little rancour; and at times, it has seemed almost as if to many from both camps an unqualified support for one group of belligerents was the litmus test of commitment to the social welfare of the underprivileged. Discussion of the arguments in the principal policy contexts is thought to be an indispensable component of any course in social policy. Yet the research testing and developing them has been insubstantial, and as Richard Titmuss argued, they are among 'the most trivialized and denigrated' in 'the age of the great simplifiers' 'who polarise conflicts so as to present them as entertainment'.[1] Little attempt has been made to complicate the key arguments by taking into account the influence of contextual factors, and to explicate their assumptions about cause and effect and the consequences of policies in such a way as to derive insight from the mainstream theory of sociology, psychology, and economics. No attempt has been made to collect the range of evidence necessary to test them. Therefore it has not been possible to develop any but the crudest models exploring the consequences of alternative policies. This book is an attempt to begin to rectify these omissions.

The study treats only one context, the school meals service; though it attempts to set the issues in the context of the broader battle against poverty and its consequences. The school meals case has features which make it an appropriate case. The effectiveness of the selectivist policy

---

[1] Richard Titmuss, *Commitment to Welfare*, Allen and Unwin, London, 1968, pp. 114–15; *Social Policy*, Allen and Unwin, London, 1975, pp. 13–14.

1

for school meals was under attack from politicians and others at the commencement of the research. It had been argued for the first time that the proportion of those eligible who were taking up the free meals to which they were entitled was low. Indeed, the research was a direct consequence of our publication of some estimates of the short-fall in the numbers receiving free meals and some comments we made in Appendix 14 of the Plowden Report.[2] The latter showed that the uptake of school meals was in general lowest in areas with the greatest number of poor children; while that of school milk was highest in such areas. The difference in the pattern of uptake was attributed to charging for meals and an eligibility criterion for the remission of charges based on a means test. The comments were quoted in Parliamentary debate, stimulated a correspondence in *The Guardian*, and secured an immediate request for more information from the Department of Education and Science. The non-uptake of free meals became overnight a national political issue. Not only had social policy failed to prevent child poverty at a time of economic prosperity, as Abel-Smith and Townsend had shown,[3] but the social intervention, designed to prevent one of the most undesirable consequences of child poverty, seemed to be of only doubtful effectiveness. Further evidence from a survey undertaken by the Ministry of Social Security confirmed that uptake rates were indeed low. Whereas Davies and Reddin had estimated that two-fifths of those eligible actually took up their entitlement, the Ministry survey estimated that one-half of the children aged five years and more from families with two or more children actually received them.[4] The difference between the estimates was small, although the Davies and Reddin estimate was an imprecise order of magnitude based on a projection from the Family Expenditure Survey data analysed in Abel-Smith and Townsend,[5] while the Ministry of Social Security estimate referred to an inappropriate population. The commissioning of our study was an immediate response to the problem. The Minister responsible for the services was able to reply to Parliamentary questions that 'we have commissioned a piece of research in which the London School of Economics ... is looking at great depth at a number of sample

[2] Central Advisory Council for Education (England), *Children and their Primary Schools*, II, H.M.S.O., London, 1967.

[3] Brian Abel-Smith and Peter Townsend, *The Poor and the Poorest*, Bell, London, 1965.

[4] Ministry of Social Security, *The Circumstances of Families*, H.M.S.O., London, 1967, Table III.

[5] *The Poor and the Poorest*, op. cit.

areas, to advise us why people do not take up their entitlement'.[6]

There are other reasons why the school meals service is a good case for the examination of the arguments and the discussion of their implications for spending policies. It is a service with complex objectives spanning more than one department of state. From time to time, it is explicitly recognized that the school meals subsidy is intended to reduce the probability among children of malnutrition due to family poverty. It is one weapon of intervention among many in the war against poverty. Policy judgements should therefore be based on a broad appreciation of strategy in this war. But it is a service provided in schools, administered by education departments, and serviced by professions whose links with others involved in the battle against poverty is at best indirect. It is a context which creates abundant opportunities, if not for goal displacement, for its broader role to be neglected. The school meals case is therefore a good test of 'the coherence of the inter-departmental approach towards financial poverty' discussed by the Central Policy Review Staff.[7] Secondly, the school meals service is economically and financially important. It contributes to the ability of women to seek employment. It is itself a substantial employer. It is difficult to estimate the true opportunity cost of this labour and of the other resources consumed.

The subsidies were large when the research was initiated and they are now larger. Our *New Society* article argued that the reduction in the subsidy payment following an increase in the price of meals from 5p to 7½p might more than equal the Plowden Report's estimates of what should be spent on establishing priority areas, making essential improvements to bad primary-school buildings, and increasing the supply of nursery-school places.[8] The value of the current account subsidy in 1965/6 was equal to over two-fifths of the entire sum paid in family allowances.[9] It was equal to the sum paid out in unemployment benefit, greater than total expenditure on local welfare services, and greater than total expenditure on children's services. Capital expenditure on canteens was 9 per cent of total local authority expenditure on primary and secondary schools in 1965/6.

The growth of the subsidy was rapid, and, through its effect on the

[6] *H.C. DEB., 1967/8, 759*, Col. 614.

[7] Central Policy Review Staff, *A Joint Framework for Social Policy*, H.M.S.O., London, 1975, p. 25.

[8] Bleddyn Davies and Mike Reddin, 'School meals and Plowden', *New Society*, 11 May 1967, pp. 690–2.

[9] £63 million compared with £152 million.

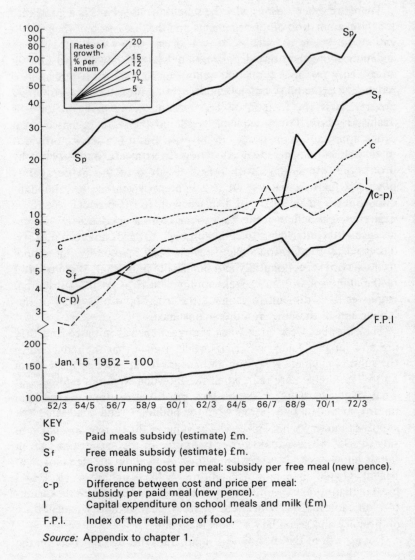

KEY

S$_p$	Paid meals subsidy (estimate) £m.
S$_f$	Free meals subsidy (estimate) £m.
c	Gross running cost per meal: subsidy per free meal (new pence).
c-p	Difference between cost and price per meal: subsidy per paid meal (new pence).
I	Capital expenditure on school meals and milk (£m)
F.P.I.	Index of the retail price of food.

Source: Appendix to chapter 1.

Diagram 1.1   Growth of costs, subsidies, and investment

rate of uptake, generated new demand for dining rooms and equipment. The growth was due to a number of factors—the growing populations in maintained schools, the increase in the proportion of each cohort that took meals, and the pricing and loan sanction policies adopted by successive governments.[10] Diagram 1.1 (and Appendix 1.1) indicates the growth of the determining factors and the consequential expansion in the service and its subsidy—or rather, its two analytically distinct subsidies: the paid and free meals subsidies. (The diagram, being semi-logarithmic, has the property that straight lines of the same slope represent the same rate of growth wherever they lie.) Because the free meals uptake rate (U_f) grew little over a decade or more, the free meals subsidy (S_f) grew at a rate $1\frac{1}{2}$ per cent per annum slower than the paid meals subsidy (S_p). (No attempt has been made to deflate the financial series to allow for inflation, although a relevant price index is shown on the diagram.) The fastest growth was for capital expenditure, made necessary to accommodate the growth in demand, stimulated (*inter alia*) by the expanding subsidy. In the mid-1950s, the growth rate was almost 5 per cent per annum. These rates of growth made more important the analysis of subsidy policy.

[10] The number of meals served depends on the number of children, the proportion taking meals and the number of feeding days (which varied slightly from year to year but which was not subject to a trend); that is:

$$m = n . \bar{u} . d$$

where m is the number of meals served, n the number of children and $\bar{u}$ the average proportion taking meals per day. Since September 1964, when L.E.A.s' individual arrangements for the partial remission of charges was replaced by a national system designed to ensure that entitlement to free meals was determined on a uniform basis, the paid meals subsidy (S_p) depends upon the relationship between the price charged for meals (p) and their cost (c) as well as on the number of children (n), the average daily paid meals uptake rate $(\bar{u}_p)$ the average proportion of days children attend $(\bar{a})$ and the number of feeding days (d), i.e.

$$S_p = (c - p)n . \bar{u}_p . d . \bar{a}$$

Similarly, the free meals subsidy depends upon the cost of the meal (c), the number of children (n), the average proportion of children attending $(\bar{a})$, the average daily proportion of these children receiving the meals free u_c, and the number of feeding days (d); i.e.

$$S_f = c . n . \bar{u}_f . d . \bar{a}$$

In fact, the Department's direct estimates of u_p and u_f depend upon a census on one day in September each year; and since the uptake rates depend on attendance rates (which are subject to some seasonal variation) as well as on the proportion of attenders who take their meal (which may also be subject to seasonal variation), these estimates may be misleading. Also calculations of the uptake rate parameters are made more imprecise by the growth in holiday meals. But for want of a more adequate method of estimating the two components of the total subsidy, we have had to base the estimates shown in the Appendix on them.

This rapid growth continues. The white paper *Public Expenditure to 1979/80* shows that by the end of the period, the cost of the school meals subsidy will be £315 million at 1975 survey prices.[11] The sum is more than one half of current expenditure on universities, one half more than is spent on teacher training, more than the current expenditure of the personal social services actually consumed by children and their families, more than four-fifths of the sum likely to be devoted to widows' pensions and industrial death benefit, and three-fifths of expenditure on family allowances and child interim benefits. As in earlier periods, the growth in the subsidy due to decisions not to adjust prices upwards sufficiently to maintain earlier commitments to reduce the proportion of the total cost of meals met from public funds will for some years be magnified by rising school populations.[12] Whatever the consequences of current policies for investment, any tendency for prices to lag behind costs during a period when rates of inflation might again be in two figures enhances the importance of the review of pricing and subsidy policies in the service.

The research

This book is organized around two issues: the analysis of causes of non-uptake of free school meals, and policy options available for developing more effective interventions. The first issue is logically prior to the second. Without an understanding of the central issues that bedevil the use of means-testing in the context, a sensible analysis of policy options is not possible. Politicians and academics alike attributed the shortfall which we had revealed to three proximate causes: (i) stigma, (ii) the absence of information about the services, and (iii) the difficulties of claiming entitlement. For instance, a document prepared by the National Executive Committee of the Labour Party stated 'where tests of means are involved, those in greatest need often fail to apply either through ignorance of their rights, dislike of the means testing procedure, or the difficulty found by the less educated and articulate in coming forward to establish their entitlement'.[13] There was disagreement about the relative importance of each of these causes. The Department of Education and Science, and some of those in the authorities in which we conducted interviews, appeared to consider that the absence of knowledge about the service was the major cause,

---

[11] *Public Expenditure to 1979/80, Cmnd 6393*, H.M.S.O., London, 1976.
[12] Ibid., p. 86.
[13] For instance, Mr Alfred Morris, *H.C. DEB., 1967/8, 759*, Col. 608.

this perception being reflected in the decision to spend £20,000 on sending out a circular to all parents in November 1967. Some of the politicians also put the main emphasis on the absence of adequate knowledge of the service and eligibility conditions. Others considered stigma to be the most important.

Assumptions about three sets of factors had a large effect on the design of the research: the key significance of a small number of the universalist and selectivist arguments in this context; the importance of factors operating differently between areas in determining the supply and demand for the service, and the relative merits of policy options; and the inefficiency of the incidence of the subsidy.

The key arguments

The essence of the selectivist prescription is that charging should be applied more widely as an instrument of resource allocation in social policy; but that the commodities thus allocated are judged by society to be of a 'merit'[14] character when their recipients are those most vulnerable in markets, so that the consumption of the poor must be safeguarded by the remission of charges. Since the vulnerability of the consumer is due to poverty, it is logical that a means test should be used as the criterion of eligibility for the remission. Selectivists argue

[14] J. G. Head, *Public Goods and Public Welfare*, Duke University Press, Durham, North Carolina, 1974. Also R. A. Musgrave, *Theory of Public Finance*, McGraw Hill, New York, 1959.

Selectivists would acknowledge that the consumption by the poor of the services is of special social importance. First, citizens can have preferences for the range of level of living of others. Thurow has demonstrated the public goods nature of the distribution of income, and the same argument is valid for the distribution of levels of living. The latter includes the consumption of commodities provided both by the private and public sector, and is more important than the former in the age of income policies and the 'social wage' (L. C. Thurow, 'The Income distribution as a pure public good', *Quarterly Journal of Economics, 89*, 2, May 1971, pp. 327–331). Although citizens may have preferences about the maximum levels of income, they are more likely to hold strong preferences about what minimum levels of living are tolerable within society. Since the consumption of social services is an important component of the social wage, their consumption by the poor (taking into account the distribution of income) can yield benefits to citizens in general that are not completely reflected in the decision-making processes of consumers. Therefore for this section of the market, some categories of service like school meals might have an element of publicness which would cause decision-making to yield an inefficient distribution of resources in the absence of intervention.

There is also a related 'merit good' argument. Politicians may believe for various reasons, some of which may be cultural, that the poor may under-estimate the probability that the failure to consume school meals will lead to malnutrition and its consequences for school performance. This was clearly an important consideration in the parliamentary debates of the 1940s, when it was argued that public understanding of nutrition was

that demand reflects the complex perception of utilities by potential consumers whose circumstances differ greatly; that the supply of services made available at any price should reflect the cost to society of producing them, and provides an incentive to potential consumers to behave in a way that will achieve the best use of social resources; that the operation of a market gives incentives to suppliers to improve their efficiency in meeting demands, incentives that are absent when the allocations are made by administrative and political decision.

Implicit in the argument are a number of assumptions. First, that the commodities themselves do not possess characteristics that makes a market system of allocation inappropriate; for instance, they are neither more non-rival nor more non-excludable than most commodities distributed through markets. Secondly, it is assumed that the market structure is such that the price yielded by it will provide an appropriate signal; for instance, that there is competition between suppliers in the markets faced by most consumers, that these markets offer a range of alternatives, that consumers are well informed about the substitutes, and that those for whom the commodity is regarded as a merit want are well informed about the rules governing the remission of charges. Again, it is assumed that demand is not extremely inelastic, that the quantity demanded depends upon the price charged, so that if the price were such that it did not reflect the real

---

limited, and that a major advantage of providing free meals would be to educate a new generation into adopting a more wholesome diet. Such arguments have recently been used with respect in particular to immigrant groups. (See Department of Education and Science, *Catering in Schools*, H.M.S.O., London, 1975.)

Professor Martin Feldstein has recently written that he detects what he calls a 'principle of categorical equity' in American writing, including that of economists. This principle 'singles out particular categories of services such as education and health care which are deemed to be fundamental interests, and asserts that the individuals' consumption of these services [*either*] should not be allowed to differ substantially, *or* alternatively such differences should not bear a strong relationship to the individuals' ability to pay'. (Our italics.) Professor Feldstein argues that Musgrave's concept of merit wants is not concerned with the distribution of consumption but with the encouragement of additional consumption that is deemed more meritorious than individuals recognize; so that while merit goods may be the subject of categorical equity, it is possible to desire greater equality of consumption while decreasing the average level. (M. S. Feldstein, ' "Wealth neutrality" and local choice in public education', *American Economic Review*, 65, 1, 1975, pp. 75–89).

Professor Feldstein uses his concept of categorical equity for the analysis of the financing of services provided collectively for the population of areas in a case in which it is a divergence from wealth neutrality that has been pronounced to be unconstitutional. When it is applied to such services in which the other form of the principle of categorical equity is appropriate, it is identical to the principle of territorial justice developed in *Social Needs and Resources in Local Services*, Michael Joseph, London, 1968. We refer to the principle of territorial justice in the concluding chapters of this book.

costs to society of producing the commodity, an inefficient allocation of resources would result. Fourthly, it is assumed that consumers' decisions reflect rational judgement about the costs and benefits of alternatives.

Therefore at the heart of the selectivist argument lies the assumption that consumers face sets of opportunities and incentives which they will seize in order to make the best of diverse circumstances. Their arguments imply that the cultural obstacles to seizing these opportunities (including the claiming of benefits) are great only for a minority. It is therefore neither necessary nor right in principle to subordinate the choice of policy instruments to the needs of those whose culture imposes such obstacles. Indeed, since the culture is assumed to have a pervasively negative influence on their welfare, it is justifiable to make its modification an aim of policy. This culture is necessarily transmitted inter-generationally but not necessarily intra-familially: it need not be the same families that will tend to be the least adaptable if some cultures have a higher probability than others of causing some families to respond inadequately to incentives.

Universalists attack each of these assumptions. They argue that the commodities have characteristics that make their allocation through markets inappropriate: for instance, that private decisions greatly affect public welfare in ways that do not influence private decisions, or that some of the factors that influence demand interfere with the rationality of consumers; and that there must inevitably exist dangers of monopoly both because the costs of time and transport limit the geographical scale of markets, and because there exist economies of scale in the provision of services of a character that makes them similar to those industries that Robertson called 'octopoids'.[15] Again, they might argue—although they appear not to have done so, because they rarely discuss the consequences of market interventions for allocative efficiency—that the elasticity of demand is less than that for most non-merit goods because they are the subject of so many special exemptions, so that provision free of charge would cause less distortion than it would in most markets.[16] Also they argue that the capacity to claim entitlements of those for whom the services constitute merit goods is more limited than is generally thought. For instance, Richard Titmuss attacked the residualists for over-estimating 'the potential of the poor,

[15] D. H. Robertson, *The Control of Industry*, Nisbet, London, 1923.

[16] Instead, they argue that the widespread exemptions reduces the budgetary consequences of increasing charges. See R. A. Parker, 'Charging for the social services', *Journal of Social Policy*, 5, 4 October 1976, pp. 359–74.

....hout help, to understand and manipulate an increasingly *ad hoc* society'.[17]

Indeed, the universalists seek to change the focus of the argument. The selectivist argument is one about instruments—about using price mechanisms supported by the remission of charges for those who satisfy the requirements of a means test, as a device for increasing the efficiency with which ends are achieved. Their writings show a concern for matching means to declared ends, an efficient balance of government expenditures between services, the adjustment of supply to a variety of needs that are continually changing, and what Burton Weisbrod calls 'vertical efficiency' in the supply of resources, a crude indicator of which would be the proportion of benefit received by those who are needy.[18] The universalists propose a wider goal for social policy. They question whether the numbers who perceive themselves to be relatively deprived is diminishing, and whether there is taking place an *embourgoisement* that is replacing fraternalistic and co-operative values by individualistic and competitive ones. Thus, in contrast with the residualists, or rather the contractionist residualists, who argue that social trends have reduced both the political pressure and the need for major state commitment to anti-poverty policy, the universalist argues that social policy is necessary to reinforce social cohesion in a system still dominated by fraternalistic and co-operative values. Only thus can a perception be created that the existing order can adequately improve social justice. Social policy is to be justified as much by its contribution to the sense of cohesion in society, to the implicit or explicit social contract, as by the attainment of the narrower ends of particular policies. Some of the universalists set this argument in the context of the theory of exchange. Boulding postulates an 'integry' of transactions involving unequal exchanges, a system parallel to the 'economy' which consists of transactions in which exchanges are equal.[19]

The universalist holds that the inequalities of exchange of social policy are functional to society. However, the work ethic asserts the

[17] Richard Titmuss, *Commitment to Welfare*, Allen and Unwin, London, 1968, p. 21.

[18] Burton Weisbrod, 'Collective action and the distribution of income: a conceptual approach', Reprint Series, 34, Institute for Research on Poverty, University of Wisconsin.

[19] K. E. Boulding, 'The grants economy', in *Collected Papers*, Colorado Associated Universities Press, Boulder, Colorado, 1971, II. Boulding argues that the integry is concerned with such factors as status, identity, community, legitimacy, loyalty, and trust. 'The grants economy ... [the integry] ... is not merely a rough measure of the integrative system; it is also in considerable part a creator of integrative relationships' (Ibid., p. 479).

contrary. The receipt of a means-tested service symbolizes the inequality of exchange, and so symbolizes the conflict between the social policy ethic and the work ethic. It is for this reason, argues the universalist, that the evil repute of the means test is in some circumstances powerful, pervasive, and ineradicable. Receiving a means-tested service inevitably leads to a loss of self-esteem and the stigmatization by others, because it creates a conflict between the work ethic and obtaining benefits which the potential claimant thinks that he (or the dependant for whom he is claiming) needs; and so causes that disjunction between ends that are socially approved and means that are socially prescribed that is the hall-mark of Mertonian anomie. In the school meals case, the means test punishes the eligible claimant by forcing him to lose esteem if he is to claim an entitlement to fulfill his duty as a parent pursuing the best interests of his child. It punishes the eligible non-claimant by causing him to neglect his child's interests. It undermines the sense of legitimacy of society among those whose means place them just above the margin and causes them to be more receptive to the ideas of those who argue that abuse of the system of benefits is widespread, and that recipients are morally unworthy. Thus means tests are not just incompatible with the reinforcement of social integration that is possibly the prime objective of social policy, but are positively divisive. The loss of belief in the legitimacy of the social order that means tests generate fosters an instrumental attitude to society as a whole, the resentment if not exploitation of society, a sense of satisfaction in 'getting one over on them'.

If the work ethic is so strong that the disrepute of the means test is an inevitably powerful consequence of the inequality of exchange, social policies cannot be justified merely by their efficiency in attaining the more specific goals of intervention. By asserting that the reinforcement of social integration is of major (if not of prime) importance among the goals of social policy, the universalists introduce an externality argument that cannot be tested by conventional economic analysis. Moreover, if the work ethic is so strong as to make dis-

---

To the argument that the integry promotes social cohesion, the residualist would reply that if the integry grows faster than the economy, there is evidence to suggest that beyond some point the further growth will diminish, not enhance, integration. They argue that the growth in the integry is achieved at the expense of growth of the economy—that it is the economy that provides the basis for satisfying the expectations raised by political promises to enlarge the integry, and that the unfulfilled expectations of a high grant economy can be damaging to social cohesion as the absolute and relative deprivation of a low grants society with greater 'value stretch'.

reputable the recipients of many of the flows of the integry, their justification cannot depend upon 'want-regarding'[20] criteria alone. There are at least two ways in which universalists resolve the contradiction between their argument that the work ethic is strong and pervasive, and their prescription that social policy should be based on an ideology that conflicts with it. One is to argue (paternalistically) that want-regarding principles should not be of primary importance in social policy: a reliance on want-regarding criteria is decried as hedonism. Some social policy writers define the area of social policy as an enclave, a sector in which 'ideal-regarding' criteria should have greater importance in relation to 'want-regarding' criteria; it being assumed that economic policy is more influenced by want-regarding criteria. More typical is the second method: to de-emphasize the conflict between the work ethic and their principles. They argue that many benefits are principally a form of redistribution from one stage of a citizen's lifetime to another, or a compensation for diswelfares that arise as an inevitable consequence of social progress or for bad luck in an unpredictable world; that problems of allocation and the misuse of welfare are a result of remediable structural weaknesses of its organization and that what amount to high marginal rates of taxation of the poor have a more serious effect on their perceptions of welfare and its recipients than on their behaviour in the labour market or work-place. Such universalists argue that leaders of opinion should promote the belief that the implications of the work ethic do not directly contradict the principles of the universalist's ideology. At most, the salience of the former is oblique.

There are other critical essays that review universalist and selectivist writing.[21] Here it is necessary merely to pick out those arguments which we considered to be of key importance in the school meals case and such that we could collect data for their examination. Viewing the general arguments in the school meals context suggested four perspectives that influenced the collection and analysis of data.

(i) Central to the universalist argument is that the stigma induced by the means test deters the eligible from claiming their entitlement. However vertically efficient the incidence of the subsidy of a means-tested service might look, it is inevitably inefficient in that the potential for stigma of the means test deters many of those in need from

[20] Brian Barry, *Political Argument*, Routledge, London, 1965.
[21] Critical reviews include Mike Reddin, 'Universality *versus* Selectivity', *Political Quarterly*, *40*, 1 January 1969, pp. 12–22.

applying. Little can be done to make the means test more acceptable and hence a more efficient instrument, so powerful is (a) the symbolic 'meaning' of the means test to potential claimants or (b) their expectations about the probability of stigmatization by others, or (c) since claimants 'learn' meanings from encounters with them, the perceptions of those having contact with potential recipients and on whom depends the distribution of the services. Citizens use a moral vocabulary to discuss the meanings of giving and receiving services. Indeed, in the special case discussed in *The Gift Relationship*, Richard Titmuss argued that 'their view could not be expressed in morally neutral terms'.[22] The perception that the poor receives more from society than he contributes to it is central to the moral issue. The self-respecting citizen is unwilling to put himself in a situation in which others may perceive him thus: he cannot easily be persuaded to see the situation to be other than reflecting the inequality of exchange; and/or is unconvinced that those (like employers or teachers) who will know who receives the benefit will perceive recipients differently.

This universalist argument provided a focus for policy debate. Indeed, during the six or seven years that followed the rediscovery of child poverty and (later) the discovery of low rates of take-up of means-tested services, the principal concern came to be that uptake was too low for the free meals scheme to be considered successful. The concern was widespread, though articulated mainly by Labour members who used evidence of low uptake as a weapon against selectivist policies, the low uptake being thought to result from dis-welfare created by the selectivist free meals scheme for people eligible to benefit from it. This is well illustrated from the speech in the Adjournment debate on *The School Meals Service (Selectivity)* by Alfred Morris. His argument ran thus;

> More and more people are urging a change towards increasing selectivity in the social services ... Opposition members have been especially strident in their condemnation of the universal principles of social security overall irrespective of means. They argue that universality is outdated and help must be concentrated on those whose needs are greatest ... but we have had selectivity in the school meals service for many years ... It is estimated that last year 660,000 children were entitled to receive free meals, but well over 300,000 of these children refused to take free meals. They refused according to Press reports of enquiries undertaken by Chief Education Officers because their parents were sensitive to taking charity ... It is not only the parents who felt sensitive about

[22] Richard M. Titmuss, *The Gift Relationship*, Allen and Unwin, London, 1972, p. 13.

existing arrangements for free meals ... some of the children who can pay their way in school sometimes take pride in comparing themselves with the poorer families who cannot do so ... It is for the advocates of selectivity to show how their system can work without humiliating those, including children, whom selectivity is said to be intended to help.[23]

(ii) More fundamental than the argument about the consequences of stigma for the probability of an eligible person claiming the benefit was the second key universalist argument, that attitudes to society are damaged by the existence of a system based on means tests to establish eligibility; that means tests are an intrinsically divisive policy instrument, and as such, incompatible with a perception of social services as not merely 'utilitarian instruments of welfare' but also as 'agents of altruistic opportunities'[24] reinforcing the integry.

(iii) Although stressing the integrative aims of social policy, few universalists would deny the relevance of objectives specific to individual services. The school meals service is the subject of government statements about objectives that are unusual for their clarity. Statements were frequently made by ministers during Parliamentary speeches in the 1940s. Combating malnutrition was clearly the principal aim, and the risks of malnutrition were perceived to be associated with family poverty. Thus free school meals, family allowances, and some other cash benefits were considered in relation to one another.[25] Indeed, the level of family allowances was set at a level lower

[23] *H.C. DEB., 1967/8, 759*, Cols 6706–10. This debate, like that following the statement by Patrick Gordon Walker on the Family Endowment Scheme, also focused on members' perceptions on the way the principles of universality and selectivity had been applied. (*H.C. DEB, 1966/7, 751*, Cols 57–9.) Lena Jeger congratulated the Minister on maintaining the principle of universality (Col. 59). Mervyn Pike attacked the statement 'for putting aside good selectivity and accepting universality' (Col. 59). Edward Heath attacked it on the grounds that more than 50 per cent of children would receive less help than they needed because of the priority given to universal family allowances (Col. 61).

[24] *The Gift Relationship*, op. cit.

[25] *H.C. DEB., 1943/4, 404*, Col. 1116. See also *H.C. DEB., 1943/4, 387*, Q. 285; *H.C. DEB., 1943/4, 388*, Col. 1149; *H.C. DEB., 1943/4, 424*, Col. 1804; *H.C. DEB., 1943/4, 425*, Q. 23; *H.C. DEB., 1944/5, 42*, Cols 1115 and 1149; *H.C. DEB., 1945/6, 433*, Col. 2052; Board of Education, *Circular 1629*. This was equally true in the late 1960s. The Minister's statement on the Family Endowment Scheme related charging and means-testing in school meals to a policy for school and welfare milk, rent, and rate rebates, housing subsidies, income tax allowances for children, family allowances, and improvements to what he called 'social capital' in such deprived districts as educational priority areas. The statement commenced with the words: 'The problem of family poverty is complex and there is no simple or single solution to it...' (*H.C. DEB., 1966/7, 751*, Col. 57).

than that recommended by Beveridge because it was intended that school meals should be universally available free of charge, despite the protests of such persons as Eleanor Rathbone who argued, *inter alia*, that it was twice as expensive to provide meals at school than at home.[26] Other objectives such as social and nutritional training were also discussed, but these were clearly secondary.[27] However, the social changes of the last three decades would make the unquestioned acceptance of the policy objectives naïve. It is naïve to apply the aims specified in the 1940s for the service to evaluate its contemporary achievements. It is therefore necessary to review the objectives of the service. To do this, it is desirable to investigate the causes of variation in consumer demand.

(iv) The universalist literature does not contain an extensive critique of pricing as a means of providing incentives to consumers and signals to suppliers that encourage and enable them to use resources more effectively.[28] Indeed, the critiques of policy arguments about charging for social services show the virtual absence of the economist's normative theory of pricing from the appreciative judgements of politicians and higher administrators.[29] However, such arguments are central to the selectivist arguments in the academic literature, although they reflect only crudely the sophistication of the contemporary normative theory of pricing developed by theoretical economists.

These were the four key arguments uppermost in our minds when designing the collection of data. They remained of importance to our policy argument throughout its development.

[26] *H.C. DEB.*, *1943/4, 404*, Col. 1172.

[27] Some of the arguments now appear unrealistic. Given good surroundings, the Parliamentary Secretary to the Board of Education argued in 1946, the meal could have many beneficial effects: 'where flowers and other decorations are used in the dining room, it helps to develop a sense of beauty and to teach a consideration for others, and promotes a sound social spirit in the school' ... as it had done 'in the public schools and at older universites' (*H.C. DEB., 1946/7, 436*, 333). Professor Titmuss indicated the importance of social training in his history of social policy during the war. (Richard Titmuss, *Problems of Social Policy*, Longmans, London 1950, p. 44.)

[28] An exception is David Collard's Fabian pamphlet, which lists the *caveats* entered by economists to the elementary normative theory of pricing. See David Collard, *The New Right: a critique*, Fabian Society, London, 1968.

[29] See R. A. Parker, 'Charging for social services', op. cit.

The importance of local factors

The political argument (and some of the academic comment) implied that generalizations about the relative impact of the three proximate causes would hold equally for children with similar backgrounds in Newcastle as in Plymouth, in Essex as in Cardiganshire. To us it seemed that this was an important example of a more general process by which the degree of territorial justice was determined. We expected the authority itself to have a substantial influence on the balance of influence between causes. In particular, our work on the theory of territorial justice for other local authority social services[30] had led us to expect that the variations which we had observed between authorities were not merely the reflection of variations in the characteristics of areas and their populations. Earlier research had suggested that the policies implicit in the ways authorities provided services had a powerful influence on demand, and so on uptake. We argued that such policies would be likely to influence the attitudes of actors at the points of contact with consumers. Such an argument seemed entirely compatible with the research on the school meals service itself which we had undertaken before this project was started.[31] In particular, it squared well with the result that not more than 50 per cent of variation in the free meals uptake rate among county boroughs and 25 per cent of the variation among counties could be explained by statistical models using poverty correlates.

There is little basis for accepting the conventional wisdom that local variations mainly reflects the values of local citizens. Indeed, I have recently argued elsewhere, the evidence accumulated by British political scientists and others implies that the nature of British local politics is such as to insulate the authority both from pressures that might stimulate a response to local needs and from the stated preferences of the electorate.[32] Consumer demand exercises an effective antidote in a few local authority services. Generally local authorities are area monopolists experiencing little competition from alternative providers in their areas. Where alternative providers exist, they are not regarded as rivals

[30] Bleddyn Davies, *Social Needs and Resources in Local Services*, Michael Joseph, London, 1968.

[31] Bleddyn Davies and Valerie Williamson, 'School meals—shortfall and poverty' in *Social and Economic Administration*, 2, 1 January 1968, pp. 3–19.

[32] Bleddyn Davies, 'On local expenditures and a standard level of services' in Bleddyn Davies, 'Determinants of Variations in Expenditure and the Measurement of Need', *Report of the Committee of Enquiry into Local Government Finance, Memoranda of Evidence*, H.M.S.O., London, 1976, Appendix 10.

for custom, since there is no precise equivalent to profits as an indicator of success.[33] If the school meals service is similar to most British local government services, the implicit policies and behaviour of the principal actors in the local socio-spatial system are likely to be insensitive to variations in the values of citizens.

The characteristics of the school meals service reinforce rather than weaken these general features of British local government. Above all the school meals service is politically invisible. The service is a small part of the work of a large department. It became clear during the interviews in local education authorities that in most authorities, the highest level with real administrative contact with the service in the organization was an assistant education officer. The service is only indirectly relevant to the main objectives of the department as a whole as these are perceived by the most important professionals and politicians.[34] It therefore seemed quite likely that local variations in the national policy paradigms for school meals would consolidate and grow stronger over time; and that the national paradigm would be dissonant with the increasingly systematic local variations in percep-

[33] The analogy between firms and local authorities is discussed at greater length in Bleddyn Davies et al., Variations in Services for the Aged, Bell, London, 1971, pp. 22–3. Some British economists follow the Americans and take the opposite view, relying on migration to provide a sanction in the competitive process. An early example is D. S. Lees, 'The place of local authorities in the public economy' in Public Administration, 39, 1, Spring 1961, p. 32.

[34] Indeed, it is clear that this is a service for which most of the general theories put forward by political scientists have little to contribute to the explanation of the pattern of variation. The electoral process and party competition arguments of the type put forward by Dahl, Dahl and Lindblom, and Downs seemed irrelevant; (see Robert Dahl and C. E. Lindblom, Politics, Economies and Welfare, Harper and Row, New York, 1953); Anthony Downs, An Economic Theory of Democracy, Harper and Row, New York, 1957; J. Schumpeter, Capitalism, Socialism and Democracy, Harper and Row, New York, 1947. Models of the type used in the Variations books failed to discover any political influence. Indeed the Layfield evidence (op. cit.) suggests that much of the British political science literature may have exaggerated the influence of crude party strength on outputs. There is no reason to believe that the Who Governs? approach has any more salience to this than it has to most other British outputs. (See Robert Dahl, Who Governs?, Yale University Press, New Haven, Connecticut, 1961.)

Despite the political local activities of local Child Poverty Action Groups (C.P.A.G.s) our interviews provided little reason to think that interest groups had a significant influence. (See Theodore Lowi, The End of Liberation, Norton, New York, 1969; F. F. Piven and R. Cloward, Regulating the Poor, Pantheon Books, New York, 1971.) Similarly there was little evidence of continuing partisan mutual adjustment at the national level; and the context proved not to provide support for the general community power approach with its emphasis on community characteristics affecting the behaviour of authorities as political organizations and thus outputs—the type of approach described succinctly by the diagram in Terry Clark's Community Power and Political Outputs, and exemplified in this country by Noel Boaden's Urban Policy-

tions of the services due to variations in the implicit policies of authorities.

A more precise causal argument underlay the design of the research. First, we argued that the implicit policies and behaviour of the authority were less influenced by other causal factors entering into our argument than were these factors influenced by local policies. The policies would affect such influential actors at the consumer interface as head teachers, teachers, and education welfare officers. The attitudes and actions of these actors and the supply policies themselves would influence the experience that consumers would have of the services. Such experience would in turn affect consumer attitudes towards the service, not only among those who had had themselves been exposed to the service, but also among others having close contact with them. Experience of the services and the attitudes formed towards them would influence behaviour; but as will be made clear in the sections of the analysis elaborating the argument, we would not suggest that any of these variables are entirely determined in this way. For instance, the actors are much influenced by professional values.

Making and the *Variations* studies. (See Terry Clark, *Community Power and Political Outputs*, Sage, Beverly Hills, 1973, p. 3; Noel Boaden, *Urban Policy-Making*, Cambridge University Press, London, 1971; and Bleddyn Davies, *Variations in Services for the Aged*, op. cit. and *Variations in Children's Services among British Urban Authorities*, op. cit.)

What seemed to be of greater relevance were the coral island theories of the growth of policy interventions like those of MacDonagh, Webb, or Thoenes. (Oliver MacDonagh, *A Pattern of Government Growth 1800–60*, MacGibbon and Key, London, 1961; Sidney and Beatrice Webb, *English Local Government*, Longmans, London, 1927–9; Piet Thoenes, *The Elite in the Welfare State*, Free Press, New York, 1966.) It was not that there was a complex learning process in the policy context (V. O. Key, *The Responsible Electorate*, Harvard University Press, Cambridge, Mass., 1966); H. Heclo, *Modern Social Politics in Britain and Sweden*, Yale University Press, New Haven, 1974. Not surprisingly, perhaps, there was little evidence of feedback during the period, which preceded the establishment of P.E.S.C. and the C.P.R.S. Instead it was the degree to which the process of government worked to reinforce incrementalism that was of interest. This incrementalism was reinforced because fundamental issues were not defined and faced by actors in the process, although the government exercised control by setting increasingly tight standards (like eligibility criteria). There seemed to be little of the subtlety of central–local relations described in this country by Griffith, more extensively explored on the continent by Tarrow and Aiken and in the United States by Roig; and controlled in statistical models for France by Jacqueline Becquart-Leclerc. (See J. A. G. Griffith, *Central Departments and Local Authorities*, Allen and Unwin, London, 1965; Sidney Tarrow, for instance in 'Local constraints on regional reform: a comparison of Italy and France', *Comparative Politics* 1974, 1–36; J. C. Becquart Leclerc, *Paradoxes du Pouvoir Local*, La Foundation Nationale des Sciences Politiques, Paris, 1975; Michael Aiken and Roger Depré, 'Policies and policy outputs: a study of city expenditures among 196 Belgian cities'; and C. Roig, 'L'évolution de la planification urbain aux Etats Unis', *Actualité économique*, 1967, 3 and 4, 1968, 2.)

The professions concerned contain many who would be classified as 'locals' rather than as 'cosmopolitans' and so would reflect regional values as well as values reflected in the implicit policies of authorities. Similarly people's experiences of the services are influenced by many factors other than those postulated in the argument. Their service-specific attitudes reflect more general attitudes and ideologies. Again we expect additional factors to affect their actual behaviour, particularly the sex and age of the children. There is a great deal of evidence that puberty may have an effect on girls' perceptions of the advantages and disadvantages of taking up the service, since they may be more conscious of their diet and more sensitive to stigma. Older boys were also expected to be more sensitive to stigma than younger boys. Both girls and boys may be more than likely not to take up the service as they grow older, because their home and the school may be more distant from one another. The free meals service is a form of social security administered by education departments and the schools. It is associated in people's mind with education and the schools themselves. We therefore postulated that there may be a connection between attitudes to education and the school and school meals. Indeed all three sets of attitudes may be manifestations of the same complex of social characteristics, specific circumstances, and the consequences of important events. Something connected with the school meals service may colour a child's or its parents' attitude to the school or *vice versa*.

The design of the research reflects these arguments in various ways. Since we expected causal processes to operate differently as between authorities, such data as there were for authorities were thoroughly analysed, using multivariate techniques; employees of the L.E.A.s were interviewed; and social surveys were conducted in those authorities where the actual free meals uptake rate contrasted with the rate predicted from their poverty correlates.[35] Areas in which the free meals uptake rate was a great deal higher than that predicted by the Davies and Williamson models were called 'over-achieving' areas. 'Under-achieving' areas were those whose uptake rates were lower than those predicted by Davies and Williamson. Interviews with employees of the

[35] We had previously established that free and paid meals uptake rates were correlated, so that in adopting a research design built around the contrast between what we called 'under-achieving' and 'over-achieving' authorities with respect to their free meals uptake rates, we would also obtain a design which allowed some contrast between 'under-' and 'over-achievers' with respect to their paid meal uptake rates. See Davies and Reddin, 'School Meals and Plowden', op. cit., 691.

local education authorities—chief education officers or their assistants, chief education welfare officers, education welfare officers, head teachers and teachers—were conducted in 'under-' and 'over-achieving' towns. These interviews were intended to discern any striking explanations of under and over-achievement connected with the L.E.A.s' manifest or implicit priorities and the way the delivery of school meals was organized. Also undertaken in these authorities were analyses of data on attendance rates, the administrative consequences of the Minister's circular of November 1967 to parents, and the characteristics of the new and older free meals recipients. A study of the sensitivity to changes in labour market indicators of changes in free meals uptake rates was undertaken in forty-eight authorities.[36] Surveys were undertaken of mothers in two large towns whose functions in each of the regions of which they were a part were similar. One town was an over-achieving area, the other an under-achieving area.

The main collection of data was the survey of mothers. The questionnaires contained questions on attitudes at varying levels of generality. Some of the attitudes were intended to indicate attachment to broad ideologies; for instance, ideologies underlying perceptions about the causes of poverty. Less general were questions about attitudes to means-tested services as a group. More specific still were questions about attitudes to the free meals service and the school meals service as a whole. Also included was a battery of questions about parents' and children's attitudes to, and experiences of, school and education in general. The battery was drawn up in such a way as to permit factor analysis. In order to facilitate the comparison of our results with those of other investigators, we used many of the same questions in this battery as were used in the survey reported by Roma Morton-Williams in Appendix 3 of the Plowden Report.[37] (Our criteria for the selection of questions were their face validity and loadings in the factor analysis reported there.) By including questions of varying levels of generality with respect to ideology and varying specificity with respect to the school meals service, we hoped to test and then make use of the generalization that more general attitudes—enduring dispositions of persons which organize the psychological orientation towards a class of phenomena—influence perceptions of a specific con-

[36] Bleddyn Davies *et al.*, 'Some constraints on school meals policy', *Social and Economic Administration*, 5, 1, January 1971, pp. 34–52.

[37] Roma Morton-Williams, 'The 1964 National Survey', Appendix 3 of Central Advisory Council for Education (England): *Children and their Primary Schools*, II, op. cit.

text to a greater degree than *vice versa*. By this means, we intended to unravel the complex network of causal relations within each L.E.A., and relate the approximate causes (stigma, ignorance, and difficulty in handling the service) to broader sociological explanations of behaviour.

Since some of the arguments relate attitudes on whether people do or do not take meals to the sex and age of the child, a sample design was chosen which would give equal numbers of persons with each combination of the causal attributes.[38] Since the best sampling frame available was the school register and very different proportions of children pay for meals, have them free, and do not take meals, a sample design was chosen which would produce roughly equal numbers in each of the three groups.[39] This procedure yields a design that is optimal for making estimates for each group of children classified by uptake characteristics and for comparisons between such groups in the two areas; but it is not one that is optimal for yielding estimates for the population as a whole.

The inefficient incidence of the subsidy

Our earlier analysis had convinced us that the incidence of the subsidy was inefficient.[40] The results also suggested that the aims specified for the services by Ministers may not have been the most important to some groups of consumers, or indeed those local authority personnel who played a major part in determining the nature of the service

[38] This is virtually a factorial design. (See W. G. Cochran and G. M. Cox, *Experimental Designs*, Wiley, New York. 1964, Ch. 5.)

[39] The proportions of children on the registers taking free meals, paying for them and not taking meals on the day of the September count 1967 was as follows:

	Dining rate		Non-dining
	Paid meals	Free meals	rate
'Under-achieving' authority	55%	6%	39%
'Over-achieving' authority	60%	12%	18%

(The paid meals rates have been subsequently rounded, and the last column treated as a residual, so as to conceal the identities of the authorities.)

The overall response rate—completed interviews as a proportion of the number of sampling units sent a letter by the L.E.A.s requesting permission to approach them—was 79.7 per cent.

[40] Bleddyn Davies and Valerie Williamson, 'School meals—short-fall and poverty', op. cit., and Bleddyn Davies, 'The cost effectiveness of education spending' in Peter Townsend, ed., *Social Services for All?*, Fabian Society, London, 1968, pp. 49–60.

actually provided. For instance, one of our papers suggested that women's working appeared to be a factor associated with high uptake rates of paid meals. This suggested that some consumers may take up the service as much because they wanted their children looked after during the lunch breaks as because they valued the nutritional quality of the meal or any social training that the service aimed to provide. The service might not be meeting the aims for which it was conceived, although the function which it performed might be worthy of the subsidy which the service received. Clearly, sensible policy decisions would require an evaluation of the patterns of consumption of the service both in relation to these actual functions it performed and to those it was intended to perform. The cost-effectiveness analysis that was needed should take into account a broad range of consequences. Only a narrow range of ecological data was available for such an analysis. Moreover it was not the data which would seem to be most salient to it. It was clear that survey data was required both to confirm the general inference about the inappropriateness of the current incidence of the subsidy and to explore the latent and manifest functions of the service.

Survey evidence demonstrating the inefficiency of the incidence of the paid meals subsidy as between children from families of different incomes and sizes was obtained from the Family Expenditure Survey.[41] It implied that among smaller families, the higher the household income, the larger tended to be its expenditure on school meals; and thus, the higher the subsidy it enjoyed. The evidence is ambiguous for larger families, the correlations being in opposite directions in the two years. However, given household income, the bigger the household size, the bigger tended to be the expenditure per child. In this respect, at any rate, the subsidy was a relatively efficient one. But on the whole, looking both at the individual and area incidence of the subsidy, these figures suggested that the incidence of the subsidy was inefficient by the criteria implicit in the purpose of the service as it was officially prescribed.

It was because we were convinced that the incidence of the subsidy as a whole (and its paid meals component in particular) was inefficient that we broadened the objectives of our data collection to include evidence which allowed an exploration of the factors affecting the demand for paid as well as free meals.

---

[41] We were grateful to the Central Statistical Office for making available these unpublished data. There were published in the two tables in Bleddyn Davies, 'The Cost-effectiveness of education spending', op. cit.

Appendix 1.1 The Growth of the School Meals Service, England and Wales

Financial Year (1.4–31.3)	1 n (millions)	2 U_p (%)	3 U_f (%)	4 U_t (%)	5 m (millions)	6 e (£m)	7 p (pence)	8 c (pence)	9 (c−p) (pence)	10 S_p (£m)	11 S_f (£m)	12 S_t (£m)	13 I (£m)	14 F.P.I.
1952/3	5.76	—	—	51.3	596	43	2.92	6.9	3.9	—	—	27.6	2.6	106.1
1953/4	5.95	40.9	4.2	45.1	549	42	3.75	7.4	3.7	20.8	4.3	25.2	2.5	111.0
1954/5	6.11	41.8	4.0	45.8	576	47	3.75	7.8	4.1	24.7	4.6	29.2	3.1	115.2
1955/6	6.25	44.7	3.6	48.3	610	54	3.75	8.2	4.5	30.5	4.6	34.1	3.6	123.6
1956/7	6.39	44.5	3.4	47.9	644	61	4.0	8.8	4.8	33.7	4.8	38.4	4.5	126.4
1957/8	6.21	42.4	3.5	45.9	596	62	5.0	9.5	4.5	31.2	5.4	36.6	5.3	131.4
1958/9	6.47	44.1	3.7	47.8	620	66	6.0	9.7	4.7	33.7	5.8	39.5	6.0	132.4
1959/60	6.51	45.8	3.9	49.7	685	72	5.0	9.5	4.5	35.1	6.3	41.5	7.1	133.0
1960/1	6.50	48.6	3.8	52.4	689	75	5.0	9.9	4.9	39.1	6.2	45.2	7.4	133.0
1961/2	6.58	50.4	3.6	54.1	732	81	5.0	10.2	5.2	43.7	6.2	49.8	7.7	136.1
1962/3	6.51	52.1	4.0	56.1	742	86	5.0	10.5	5.5	47.2	6.9	54.1	8.3	140.3
1963/4	6.51	54.7	4.4	59.2	781	90	5.0	10.4	5.4	48.8	7.6	56.3	9.0	143.0
1964/5	6.58	57.9	4.3	62.2	851	101	5.0	10.7	5.7	55.6	7.9	64.3	10.1	150.0
1965/6	6.67	60.7	4.6	65.4	881	111	5.0	11.6	6.6	64.5	8.3	72.9	9.8	155.0
1966/7	6.81	63.5	4.8	68.4	915	124	5.0	12.0	7.0	75.2	9.7	84.8	14.5	159.8
1967/8	6.97	63.7	5.8	69.5	1,021	136	5.0	12.3	7.3	79.8	12.3	92.1	10.3	162.0
1968/9	7.16	58.4	11.7	70.1	1,020	143	7.5	13.0	5.5	57.5	27.2	84.7	11.1	170.2
1969/70	7.38	62.0	8.0	70.0	1,020	154	7.5	14.0	6.5	71.9	20.0	91.9	9.9	188.5
1970/1	7.59	59.6	8.3	67.9	1,044	172	8.75	15.4	6.65	74.4	24.0	98.4	10.4	199.3
1971/2	7.79	49.5	10.3	59.8	943	192	12.0	19.2	7.2	69.7	38.6	108.3	12.0	218.7
1972/3	7.93	53.3	10.7	64.0	1,026	229	12.0	21.1	9.1	92.8	43.2	136.0	13.9	239.2
1973/4	8.19	56.4	9.7	66.1	1,079	287	12.0	25.3	13.3	140.5	45.7	186.2	13.4	275.5

Notes on columns:

Column	Symbol	
1	n	Number of children present in maintained schools making the autumn school meals count on the autumn day on which the count takes place.
2	U_p	Paid meals uptake rate: the proportion of children present in maintained schools on an autumn day taking a school meal for which they have paid.
3	U_f	Free meals uptake rate: the proportion of children present in maintained schools on an autumn day receiving a school meal free of charge.
4	U_t	Total uptake rate: the proportion of children present in maintained schools on an autumn day receiving a school meal.
5	m	Number of meals served during the financial year.
6	e	Total current expenditure on meals. This includes parental contributions and gross expenditure on meals in non-maintained schools.
7	p	The price charged for meals. The prices for 1952/3 and 1956/7 are averages over the financial year.
8	c	Gross running cost per meal: the subsidy per free meal.
9	$(c - p)$	The difference between cost and price per meal: the subsidy per paid meal.
10–12	S_p, S_f, S_t	Estimated paid, free and total meals subsidy respectively. These estimates are based on the assumption that the autumn count uptake rates are representative of the relative sizes of the two groups taking meals over the year. If this assumption were relaxed, they would remain adequate indicators of the relative rates of growth of the two components of the subsidy as long as any seasonal variation there may have been in the ratio $U_p : U_f$ was similar throughout the period. This latter assumption may well have been invalid in 1967/8 and 1968/9. The estimates were computed using the following formulae:

$$S_p = \frac{\left(\dfrac{U_p}{U_t} \dfrac{c-p}{c}\right)}{\left(\dfrac{U_p}{U_t} \dfrac{c-p}{c}\right) + \dfrac{U_f}{U_t}} \cdot S_t \qquad \text{and} \quad S_f = S_t - S_p$$

13	I	Capital investment: capital expenditure financed from revenue or from loans on school meals (and milk) services.
14	F.P.I.	Index of food prices. The food element of the Retail Price Index (and before 1956, the Interim Index of Retail Prices) as at mid-September each year. January 1952 also.

Sources: Cols 1–8, Department of Education and Science, Statistics of Education, V, Finance and Awards, H.M.S.O., London, annual.
Col. 14, Central Statistical Office, Monthly Digest of Statistics, H.M.S.O., London.

PART I: THE SURVEY

2 School Meals and the Consumer

The arguments of the politicians showed that the schools meals service has always been regarded by governments primarily as a weapon in the war to save children from the most pernicious consequences of family poverty. However, this is not its sole *raison d'être*. During the war years, for instance, ministerial statements gave some importance to social training of various kinds. This is a service whose political legitimacy has been well established by its long history—indeed a service that has been made sacrosanct and practically inviolable in the eyes of many because of its association with the political heroes of the early struggles of the British Labour Party. Moreover, *rien ne dure comme le provisoire*. The very longevity of the service has allowed subordinate goals to multiply and gain in importance.

The acceptance that came of long usage was accompanied by a loss of interest in the critical evaluation of its effectiveness by the legislature and those whose perceptions are dominated by it, particularly the higher civil servants, the 'production engineers of the parliamentary process' as Lord Armstrong has called them. The loss of interest gave increased power to those employed in the service to fashion and define goals quite unrelated to the war on poverty. In some cases it is the higher civil service itself who uses such a context to satisfy their needs. In this case, possibly because the number of higher civil servants involved was too small, it was such professional groups as the school meals organizers whose interests affected the implicit goal structure of the supplying organization. The way which such goal displacement can serve the needs of professionals when political control is weak has been well described for other contexts. However, it is not our concern here to analyse the content and form of the displacement of goals by interest groups in the supplying organizations. Our concern is with the goals defined by society through the political process and with the latent functions performed by the service as revealed by consumer behaviour and attitudes. Chapter 1 has described the former. This

27

chapter is concerned with the latter, and also discusses the political acceptability of some meta-policies for school meals in the light of respondents' reactions to them.

How consumers perceive the service, and how they behave when faced with some degree of choice about consumption, can both be legitimate bases for inference about the functions the service performs. Neither form of evidence is sufficient to provide a picture detailed or balanced enough to contribute the contextual understanding necessary for policy analysis. Behaviour is an inadequate guide to perceptions and preferences. For it to be otherwise requires of the population studied a high degree of adaptation to changing opportunities and circumstances. It requires them to operate a calculus of self-interest which would be rational only if it is judged highly probable that the pursuit of a strategy would usually be rewarded with the expected consequences. Some argue that many of the worst off do not perceive their world thus.[1] Moreover for such behavioural evidence to be a good basis of inference requires the existence of a very real freedom of manoeuvre. It is arguable that many—particularly again the worst off —lack effective choice. Yet it would be equally naïve to assume that direct questioning, using a tightly structured instrument, can always yield a better basis for inference. The discussion of this chapter therefore relies both on respondents' statements about their behaviour and their expressions of opinion and attitude.

The principal behavioural variables available to us are (a) whether or not school meals are received; and if received, whether they are paid for or obtained free of charge; and (b) how the consumers responded to an increase of one-half in the price of meals. The responses of consumers to price changes yield as much information about the functions of the service as the patterns of variations in uptake. They provide evidence about consumers' re-evaluations of the service; particularly when the price increase is substantial.

Section 1 analyses mothers' statements about the advantages and disadvantages of consuming school meals. The response to the price change is the subject of Section 2. Section 3 discusses the opinions of mothers about alternatives to school meals, and their attitudes to alternative policies for school meals.

[1] See Chapter 4.

1. Advantages and Disadvantages Receiving School Meals

(a) Advantages (Table 2.1)

The schedule contained several questions intended to inform us about the ways in which respondents thought the service useful. In particular all respondents were asked about the advantages and disadvantages of taking school meals. Six open-ended questions were asked; three about advantages, three about disadvantages. It seemed important to distinguish perceptions of advantages to the child from perceptions of advantages to the child's mother. Because the norms that govern motherhood exalt self-sacrifice, we expected the mothers interviewed to overstate the importance of advantages and disadvantages to the child as compared with advantages and disadvantages to the mother herself and the family as a whole. However, we did ask the mothers what, in their opinion, was the single most important advantage of receiving school meals, and similarly we asked them what was the single most important disadvantage of doing so. The respondent was asked to focus her judgement about advantages and disadvantages on the situation of the named child. By this means we sought to obtain from a population of respondents a more faithful reflection of the variety of evaluations of the situation than if we asked a question without postulating a specific context.

Advantages to the Child

The first section of Table 2.1 summarizes the results.

(a) Scrutiny of the questionnaires revealed that as well as an interest in the meals themselves, mothers saw the service as saving their children from lunchtime travel and its associated fatigue, danger, and expense. Some also perceived that the taking of school meals allowed their children to participate in the lunch-time recreations provided by the school. The nutritional interest was not in general associated with statements about the convenience of saving travel time. The table shows some interesting patterns of variation between meals groups in the statements of mothers about these two types of benefits. Among payers, the convenience benefits were more frequently mentioned than the nutritional benefits. The same was the case among non-takers. However, among

Table 2   Mother's opinions about the advantages of the named child taking school meals

	Non-takers		Payers		Free meals receivers	
	U*	O*	U*	O*	U*	O*
	%	%	%	%	%	%
(a) Advantages to the named child						
1. Provides regular and at least satisfactory meals	20	15	35	31	42	38
2. Saves travel time and fatigue and/or provides recreation time and/or safer	25	33	45	58	31	42
3. Improves table manners and/or makes child familiar with more varied dishes	5	3	3	1	4	5
4. Other (includes advantages to mother stated in error)	2	0	0	0	3	0
5. No advantage stated	48	50	15	10	10	15
Number of respondents	77	68	79	79	68	81
(b) Advantages to the mother						
1. Safety of child	5	4	4	5	6	6
2. Less work for mother	35	26	25	27	47	48
3. Freedom of mother to work	14	13	44	37	9	9
4. Cheaper	4	7	1	2	10	17
5. Other	2	4	9	6	13	14
6. No particular advantage	49	44	16	22	15	10
Number of respondents	77	68	79	79	68	81
(c) Most important advantage						
1. Provides regular and/or varied and/or satisfactory meals	17	15	42	35	47	46
2. Saves travel time and/or fatigue, and/or provides recreation time and/or safer	19	15	34	34	32	19
3. Improves table manners and/or makes child familiar with more varied dishes	4	3	4	3	5	2
4. Less work for mother	14	15	6	5	3	10
5. Freedom for mother to work	2	6	12	12	2	2
6. Cheaper	2	3	3	1	2	2
7. No particular advantage	40	41	11	10	9	10
Number of respondents	77	68	79	79	68	81

Note: U denotes the 'under-achieving area', O the 'over-achieving' area.

the free meal receivers more weight was accorded to the nutritional benefits. Indeed, in the under-achieving authority, a higher proportion of mothers quoted nutritional benefits than quoted convenience advantages—a relationship whose significance will become clearer later in this chapter. To a high proportion of free meal receivers, the service is important because it performs the functions most closely salient to its role as a weapon in the war against the malnutrition consequences of family poverty. But even among free meal receivers, it was a minority of mothers who thought that an important enough advantage to mention to the interviewer.

(b) Substantial minorities did not claim any particular advantages to the named child of receiving school meals. This was particularly so for non-taking children. What the table suggests, therefore, is an acceptance of the benefits of the service subject to the satisfactory outcome of a calculus of advantage, rather than enthusiasm for proselytizing its virtues. This is an inference which receives the support of much other evidence in the survey. The evidence that mothers assessed the costs and benefits is that a substantial proportion responded to price changes, and, as we shall see below, did so in a manner that appeared to a high degree 'rational', given their circumstances. Mothers evaluated the price of the meal against alternatives, and for many, the 'consumer's surplus' was not large.

The survey provided a great deal of evidence that mothers perceived the service as useful. First, it shows that most mothers would have preferred to have their children take school meals. As many as nine out of ten mothers whose named children received free meals would have liked their children to have had school meals. More than one half of all mothers of non-taking named children would have preferred them to do so, although the first part of the table shows that the mothers of non-takers were the least likely to want their children to take school meals. Secondly, even among non-takers, most named children had received school meals for more than a term during their school career. This was true of more than one in every two children currently not taking school meals in each authority. The continuity with which they were taken is striking. In the under-achieving authority one out of two named children in each of the receiving groups had received school meals continuously since starting school. In the over-achieving authority, three out of every four had done so. Indeed, a high proportion had received their first school meal within their first year at school and had continued to receive it without break thereafter. Two out of every three children currently receiving school meals had first consumed them before the age of seven. Almost all mothers intended that the named child should continue to receive school meals until the end of their school life, circumstances permitting, and almost all children consumed school meals five days a week.

Thirdly, the relative unimportance of nutritional considerations among mothers' replies was not evidence that they thought badly of it. Respondents were asked about the quality of the food and the cooking. Only a minority thought them bad. Indeed among free meals recipients as few as 4 per cent thought them so. It is not surprising that those who valued them for their nutritional benefit should have thought well of their quality. Neither is it surprising that mothers in the group that contained many who could see few advantages in taking meals were more likely to denigrate them: as many as 14 per cent of non-takers thought them bad. That almost twice the proportion of non-takers as payers thought the quality of the meals bad was no doubt partly due to the rationalization of their non-consumption, but we have no reason to question that it was also partly due to a real difference in perception. Most respondents were satisfied with the quantity served; though one mother in five complained that too little was served to satisfy the appetites of her children.

(c) What was it then that distinguished the non-takers? As might be expected, they were on average worse off than payers. But it would be quite wrong to assert at this stage that their behaviour was entirely dictated by financial motives, even though the reason why they appeared to be less enthusiastic about the service was because they might have been rationalizing their non-consumption to some degree. There is evidence that other factors had an important influence. The survey yields factual evidence that the consumption of meals was less of an advantage to them. First, a higher proportion lived within walking distance of the school. The proportions for the under- and over-achieving authorities were 75 and 60 per cent: those for payers were 54 and 56 per cent. Secondly, 90 per cent and more of named children not taking school meals had their lunch at home in both authorities. (As one might predict from our argument that supply influences demand, the proportion was higher in the over-achieving authority.) Thirdly, a lower proportion of the mothers of non-takers worked.

(d) Few mothers rated social training to be important. Indeed a quite substantial proportion thought the supervision of meals was inadequate. As one expects from the other results, the proportion thinking so was again lowest (8.5 per cent) for recipients of free meals and highest (18.3 per cent) among non-takers. However, not all mothers in these minorities considered that the presence of teachers was necessary to provide adequate supervision, since between 80 and 90 per cent of mothers thought that other helpers could supervise meals as adequately as teachers. It seems that mothers do not expect much social training from the service. The paternalist and patrician idealism of the Minister quoted in Chapter 1 would seem utterly unreal to these mothers one-quarter of a century later.

(e) Non-takers in the under-achieving authority were about as likely to see important advantages as were non-takers in the over-achieving authority. There is no sign either that more of the former saw advantages but were deterred from consuming by other factors; or, conversely, that they saw the service as less attractive. The single tabulations imply that non-takers in the two areas were similar with respect to correlates of deprivation—for instance proportions with low household income, from one-parent households, of low social class, of households with an unemployed head, or with a mother born outside the British Isles.

Advantages to the Mother

An examination of the answers to the open-ended question suggested that the codes listed in the table provided an adequate description. The regression analyses on which some of our earlier papers were based suggested the importance of mothers' employment. This was clearly reflected in the answers to this question also. The regression analyses also examined the consequences of price changes for uptake rates. The results suggested that mothers based their decision in part on the relative costs of the school meals and alternative provision. The costs not only include direct expenditure on the meals themselves and the food otherwise consumed at home, presumably reflected in row 6 of the table, but also other expenditures like the costs of collecting and returning children who have to be accompanied, and various opportunity costs of doing so. That such costs may often dwarf the direct expenditures on food is no doubt one reason for the relatively low proportions of mothers quoting cheapness as an important advantage, and the relatively high proportions specifying less work for the mother.

As was evident from the first section of the table, higher proportions of the mothers of non-takers saw no particular advantage to themselves in the named child taking school meals. Secondly, the table reveals a most interesting contrast between the perceptions of the mothers of non-takers and those of other children. Whereas the reason most frequently given by the mothers of payers was freedom for the mothers to work, the reason stated most frequently by mothers of the non-takers and free meals receivers was the reduction in the amount of work for the mother herself. The mothers of payers were indeed more likely to be in employment than others. Whereas two-thirds of the mothers of payers were in paid employment, this was so of less than two-fifths of the non-takers' mothers. (On average, only one in four mothers of free meals recipients were in paid employment.) Moreover, payers' mothers tended to work longer hours than non-takers' mothers. Twice the proportion of the former than the latter worked twenty hours per week or less. Thus it appears that mothers' employment was an important influence on the probability of their children taking school meals, but of course it was only a proximate cause of their consumption behaviour. It was itself an outcome of a complex process involving such factors as the number of dependent children in the family and other aspects of household composition, the employment possibilities open to the women concerned and the income earned by other members of the household.

Few of the payers' mothers referred to the relative cheapness of school meals. Higher proportions of non-takers' families did so. The highest proportions were the recipients of free meals. (Possibly mothers with low incomes attached a lower implicit valuation to the less obvious costs mentioned in the first paragraph.) This reflects the relative prosperity of the groups. However, in itself, a judgement about the food costs of alternative ways of providing comparable meals did not appear to be a major influence on the consumption decision.[2]

Most Important Advantage

In this question, an attempt was made to gauge the relative importance of the principal items. Again, non-takers were more likely than others to see no particular advantage to accrue from the named child taking school meals. The third, unlike the second section of the table, suggests that non-takers' mothers were more likely than others to see the most important advantage of their named child taking school meals to

[2] Bleddyn Davies and Valerie Williamson, 'School meals: short-fall and poverty', *Social and Economic Administration, 2,* 1 January 1968, 3–19; Bleddyn Davies *et al.*, 'Constraints on school meals policy', *Social and Economic Administration,* 5, 1, January 1971, 34–52.

be the reduction of work for themselves. It was the mothers of free meals recipients who were most likely to name this as being the most important advantage to themselves.

In the overall assessment reported in the third section, mothers appeared to attach more importance to the nutritional function than the other main source of benefit to the child. The results of the two

Table 2.2   Mothers' opinions about the disadvantages of the named child taking school meals

	Non-takers		Payers		Free meals receivers	
	U %	O %	U %	O %	U %	O %
(a) Disadvantage to child						
1. Dislike of some or all meals	21	25	10	5	10	3
2. Insufficient quantity	2	3	2	0	5	4
3. Inadequate quality	5	3	2	2	0	3
4. Incompatible with religious observance	7	8	0	0	0	0
5. Other (including disadvantages to respondents)	11	5	5	2	0	1
6. No disadvantage volunteered	56	41	86	90	84	91
Number of respondents	77	68	79	79	68	81
(b) Disadvantage to mother						
1. Mother enjoys company and/or would not otherwise cook	5	4	4	0	5	3
2. Expense or value for money	4	8	8	3	0	0
3. Other (including disadvantages to named child)	10	9	2	9	2	1
4. No disadvantages volunteered	80	79	79	96	92	96
Number of respondents	77	68	79	79	68	81
(c) Most important disadvantage						
1. Dislike of some or all meals	7	17	9	3	7	1
2. Insufficient quantity	4	3	3	0	3	0
3. Inadequate quality	5	2	1	3	0	1
4. Incompatible with religious observance	4	6	0	0	2	0
5. Mother enjoys company and/or would not otherwise cook herself a meal	6	2	4	0	3	0
6. Expense or value for money	5	6	5	3	2	0
7. Other	5	7	0	3	0	1
8. No disadvantages stated	64	11	77	90	84	97
Number of respondents	77	68	79	79	68	81

Note: U denotes the 'under-achieving area', O the 'over-achieving' area.

sections are alike in the high proportion of the mothers of both receiving groups who attributed the principal advantage to the child.

(b) Disadvantages (Table 2.2)

Disadvantages to Child

The literature suggests several reasons why children from the poor large family might be expected to dislike school food.[3] Additionally, the survey areas were so chosen as to contain substantial numbers of people whose religion would proscribe some items likely to be served at school. Most of those who replied did not state any disadvantages either for themselves or for the named child. This was least the case for the mothers of non-takers. It is quite consistent with the replies to the question about advantages, since higher proportions of non-takers than of mothers of other groups saw no advantages in consuming school meals. The most important disadvantage named was that the child disliked some or all of the meals. The proportions whose children disliked the meals were much the same among the two recipient groups, but much higher among non-takers. The pattern is not to be explained by the age structure of non-taking named children, since this was controlled in the sample design.

Disadvantages to Mothers in Named Child Taking School Meals

Respondents saw few disadvantages to themselves in the named child receiving school meals. A small and roughly similar proportion of each group would miss the child's company at lunch-time. Perhaps the respondents understated the importance of the costliness of the meal. The price increase had a considerable effect on the uptake rate, contrary to what one would infer from the second section of Table 2.2. This was more strongly felt by the families of non-takers than those of payers; in the over-achieving authority, 17 per cent of non-takers' families contained children who stopped having school meals when the price went up to $7\frac{1}{2}$p; in the under-achieving authority the proportion was 12 per cent. Even in the over-achieving authority, where the effects on children in payers' families were much greater, only 6 per cent of families contained children who stopped having school meals at that time. The proportion of free meals receivers' families with such children is one quarter that for non-takers' families.

[3] Hilary Land, *Large Families in London*, Bell, London, 1969.

Main Disadvantage of Named Child Taking School Meals

It appears that few respondents perceived disadvantages that were important enough to discuss. Again the disadvantages to the child were more frequently stated than disadvantages to the mothers. The costliness of the meal would appear to be more important than mothers suggested, judging from the elasticity of demand.

In general, then, mothers thought well of the service, but were not primarily interested in its contribution to the diet of their child. What appeared important to many mothers was a service that allowed the children to have some food at school at lunch-time, thus enjoying a more satisfactory period of recreation and avoiding the dangers and fatigue of travelling home. It was particularly important to working mothers.

2. Price Change and Uptake

The price charged is the principal policy instrument used to control consumption. It is therefore an essential prerequisite for policy discussion to understand better the consequences of raising prices for those who consume and therefore benefit from the school meals subsidies. Some three months before our survey interviews were conducted, the price of the school meal was raised by one half. This was large enough to force a reconsideration of the benefits of consumption, even in a service where consumption habits had been well established during a decade in which the price was not changed. In this section we explore the consequences for uptake of this change in price.

The Technique of Analysis

The preliminary counts and tabulations which we have already discussed provided a good basis for judging what factors were likely to affect response. Further analysis was needed to indicate the relative importance of such factors and the form of the relationships between the factors and the response. The discussion that follows explores this, using the procedure known to survey analysts as 'elaboration'.[4] Elaboration has been conducted using an algorithm that simulates the search activity of the social survey analyst at the exploratory phase of his work. The algorithm searches for, selects, and shows the best predictor of variation in the dependent variable within a population

[4] M. Rosenberg, *The Logic of Survey Analysis*, Basic Books, New York, 1969.

group in each of a series of steps. Unlike regression analysis, for instance, it allows the choice of different variables for different groups, and is therefore a good search technique for use in situations where the analyst expects to find different factors to be causally important for different groups of people, or for people whose circumstances are different. The technique is also useful for exploration because it does not assume that the relationship between causal factors and response is necessarily linear. The most important results are shown in tree diagrams which show the mean, standard deviation, and the number of observations in each group created by the operation of the algorithm.[5]

The Causal Factors and Predictor Variables

The explanation of the consequences for uptake of price changes must certainly take levels of family income into account, and with it the mother's employment status, since an income which consists only of the earnings of a father reflects a higher real standard of affluence than the same income earned both by the father and the mother of children of school age and younger, although we have no data (and lacked much convincing evidence from the work of others) which we could use to make any judgement about the equivalence of household incomes based on the earnings of one or both parents. Similarly, household income itself is an inadequate indicator of standard of living not only because it ignores wealth, the stability of income, and expected flows of incomes, but also because it takes no account of variations in factors generating a need for differing expenditure, and in particular, variations in the number of dependent children in the family. The nearest to a concept of income standardized by expenditure needs available to us is 'standardized income'. Standardized income is the difference between assessed income and the income required for eligibility for free meals for all the relevant children.

The potential for living standards of income is clearly likely to affect attitudes to the service, as are the demands made by such aspects of the manner of earning it as the number of hours of work undertaken by the mother. However, such attitudes are of interest in their own right; partly because they are likely to reflect aspects of culture which have little to do with current incomes, and partly because they are the

[5] The technique is explained in J. A. Sonquist and J. N. Morgan, *The Detection of Interaction Effects*, Michigan Survey Research Centre, Institute of Social Research, Michigan, 1970.

most direct evidence we have about the latent function of the service and its subsidies. The main direct evidence of attitudes collected in the survey consists of the answers to the six open-ended questions about mothers' perceptions of the advantages and disadvantages to the named child and to themselves of the named child taking up school meals. (See Section 1 of this chapter.) An attempt was made to assess the degree of importance the mother attached by asking what *particular* advantages and disadvantages were perceived, and also by asking what the most important advantage and disadvantage was. The coding of the advantages reflected our interest in the latent functions of the service: nutritional advantages formed one code; child-minding (for instance, while mothers were at work) formed a second; a propensity to see it as a creative part of schooling (in the form of socialization or recreation) was a third; a perception dominated by the relative cost of a school dinner and an equivalent meal outside or at home was a fourth; and an uninterested reply formed a fifth. (In contrast, the disadvantages were coded so as to distinguish mainly specific grievances— a dislike of the meal or other aspects of the meals service; a dislike of the meals context on social grounds (like the danger of acquiring bad table manners); religious taboo; its costliness; and (again) a lack of interest. Only two of these directly indicated the latent functions of the service.

The other data about parents' perceptions of the service used were a set of questions intended to illuminate the importance of supply factors within the control of the school meals service itself. Mothers were asked whether they thought the food (its type and cooking) good, bad, or indifferent; whether they thought enough, too much or too little food was provided; whether the dining accommodation used was adequate; whether the meals were adequately supervised. Only one code in each of the advantage and disadvantage questions overlapped these to any degree.

The main factors ('standardized income' and mothers' employment) are not the only contextual factors thought likely to affect attitudes and decisions. The real cost of the meal to most mothers is its price and the cost of travelling (including the value of the time spent by the child and the mother in such travelling), less the cost of what alternative provision is considered adequate. Whether or not the family had a child of under school age at home was considered to be a major factor in the cost of a meal at home and an important contextual influence on mothers' attitudes. Finally, since uptake rates were very different in the two areas, and the social consequences of price changes might be ex-

Table 2.3 Predictor variables used in the AID analysis of the effects of price changes and levels*

	No. of groups	Variable Codes	Short title
Area	2	Over-achieving	OVERACH
		Under-achieving	UNDERACH
Standardized income group	4	1. Eligible on income grounds	SIG
		2. Not eligible on income grounds but less than £2 per week above that level	
		3. £2 and less than £4 a week above that level	
		4. £4 or more a week above the eligibility level	
Mothers	3	0. Not in employment	MOTHEM
		1. In employment not more than 24 hours a week	
		2. In employment more than 24 hours per week	
Young child at home	2	1. A dependent child of less than school age at home	DEPCHLD
		0. No such child at home	
Food inadequate	2	1. Food thought bad	FDINAD
		0. Food not thought bad	
Enough food	2	1. Food thought insufficient in quantity	ENFD
		0. Food thought sufficient in quantity	
Accommodation inadequate	2	1. Accommodation thought inadequate	ACCOMINAD
		0. Accommodation not thought inadequate	
Supervision inadequate	2	1. Meals supervision thought inadequate	SUPERVISINAD
		0. Meals supervision not thought inadequate	
Particular advantages to named child	5	0. Nutritional	ADVCHLD
		1. Child-minding	
		2. Child socialization or recreation	
		3. Financial	
		4. None in particular	
Particular advantage to Mother	5	0. Nutritional	ADVMOTH
		1. Child-minding	
		2. Child socialization or recreation	
		3. Financial	
		4. None in particular	

Table 2.3—cont.

	No. of groups	Variable Codes	Short title
Most important advantage	5	0. Nutritional 1. Child-minding 2. Child socialization or recreation 3. Financial 4. None in particular	MIMPADV
Particular disadvantage to named child	5	0. Character of meals or service 1. Social 2. Religious taboo 3. Costliness 4. None in particular	DISCHLD
Particular disadvantage to Mother	5	0. Character of meals or service 1. Social 2. Religious taboo 3. Costliness 4. None in particular	DISMOTH
Most important disadvantage	5	0. Character of meals or service 1. Social 2. Religious taboo 3. Costliness 4. None in particular	MIMPDIS
Travelling time school to home	2	1. More than median travelling time 0. Median travelling time or less	TRAVTIM
Cost of travel school to home	2	1. More than median 0. Median or less	TRAVCOST
Low social class	2	1. Father in social class V 0. Father not in social class V	LSCD
Hindu, Moslem or Sikh	2	1. Hindu, Moslem or Sikh 0. Not Hindu, Moslem or Sikh	REL
Child orientation positive instrumental attitudes to education	2	1. Higher than median score 0. Median or lower score	EDID

*Analyses discussed in Section 3(b) of this chapter also had as possible predictors EXP, IRPSD, and OSPSD. These variables are defined in the Glossary, p. 253. Additionally the consumption status of the named child was used as a predictor.

pected to vary with uptake rates, it was thought that area might be a predictor.

The predictor variables used are defined in Table 2.3. Since some of the variables are complex, and since it is not feasible to state long titles in the boxes on the diagrams, and variable numbers are not easily remembered, short titles have been given to each of the predictors. These are listed in the third column of Table 2.3. In order to assist readers unfamiliar with the method of presentation of the results, the final groups of Diagram 2.1 are fully defined in Table 2.4. A comparison of Diagram 2.1 with Table 2.4, making reference to Table 2.3, will make clearer the interpretation of this and subsequent diagrams. The

Table 2.4   The definitions of final groups in Diagram 2.1

Group	Definition
4	Mothers who considered the most important disadvantage (MIMPDIS) of taking meals to be the character of the meals service, social, or conflicting with a religious taboo (codes 012); and who claimed a particular advantage to the named child in taking them (ADVCHLD) codes other than 4).
7	Mothers who considered that the food was insufficient in quantity (ENFD code 1), *and* who either thought costliness to be the most important disadvantage or reported no particular disadvantage (MIMPDIS, codes 3 and 4), *and* who named a particular advantage to the child in taking school meals (ADVCHLD, codes other than 4).
16	Mothers whose household income was below the eligibility level (SIG, code 1) *and* whose named child incurred less than the median travel cost to the school (TRAVCOST, code 0) *and* who either named no form of advantage to the child as most important or who named as most important financial or nutritional advantages (MIMPADV, codes 3, 4, 0) *and* who considered the quantity of food served sufficient (ENFD, code 0) *and* who either thought costliness to be the most important disadvantage or reported no particular disadvantage (MIMPDIS, codes 3 and 4), *and* who named a particular advantage to the child taking school meals (ADVCHLD codes other than 4).
17	As for group 16, save that household income exceeds the eligibility level.
12	Mothers without a dependent child living at home (DEPCHLD, Code 0) *and* who stated that the most important advantage of the named child taking school meals was either that he was cared for or that he benefited from the socialization with others or recreational pursuits (MIMPADV, codes 1 and 2) *and* who considered the quantity of food served to be sufficient (ENFD, code 0), *and* who either thought that costliness to be the most important disadvantage or reported no particular disadvantage (MIMPDIS, codes 3 and 4), *and* who named a particular advantage to the child in taking school meals (ADVCHLD, codes other than 4).
13	As for group 2, save that a dependent child living at home.
8	Mother from underachieving area (UNDERACH) *and* who saw no particular advantage to the child in taking school meals (ADVCHLD, code 4).
9	As for group 8, but from overachieving area (OVERACH).

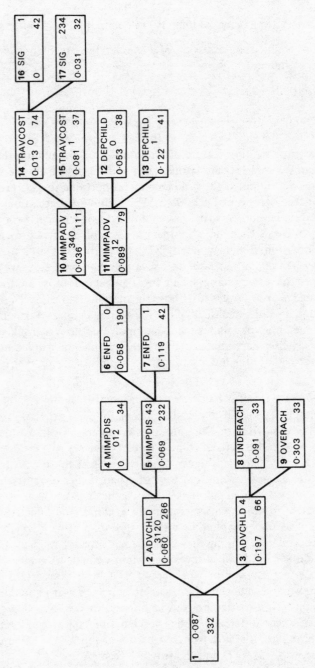

Diagram 2.1 Whether or not any of the children stopped having school meals when the price went up to 7½p

diagrams code 1 the possession of a characteristic or high scores on a dummy variable.

Results

(i) The probability that one or more children stopped having school meals when the price went up from 5p to 7½p (Diagram 2.1)

(a) The most striking feature of Diagram 2.1 is the unimportance of SIG (Standardized Income Group). In order to investigate the reasons for this, we examined the gradients in proportions for SIG groups in each analysis group of Diagram 2.1. This showed that SIG has effects that are weak but pervasive. SIG 1 mothers had higher proportions giving up meals than SIG 2 mothers in each of the group formed by the elaboration. Similarly much higher proportions of SIG 3 than SIG 4 mothers had one or more children give up school meals. As we argued in 1971, the price changes had most effect on those in the well-populated income groups just above the margins that define eligibility.[6] Although it would be difficult if not impossible to unravel the net effect of income on uptake under the assumption that no free meals existed, we display elsewhere evidence suggesting that income had the expected effect throughout the income range and in spite of the existence of free meals.

(b) One would also have expected MOTHEM to be important in the explanation. The gradients in proportions for each MOTHEM group for every analysis group in Diagram 2.1 were examined. In group 2 and most of the groups derived from it, those families whose mothers were out of employment had higher proportions than those with mothers in part-time employment, and the latter had higher proportions than those with mothers in full-time employment. The gradient was at its steepest in group 5, where MOTHEM was almost as effective a discriminant as the variable that split the group, and with which it was clearly correlated. Among those who named an advantage to the child but could see no disadvantages important enough to name, whether or not a woman was at work could well be an important factor. MOTHEM was not independent of SIG. It is in such a group as this that one might have expected both to be important. We have already seen that there was a difference in the expected direction between SIG 3 and SIG 4 means in most groups derived from group 2—the same groups as those in which we found the MOTHEM gradients.

(c) Despite these caveats, the impression yielded by these results is

[6] Bleddyn Davies *et al.*, 'Some constraints on school meals policy', op. cit.

that the amount of consumers' surplus derived from consuming school meals at the price of 7½p was strongly influenced by immediate contextual factors—whether mothers saw any important advantages to the child in consuming them, whether they had sufficient interest in the service to discuss inadequacies in the actual provision, whether it was expensive for the child to return home for lunch, or whether there was a child of pre-school age at home for whom a meal had to be prepared irrespective of whether the named child ate at home or at school. For instance DEPCHLD split group 11; and the analysis of residuals shows that TRAVTIM may well have had an effect on group 3 in the direction expected.

(d) The domain of variables which reflect impressions of those aspects of the quality of the school meals service that is controllable by the service itself—BADFD, ENFD, ACCOMINAD, SUPERVISINAD—did not, in general, have the expected effect, though the tabulation of the residuals suggests that ACCOMMODINAD may have had an effect in both groups 11 and 3. The apparent effects of ENFD on group 5 and in final group 3 are in the direction opposite to what one would expect if ENFD were an indicator of this aspect of the quality of the food, rather than a reaction determined by subjective circumstances. Its importance in these results may well reflect the fact that the children most likely to have stopped taking when the price rose were those who had inadequate breakfasts—that they were hungrier than others.

Several conclusions may be drawn. First, income standardized by family composition did not have the powerful pervasive effect one might anticipate; but it had an effect in the expected direction on those whose incomes were at the margin of eligibility. The employment status of the mother was important only to some groups. Secondly, the most immediately powerful factors influencing the decision whether or not to continue to receive school meals at a higher price were contextual. Those that were controllable by the school meals service itself were not important among these factors, and neither were factors likely to be influenced by the gatekeepers whose influence we shall be discussing in the next chapter.

(ii) Probability that there would be times when the children could not have a school meal when the price was 5p (Diagram 2.2)

The large price increase made families, who would have received considerable consumer's surplus at the lower price, marginal. Moreover because only two-fifths per cent of free meals receivers would have been receiving free meals before 1966 when the price was raised to 7½p, the heavy representation of receivers of free meals in the groups would make less difference to this variable than to that based on the question ascertaining the number who had children who did not continue to receive school meals when the price was increased to 7½p.

Table 2.5   Type of meal that receiving children would receive if school meals not provided

	Snack[1] %	Cooked meal[2] %	Packed lunch[3] %	No meal[4] %	Various[5] %	Total %
Under-achieving authority						
Paying	18	44	35	0	3	100
Free	47	44	6	0	3	100
Over-achieving authority						
Paying	47	38	10	2	3	100
Free	50	37	8	0	5	100

Key [1] Snack (e.g. soup or beans on toast)—eaten at home.
     [2] Cooked meal (e.g. meat and vegetables)—eaten at home.
     [3] Packed lunch/sandwiches—not eaten at home.
     [4] 'Would not have any lunch.'
     [5] Varies (e.g. sometimes cooked meal, sometimes snack, etc.).

(a) SIG was the best predictor, the gradient of proportions by SIG class being what one would expect. Again proportions for SIG classes were separately examined for each of the analysis groups in the diagram. In each group where there was more than one SIG class present, there was a gradient in the expected direction. Moreover, the steepness of the SIG gradient was unaffected by ACCOMINAD.

The results throw some light on the different motivations of income groups. Among those eligible on income grounds, the mothers who were most likely not to take school meals were those who saw the main advantage of taking school meals to the child to be the quality of the meal; 64 of the 65 in group 5 quoted nutritional advantages to be most important. In contrast, 46 of analysis group 4 mothers saw the main advantage to the child to be that it was being looked after; 47 saw

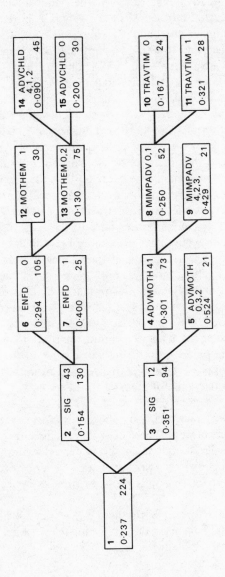

Diagram 2.2 Whether or not there were times when the child could not have school meals when the price was 5p

this as the main advantage to the mother, and 41 saw it as the main advantage overall. Another 22 of the group 4 mothers saw no particular advantage to the child, 21 seeing no particular advantage to the mother either, and 16 seeing no particular advantage overall. Those who saw the advantage to be child minding had the lowest proportions. Moreover, it is likely that analysis group 5 mothers were worse off than analysis group 4 mothers, since a higher proportion of them—26 as compared with 20 per cent—worked, and a much higher proportion of them worked full-time, yet only achieved a low (SIG 1) household income. (The table quoted earlier from the Plowden Report,[7] showed that the proportion working full-time varied more with father's income among the badly off than the proportion working part-time.) This interpretation also makes sense of the otherwise puzzling interaction effect between travel time and perceived advantage to the child. If group 3 mothers were really worse off than group 4 mothers, children would have been more likely to eat at home if their mothers were not working, and if their home was not too far away (and the cost of getting there was not too great). In practice, this might well have been mainly children of primary-school age. As one might expect if it reflected children's tastes to a greater degree, it was the secondary-school children from analysis group 4 who tended to miss meals more often, or who were more reluctant to seek free meals. Within analysis group 4 itself, the worse off nutritionally may have taken up school meals less regularly, judging from the direction of the gradient of proportions for ENFD.

If we are correct in seeing reluctance to claim free meals as an important causal factor among those eligible on income grounds, potential recipients would have been more reluctant to have recourse to the free meals alternative in the under-achieving area. That the group 3 proportion for UNDERACH was some 7 percentage points higher than that for OVERACH provides some evidence in support of this.

Ironically, therefore, it is the neediest, whom we have seen to be those who would have used the service for the reason it was provided, who were the least likely to take up school meals at a time (like 1975) when paid meals enjoyed a subsidy of 60 per cent of their cost. The pattern is somewhat different among the better-off. Those who see the principal advantage to be broadly child-minding in character were the most likely not to have had school meals from time to time. But again the situation was not without its irony. It was those who

[7] Central Advisory Council on Education (England), op. cit.

saw no particular advantage in taking up the service who had the lowest proportions unable to afford meals on occasion.

(b) The employment variable, MOTHEM did not split groups. Among mothers not eligible on income grounds alone, the proportion for part-time workers is far lower—12 percentage points—than that of other mothers. This is partly due to the complex pattern of association between full- and part-time work and low income shown (for instance) by Table 10 of Appendix 3 of the Plowden Report.[8] Broadly the same pattern of association holds also among those eligible on income grounds, most of whom would have been receivers of free meals by the time of the survey.

We may summarize the principal features of results thus:

1. Standardized income was the best and most pervasive predictor.
2. Among those eligible on the income criterion alone, the children most likely not to take school meals were those whose mothers thought the main advantage was nutritional.
3. It would seem that it was a characteristic of clients and their circumstances rather than controllable features of the service that appeared to be important.

3. Consumers and the Political Alternative Policies

The consumers of school meals may be heterogeneous and unorganized, but they are extremely numerous. Disgruntlement with changes in school meals policy could have substantial effects on the diffuse support on which a government depends for its re-election. Just what policy changes could on balance add to or diminish this support is an important issue. We have seen that most approved of as well as used the service. It is therefore important to explore more evidence about the extent, causes, and correlates of variations in consumers' surplus. The evidence discussed so far has suggested some of the factors that explain why a substantial proportion of mothers did not gain sufficiently from it for their consumption to be affected by the price change. The perceptions of mothers about what alternatives they might have adopted if their children could not take school meals is important evidence about this. It is analysed in Section 3(A). Secondly, not only self-interest, but also beliefs about what is socially just, efficient, and in the public interest are important. For this reason, we investigate

[8] Central Advisory Council on Education (England), op. cit., II, p. 104.

what meta-policies mothers approved, and who it was that supported each of the alternatives. This is the subject of Section 3(B).

(i) The Alternatives to Taking School Meals

In reply to a question about what alternative arrangements would have to be made for children to have meals at lunch time if school meals were not provided, two out of every three payers and nine out of ten receivers of free meals stated that a meal would be provided at home. The proportion of payers stating that their children would eat at home was much the same as the proportion not in paid employment, and the proportion of free meals receivers stating that the children would eat at home was greater than the proportion not in paid employment. Therefore, either some mothers would give up work or respondents were unrealistic in their answers to this hypothetical question. Of course some unrealism in the answers need not imply that their analysis would yield misleading answers—that depends on whether the degree of unrealism is associated with factors whose effect we are exploring.

Table 2.5 analyses the answers to a question about what kind of meal the named child would have received if school meals had not been provided. The results shown there do not make it clear whether the nutritional consequences were likely to be more serious for the population of one or other authority. Similarly they do not make clear whether the purely nutritional consequences were likely to be worse for free meals receivers than for payers. Again the evidence does not provide a clear basis for inference about whether it would have been the deprived that would have lost most from the withdrawal of the service, and neither does it give much indication of what factors would have influenced the alternatives chosen. We investigated the two last questions further by seeking to explain the main alternatives, using the same technique of elaboration as in Sections 2 and 3. The predictor variables used were the same and are listed in Table 2.3. Two dependent variables are analysed: whether the mother stated that a cooked meal would be the alternative, and whether the mother stated that a packed lunch would be the alternative.

A Cooked Meal the Alternative (Diagram 2.3)

(a) Those families who were eligible or nearly eligible on income grounds were the least likely to state that a cooked meal would be the alternative. This is so, even though Area was the best predictor. The

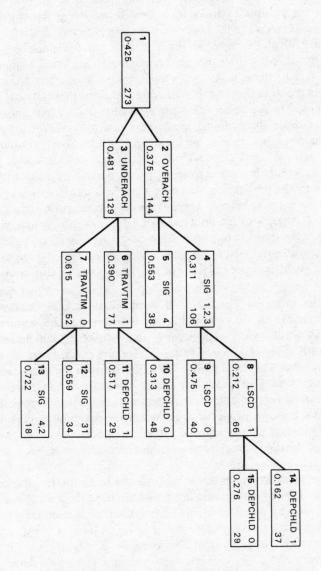

Diagram 2.3 Alternative arrangement: a cooked meal

anomalies in this relationship are more apparent than real. First it is not surprising that there was little difference between proportions among the standardized income groups in analysis group 4, since the variance of income in the lower three income groups was small in comparison with the variance in the highest of the four income groups, and since we can expect the income variable to have had a large error term. Again, there were only three persons in income group 3 in analysis group 12. In the over-achieving authority, the relationship was quite clear. In the under-achieving authority, it appeared anomalous only for those children who would have had to travel for more than a median length of time to get home for lunch (analysis group 6). For those without a younger sibling of less than school age at home (analysis group 10), standardized income seemed to make little difference to the probability of stating that the alternative arrangement would be a cooked meal. There were only seven persons in income group 4 in analysis group 11, so that the low proportion was an average over very few mothers. But perhaps we should not expect neat income gradients. Given the unreliability of estimates of household income made from general surveys, large errors were almost inevitable.

(b) One might have expected the employment variable (MOTHEM) to have been one of the principal predictors. Diagram 2.3 implies that this was not so. One might suspect that MOTHEM would have been sufficiently highly associated with Area for any effect it had to be disguised. There was not a close association between the probability of a mother working and Area; but among those working, higher proportions worked part-time in the over-achieving authority. Therefore, the difference between proportions shown in the diagram may overstate the importance of Area and understate the importance of the number of hours worked. Proportions for MOTHEM groups in each cell of Diagram 2.3 were examined.

Three predictions might have been made about the impact of MOTHEM: (i) Mothers working full-time have been expected to state the cooked meal as the alternative less frequently than mothers working part-time; (ii) mothers working full-time might have been expected to describe this as the alternative less frequently than mothers not in paid employment; and (iii) mothers working part-time might have been expected to state the alternative less frequently than those not in paid employment. The unexplained variance for each of the more populous analysis groups was examined with these three predictions in mind.

(i) In general, mothers working full-time have lower probabilities than either those working part-time or not in paid employment. There were some exceptions. The numbers in groups 14 and 20 were small. The other analysis groups, mothers working full-time, had a lower probability than mothers working part-time, as one would expect.

(ii) Only in the over-achieving area were there exceptions to the prediction that the higher proportion of those not in paid employment than full-time employed would have stated this alternative. The gradient in group 2 can be discounted because it is reasonable to assume collinearity with standardized income. The difference in proportions was in expected directions in group 9. A comparison of the proportions in groups 14 and 9 shows that it was also in the expected direction in group 15. The most interesting groups are groups 14 and 5. The numbers not in paid employment in group 5 were small, as were the numbers in part-time employment in group 14. Thus it is clear that both the standardized income and mothers' employment had pervasive effects; but in the over-achieving authority the effect of MOTHEM can only be seen where standardized income is controlled.

(iii) There is no indication that part-time employment made much difference to the ability of stating a cooked meal as the alternative. However, there may have been some slight effect disguised by the collinearity of Area with the proportion of working mothers in part-time employment.

(c) The importance of a younger sibling and travel time in the under-achieving authority again reminds us of the importance of the contextual variables. They are as important to many decisions as are the more general factors like standardized income and the mothers' employment status.

A Packed Lunch Alternative (Diagram 2.4)

One of the least expected results of the price increases in the late 1960s was the widespread adoption of sandwich-taking. It is tempting to examine the results with the benefit of hindsight to see whether they present any clues to the reason for the popularity of the packed lunch.

(a) That the better-off mothers envisaged this alternative shows the importance of class differences in tastes—and a different assessment of other costs and benefits (like malnutrition or missing cultural activities taking place in the school during the lunch break). The better off were more likely to see the packed lunch as the most satisfactory alternative. That they did so might have contributed to the subsequent

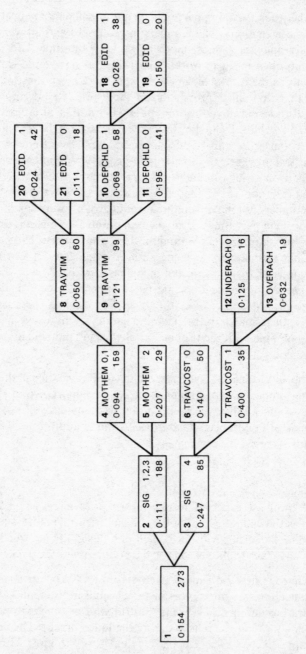

Diagram 2.4 Alternative arrangement: a packed lunch

fashion for sandwich-taking, though the positive effect of full-time work among SIG groups was also evident. (Women's working among those with low household incomes and large families may imply a low real standard of living.)

(b) The results provide some evidence that it was the secondary-school child (and others for whom travel time or travel costs would be high) for whom this was likely to seem the better alternative. Not only was travel time and travel cost the best predictor at various stages, but travel cost was also positively associated with the probability in groups 11, 10 and 18 (where the effects of travel time are already controlled), and the proportions are positively associated with travel time in group 7 (where the effects of travel costs are controlled). However, there were anomalies, as in group 6 where it would at first sight appear that TRAVTIM was negatively associated with the probability.

(c) Cultural rather than strictly economic factors were not unimportant. For instance in groups 8 and 10, EDID was negatively associated with the proportion: the more child- and education-orientated the mother, the lower the probability of seeing a packed lunch as an alternative. However, there is no evidence that this was the case in group 6.

(d) The patterns are compatible with those for cooked meal desirable. The higher probabilities among MOTHEM 0 than MOTHEM 1 groups, evident in the tabulations of the residuals, have already been mentioned. LSCD was positively associated with the packed lunch proportions but negatively associated with the cooked meal proportions.

(ii) Opinions about Subsidization Policies

Regrettably, our questions intended to discover mothers' policy preferences did not apply the techniques developed for environmental contexts to force respondents to simultaneously consider both the benefits and the opportunity costs of alternatives. Our excuse is that although the work that first developed these techniques was published long before our questionnaire was designed, it is only recently that they have been used by students outside the area for which they were invented.[9]

[9] Terry N. Clark, 'Can you cut a budget pie?', *Policy and Politics*, 3, 2 December 1974, pp. 3–32, and Terry N. Clark, 'Citizen preferences and urban public policy', *Policy and Politics*, 4, June 1976, pp. 4–140.

Our questions therefore permitted respondents both to express a preference for more benefits (like increasing the subsidy to school meals) while ignoring the consequences for taxes or alternative public expenditures. Unfortunately the questions which reminded respondents of the opportunity cost of increased spending followed rather than preceded those which asked whether they agreed with the two positions about a subsidization policy. Answers to them are therefore more likely to affect broad ideological differences than would more sophisticated questions that better reflected the costs of the alternatives.

Table 2.6   Proportions of respondents agreeing with propositions about public expenditure

Proposition	Non-takers' sample		Payers' sample		Free meals receivers' sample	
	U %	O %	U %	O %	U %	O %
That the Government should:						
1. Make more children eligible to get free school meals	38	50	35	42	54	53
2. Spend more on subsidizing the school meals service as a whole	70	54	53	43	65	44
3. Spend more on education and less on other things	78	75	78	76	72	62
4. Spend more on education and raise taxes	22	29	13	27	28	23
5. Cut taxes and reduce spending on government services	61	65	57	54	53	59

Note: All respondents answered all parts of this question.

No doubt the proportions agreeing that more should be spent on the two subsidies were higher than they would have been with questions forcing a simultaneous consideration of the benefits. Evidence of this is the difference between the proportions in rows three and four of Table 2.6 and the high proportions agreeing the proposition that taxes should be cut and public expenditure reduced. Indeed, in samples of mothers with children of school age in the late 1960s it is striking that high proportions thought that the burden of taxes outweighed the benefits of public spending. This is particularly so, since it was true of the majority of mothers of free meals receivers, and the proportions

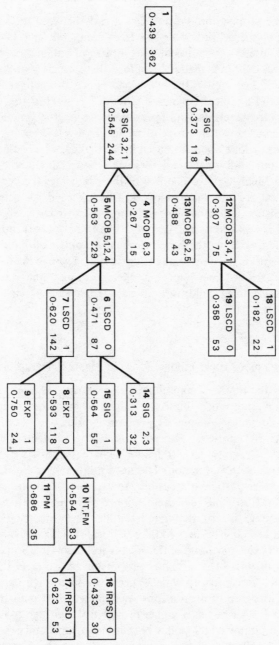

Diagram 2.5 Mother thought that the Government should make more people eligible for free meals

agreeing the proposition did not vary greatly between the six groups.

Though the questions were less than ideal, the answers to them remain of interest to political judgements about acceptability. An attempt was therefore made to explore the correlates and causes of the preferences of each of the two broad policy alternatives for school meals, extending the free meals scheme by making the eligibility criterion more generous, and spending more on the general subsidy and so keeping down the price of meals. This was done by using the same technique of elaboration used in the earlier parts of this chapter. However four additional predictors were used. These are EXP, IRPSD, OSPSD, and Meals Group. The first of these indicates the degree of experience that the mother had of the free school meals scheme. The second measures a dimension of attitudes which we have called an individualized responsibility for poverty. The third (OSPSD) indicates the pervasiveness of the mother's perception that applying for and receiving free school meals was potentially stigmatizing. These indicators are discussed and defined in Chapter 5. Meals group is the consumption status of the named child; non-taker (NT), payer (PM), or free meals receiver (FM).

A. Making more People Eligible for Free Meals (Diagram 2.5)

The higher the mothers' household incomes, the less likely they were to favour making more children eligible. SIG split the group both at the first and at the fourth stage of the working of the algorithm. Among the 362 mothers, 57.5 per cent of the eligible, 48.6 per cent of SIG 2, 47.6 per cent of SIG 3, and 37.3 per cent of SIG 4 mothers favoured this course of action. The SIG 4 mothers born in Britain and not of LSC were particularly unlikely to support an additional subsidy in this form. But higher income LSC mothers were more likely to support this policy. In this, they were more like lower income groups—no doubt their low class influenced their political socialization and so their perception of the 'meaning' of this means-tested service. Some evidence in support of this is that a higher proportion of group 19 than group 18 mothers—74 compared with 50 per cent— had high OSPSD scores; and this difference in proportions was almost great enough to have split group 12. There was a higher probability that high OSPSD scorers would have supported the policy both in SIG group 4 and other groups, although the effect of OSPSD was greater among SIG 4 mothers than among the others, judging both by a comparison of means in group

2 and 3 and an examination of the means in the final groups.[10]

If the explanation for these associations is that mothers who saw the free meals context as potentially stigmatizing thought the extension of free meals to larger numbers of children to be a method of breaking down this danger of stigmatization, one would have predicted that those who felt it most strongly would be mothers who had had experience of free meals before the circular. They would have been the mothers who had received most opportunity of seeing stigmatization. Irrespective of the context presenting the opportunity for stigmatization, one might expect them to judge stigma to have an important effect on the number of children taking up their entitlement. EXP mothers would indeed have appeared to favour making more children eligible, since EXP split group 7, and the differences in EXP group averages in all final groups were in the predicted direction. Further, if this were the reason for wishing to see more children receiving them free, and if stigmatization was perceived to be a particular danger in the underachieving area, proportions would have been higher among mothers from that area. Again, this prediction is supported by the evidence. Although Area did not split the group, the difference between Area proportions was in the predicted direction in all but one of the final groups, being larger in groups 19, 15, 17, and 11. Also, if a high proportion of mothers supported the extension of eligibility to more children because this would have reduced the danger of stigmatization of receivers, those most likely to be stigmatized for reasons additional to low income would have been the most likely to support it; mothers born in Ireland and the West Indies, for example. This prediction also

[10] This can be seen from the following table:

	OSPSD	
	High	Low
SIG 4 (Group 2)	.431	.283
Others (Group 3)	.562	.516

This table does not control for the effects of the other successful predictors. The OSPSD row means of the final groups show effects that could not have been due to correlations of OSPSD with the predictors that had defined these groups. Although the differences between OSPSD group means for groups 12 and 14 varied in the direction opposite to that hypothesized, the difference between these differences in means were much smaller than the differences between the differences for groups 14 and 15, and the difference in group 12 was greater than the differences in groups 16, 17, and 11. Indeed the high OSPSD mothers in groups 15 and 16 had lower scores than others.

appears to be compatible with the evidence. MCOB distinguished the SIG 4 British-born mothers from the others at the second stage, and the difference between MCOB means for all final groups other than group 16 were what one would expect. The high IRPS West non LSC Indian mothers of group 16 were the early settlers who were most likely to think well of the education system. One must, however, bear in mind that the numbers in the groups were small, and the situation was too complex for one to have expected the patterns to be clear. Nevertheless the amount of evidence supporting the interpretation is impressive.

B. Subsidizing the Whole Service More (Diagram 2.6)

It is clear that mothers' perception of the importance of stigma was the most important influence on their opinions. Not only was OSPSD the best predictor, but EXP—here defined as whether or not experience had been obtained a year or more before the survey—was clearly associated with the opinion; the opinion was more frequently held in the under-achieving area, and by those with the longest time to learn 'the meaning' of the services. EXP did not split categories because only a small proportion of the sample had acquired their experience more than a year previously—and the numbers were too small for the program to use the variable for splitting groups at the third stage and later. For instance group 8 contained only eleven such cases, group 9 six, group 4 nine, and group 5 nine. Nevertheless, the association with EXP was, in all cases, consistent. Also it survived successive splits. For instance, it was present within groups 19, 16, 11, and 13, where there were sufficient numbers with EXP in the group and tabulations available. Moreover, there is evidence for an interaction effect between OSPSD and EXP. Early experience had a much more powerful impact among those who believed that the effects of stigma on uptake were most pervasive. The differences between the EXP group proportions in groups 8, 9, 4, and 5 were 11, 9, 17, and 17 percentage points respectively, so that the interaction effect caused differences of approximately 7 percentage points. This interaction effect between EXP and OSPSD makes it difficult to argue that OSPSD was an attribute of the culture of the local population, and was unaffected by the implicit policies of the authorities towards the free meals scheme. Learning processes were clearly evident in other forms, it would seem. The proportion of mothers born in Great Britain was higher among high OSPSD scores. Also among the high OSPSD group, mothers born in Great Britain

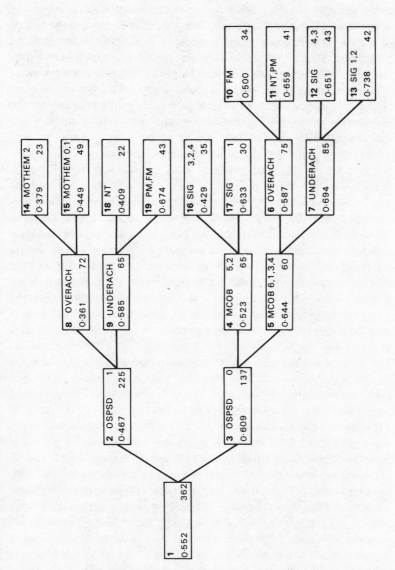

Diagram 2.6 Mother thought that the Government should spend more on subsidizing the service as a whole

favoured the policy more than the Irish or West Indians, but among those who saw stigma as least pervasive in the free meals context, the opposite was the case. In general, therefore, those who saw the receipt of free meals as potentially stigmatizing in a variety of ways perceived a high general subsidy for school meals as desirable, particularly if they had pre-leaflet experience and were from the under-achieving area.

Not surprisingly, class and income group interest was reflected. Higher proportions of those eligible on income grounds supported the proposition irrespective of their OSPSD group or their authority; and the analysis also showed that higher proportions among the high OSPSD group also did so irrespective of their country of birth or area. For one group, even with SIG controlled, LSC had a powerful enough influence to split a group. In general mothers who were not at work were most in favour of the policy—perhaps because economic pressures were not such that they identified closely with free meals receivers. Those who had high OSP scores, who lived in the under-achieving area, and who were eligible on income grounds were strongly in favour of the policy. All of those working full-time were in favour of it, as were a higher proportion of those in part-time employment than those not working at all. No doubt some of the mothers worked to avoid having their children receive free meals, and all worked because of economic pressure. The same may apply to women working part-time in group 17.

Therefore the most important generalization that can be made, on the basis of answers to the two policy alternatives analysed, is that poor mothers and mothers who were sensitive to the stigmatizing potential of the school meals context were most likely to desire the government to subsidize the service more. As we have shown earlier, the service was valued by the eligible because it provided a good and probably much-needed meal as well as because it looked after the child. Mothers who were better off saw it more as a convenience or child-minding service, valued it less highly, and would have preferred to see additional government expenditure elsewhere or a reduction in taxation. The form of the subsidy preferred by the eligible depended upon their perception of the degree and pervasiveness of the danger of being stigmatized in the free meals scheme. Those who were so sensitive may have preferred a smaller subsidy per meal, or a general subsidy, to the danger of stigmatization in the means-tested free meals scheme. But a perception that the free meals service was potentially stigmatizing was not simply determined by standardized income. Indeed the first split shown in Diagram 2.5 shows quite clearly that in this sample the mothers of families with low standardized incomes wished to see a higher proportion of children made eligible for free meals. It is unlikely that a simple random sample of mothers from the country as a whole would have yielded precisely the opposite result.

Conclusions

This chapter has shown that contextual factors, like the distance between home and school, or the presence of a younger sibling, were important determinants of uptake. Some of these factors might be judged negatively correlated with a need for meals; others might have been judged positively correlated or uncorrelated with it. To many, they were more important than standardized income or the mother's employment, and were more important than influences controllable by the school meals service and the education authority. The importance of these contextual factors is undoubtedly one important reason why a substantial proportion of those eligible on income grounds to receive free meals did not consume meals. Their importance greatly attenuates the correlation of the subsidy with need. Was it either socially just or economically efficient for families to gain or forfeit a large subsidy for a service whose consumption was so influenced by factors unrelated to the need for subsidization?

Secondly, the results imply that mothers' reactions to the policy options postulated were more pragmatic than doctrinaire. They were not merely the reflection of their self-interest; for instance, consumption status of their named child and of their standardized family income. They were such as to suggest an appreciation of some of the policy dilemmas. The results create the impression that mothers from all meals and income groups either appreciated or were close to seeing the central dilemma of anti-poverty policy—that the social expenditures intended to counteract the effects of poverty are financed by taxes levied from almost all income groups. The attitudes of mothers would not have been an insurmountable obstacle to implementing one of a broad range of policy options that could allow the service to meet its objectives more cost-effectively.

3 Applying for Free School Meals

Arguments used to explain the non-uptake of free meals mix elements of two contrasting models describing the perceptions of potential claimants. In the first, the poor claim their rights by successfully waging a war of attrition against a generally uncaring and often hostile society in conditions in which they are conscious that the odds on winning are loaded against them. Claimants see themselves to be powerless to influence their own economic status. As Cohen and Hodges wrote about the American blue collar worker of the lower-class:

> He is powerless because his bargaining power is weak; he is the most easily replaceable, the marginal utility of his contribution to the productive process is least, his skills are the least esteemed, and he has the least access to and control over strategically important information.[1]

The claimant is aware of the economic consequences for himself and his family of the circumstances of his employment, principally in what economists now describe as secondary labour markets.[2] The powerlessness of the individual is often enhanced (and partly caused) by the absence of social organizations directed towards the pursuit of the interests of the group *per se*; and the claimant is unlikely to be as influential as others in the policy-making of other pressure groups. Claimants similarly perceive themselves to be powerless over issues of less pervasive importance, like the claiming of individual benefits. They think that the processes by which benefits have to be claimed are formidably complex.

Before engaging the enemy on a front, it is necessary to evaluate the probability of victory there, and its likely costs and benefits. It is a battle in which the claimant expects victory to cause more humili-

[1] A. K. Cohen and H. M. Hodges, 'Characteristics of the lower blue collar class', *Social Problems*, *10*, 4, 1963, pp. 303–34.
[2] N. Bosanquet and P. B. Doeringer, 'Is there a dual labour market in Great Britain', *Economic Journal*, *83*, 3, June 1973, pp. 421–35.

ation than would defeat, although the act of engaging in the battle will itself put the claimant into humiliating roles. These humiliations will be of a variety of kinds, and will directly affect more than one member of the family. The humiliations are a far more important 'cost' than any effort devoted to actually making the claim, and weigh heavily on the mind during the period when the evaluation of costs and benefits is being made. The degree of the risk of humiliation, entailed during the course of the battle, and its weight in the evaluation by potential claimants, makes the decision whether or not to apply difficult, and so one likely to be substantially delayed. The evaluation is much influenced by whether the claimant can seek allies who might devise strategies and even fight with or for him. It is also influenced by perceptions about the enemies. The enemies are 'gatekeepers' who admit some and refuse others; in doing so, they apply explicit criteria that they themselves have devised, and implicit criteria which reflect their ideologies—ideologies that make them hostile to the claimant. Claimants think that gatekeepers seek to suppress demand. Partly with this aim, they conceal eligibility conditions from potential claimants. Dennis Marsden wrote: 'The local social security officials seemed to be operating informal rules to deny families the allocations for children's clothing and the replacement of household goods to which the regulations entitled them.'[3] This is so irrespective of whether the gatekeepers are those whose task is to administer service at the client interface, or to monitor the services and develop policies for them. Both are enemies, and 'they' conspire against the claimant. The claimant feels that he knows little about such eligibility criteria as exist. In order to make claiming more difficult, the enemy may force a series of costly and time-wasting skirmishes whose outcome is indecisive. Whether or not a battle is won is unlikely to be known until well after the encounter is concluded, and it is not necessarily the case that the fruits of victory will then be immediately forthcoming. The battle generally has to be re-fought periodically if the benefits are to be retained. Therefore both the costs and benefits of fighting the battle seem uncertain. Since the information about them is so imprecise, the interpretation is subjective. Partly for this reason, and partly because most of the important costs and benefits vary greatly between potential combatants, evaluations vary.

The second model has much in common with the first—the uncertainty about costs and benefits, and therefore the subjectivity of a combatant's appraisal of them, the variability of costs and benefits

[3] D. Marsden, 'The Roughs', *New Society*, *38*, 736, 1976, p. 300.

between combatants with different characteristics, the possibility that not one but several encounters will be required to determine the outcome, and the variety of actors with which the encounters take place. One crucial difference is that the encounters are with actors who at worst can be relied upon to dispense benefits but only grudgingly, and in a way that makes clear their prejudice; but at best with actors who co-operate with claimants and sympathize with them. A second difference is that claimants regard the system as neutral and at times actually on their side. A third is that it yields outcomes which claimants perceive to be predictable, given circumstances determined by objective criteria in such a way that the potential claimant does not see himself to be powerless. A fourth is that in general the potential claimant does not expect to be humiliated by others and (seeing the benefit as a right of citizenship) does not feel a loss of self-esteem in making his claim.

No one argues the validity of all the propositions in either model, far less that either model is universally valid as a whole. This is inevitable, since the models are not of causal processes (like those of Holman or Jordan),[4] but merely constitute clusters of perceptions which might be variously explained. All would agree that it is not difficult to discover large numbers of cases which would illustrate one or the other. The issues are rather whether either model fits the majority of cases, what is the quantitative importance of each, and what are the characteristics of those whose perceptions correspond in the most important particulars to the two ideal types. What proportion of mothers saw the free meals context as a battle with enemies in a hostile and unpredictable world is therefore crucial to an evaluation of the policy options available.

Part B throws more light on the beliefs and assumptions of mothers about the prevalence and causes of 'poverty', their responses to a question about what action should be taken about it, and so describes aspects of mothers' stereotypes. In contrast, in Part A an attempt is made to discover how they perceived their own experiences. It describes what mothers claimed to be their perceptions at each of three stages in the 'battle' to obtain the service. The first (discussed in Section I) is one which precedes the decision to apply. The focus of interest in this stage is the mothers' evaluation of costs, though some account is given of traumatic events that predispose mothers to apply. Section II deals with the second stage, that of the application itself. Again the focus is the subjective evaluation by mothers, but this time of their

[4] R. Holman, 'Poverty: consensus and alternatives', *The British Journal of Social Work*, 3, 4, Winter 1973, pp. 431–46; B. Jordan, *Paupers*, Routledge, London, 1973..

experiences of applying. Section 3 reports on mothers' perceptions of the reasons for the outcome. These are of interest both because the perceptions would have contributed to their evaluation at the first stage of any subsequent application, and because it was evidence that would affect the evaluations of others whom the mothers influenced. Section 4 outlines the responses of mothers to general questions about the reasons for non-uptake of free meals by those eligible for them.

The transition between stages is itself of importance, since it lays some stress on attrition as a cause of defeat. The first application is of most importance, since only a minority of the mothers of payers and non-takers had applied more than once. (On average less than one quarter had done so—much the same proportion as among the mothers of free meals receivers. As would be compatible with the argument of Chapter 1, the proportions were higher for the over-achieving authority for both the non-takers and free meals receivers.) Moreover our sample size was insufficient to study second and subsequent cycles. Therefore Table 3.1 shows the proportions 'surviving' from each stage to the next on the first occasion that the respondents considered applying.

Table 3.1   Probabilities of survival between the stages by which free meals were obtained on the first (or only) occasion on which an application was made

| | Transition from stages | | | |
| | 1 to 2 | | 2 to 3 | |
	U %	O %	U %	O %
Non-takers' mothers	27	18	86	100
Payers' mothers	10	14	67	82
Free meals receivers' mothers	75	84	96	97

Note: U denotes 'under-achieving area', O denotes 'over-achieving' area.

Part A   Mothers' Perceptions of their own Experience

The results make clear that attrition occurred mainly at this first stage. Among those who actually made an application, the probability of success was particularly high in the over-achieving authority.

I   Stage 1—The Decision to Apply for Free Meals

In this section, we examine the reasons for applying given by mothers who did not proceed to the next stage, the results of our search of data for symptoms of reluctance to apply, and mothers' statements about the traumatic events that contributed to the decision.

Table 3.2   *Proportions of families with no experience of free meals and who had not considered applying for free meals giving various reasons for not considering applying*

	Non-takers' sample		Payers' sample	
	U	O	U	O
	%	%	%	%
Income too high	26	36	50	41
Ineligible because working	7	3	5	7
Ignorance about free meals scheme	19	5	3	2
Unwillingness to reveal personal information	2	0	2	2
Pride as parents	4	8	7	12
Embarrassment to child	2	3	2	7
Disagreement with free meals in principle	0	3	2	4
Thought ineligible	17	10	17	18
Parental preference	19	10	2	0
No answer	6	26	15	16
Families who had no experience of free meals and did not consider applying %	100	100	100	100

Note: U denottes 'under-achieving' area, O denotes 'over-achieving' area.

(a) Reasons for not Applying

Mothers who had not considered applying were asked an open-ended question to discover their reasons. The results are summarized in Table 3.2. The table provides little evidence that stigma was of primary quantitative importance. The proportions imply that less than one family in ten of those who had considered applying did not do so because they were unwilling to reveal personal income or felt that applying would have injured their pride, or risked the embarrassment of their children. Substantial proportions in the non-takers' strata spoke vaguely about their 'preferences'. Some of these may have been influenced by expectations of stigma. However, our ability to make inferences was limited because it was impossible to collect data that would show the level of standardized income at the time when application for free meals was being considered. For instance, the difference between proportions of the two recipient groups who thought that income was too high probably reflects the difference in income distribution between them.

In the under-achieving authority, higher proportions stated that they did not think themselves to be eligible because of some reason that they left unspecified, or because they were at work (thus revealing a misapprehension about eligibility criteria). Similarly, higher proportions declared that they did not know much about the free meals scheme. The proportion stating specifically that their income was too high was greater in the over-achieving authority. These differences are compatible with the argument that the under-achieving authority had promoted the scheme less successfully than the over-achieving authority. The interviews conducted with teachers, head teachers, education welfare officers and other local authority officials suggested that the under-achieving authority had indeed made less promotional effort. The over-achieving authority had itself circulated parents, publicizing the free meals scheme and the eligibility criteria, before the Department of Education and Science decided to do so on a national scale. The under-achieving authority had taken no such step.

Promotion is one aspect of the effort made by authorities to secure an effective free meals service. In this, the education welfare officer (E.W.O.) is crucial. The ratio of E.W.O.s to school children was substantially higher in the over-achieving authority. Indeed, this was generally so when a comparison was made between the ratios for the over-achieving and under-achieving authorities among those visited. For this reason, cases were more frequently reviewed in the over-achieving authority, the under-achieving authority being unable to maintain the biennial reviews required by Circular 9/64. (This partly explains why our survey showed a higher rate of turnover amongst receivers in the over-achieving authority.) Moreover, as the Ralphs Report[5] has shown, the functions of the E.W.O. are extremely diverse. In the under-achieving authority, the assistant to the chief E.W.O. saw the role of his education welfare officers to be almost exclusively that of an attendance officer. (In this authority, the Victorian image was

[5] Local Government Training Board, *Report of the Working Party on the Role and Training of Education Welfare Officers*, Local Government Training Board, London, 1975.

reinforced by the Victorian high clerks' desks at which the education welfare officers worked. However, the E.W.O.s had clearly been kept abreast with some of the developments of administrative technology: biros had replaced quills.) In the over-achieving authority, the officers did not actually make the income assessments, there being a separate assessments branch of the school meals service; and there were other indications that their time was used more effectively than in some other authorities. This reflected itself in communications with parents. For instance, in the over-achieving authority, the district E.W.O. visited each secondary school in the area once a week, so being more geographically accessible to parents seeking personal contact. Similarly it was reflected in contacts with class teachers, the E.W.O. being well known in the staff room.

Secondly, variations in authorities' concern were reflected in the interviews with teachers and head teachers. In the over-achieving authority, there appeared to be a more precise understanding of the limits of a head teacher's discretion to give meals on an emergency basis. The vagueness of the head teachers' understanding probably reflected a lack of priority being given to the service by the headquarters organization. The uncertainty as well as the lack of specificity as part of a job definition could well have induced a more conservative response from head teachers—a lowering of the probability that the head teacher would think of and risk giving emergency meals. This would particularly be the case among head teachers whose own attitudes were unsympathetic. It is when their remit is most vague that the ideology of the gatekeepers themselves are most likely to influence outcomes, and when the unsympathetic head is most likely to depress uptake by postponing action until mothers and children have grown used to coping with the consequences of an emergency without free meals.

(b) Symptoms of Reluctance among those who had Applied

The questionnaire sought data about various symptoms that families were reluctant to apply—time spent thinking about applying, what mothers considered when thinking about applying for the first time, and whether traumatic events were needed to force a decision.

(i) Time Spent Thinking about Applying

For those families in the sample who had applied for free meals, a quite substantial proportion claimed that they had thought about their first or only application for a long time before applying. Substantial proportions in each group claimed that they had thought about it for what they considered to be 'a long time' before applying, the proportions varying between one person in five in the non-taking group of the over-achieving authority to two persons in five in the same group of the under-achieving authority. This area difference is what would be expected from our argument of Chapter 1. It existed also among free meals receivers who were eligible on income grounds at the time of the survey. However, more than 60 per cent of persons in each group claimed to have thought about their first application for one month or less. Only among free meals receivers was there a minority who thought about it for more than a year. The question that asked for the actual time spent waiting confirmed that among the samples of non-takers and free meals receivers, families waited longer in the under-achieving authority than in the over-achieving authority.

Whatever factors may have caused families in the sample to hesitate 'for a long time' when they first applied had lost their force by the time they had applied for the last time. It would seem that they had lost their impact most in the over-achieving area. All of those who had

Table 3.3 *Families applying for free school meals (for first or only time) by thoughts during the time when considering applying*

	Non-takers		Payers		Free	
	%	n	%	n	%	n
Area U						
(a) Stigma awareness	5	1	25	2	18	9
(b) Uncertainty about eligibility	5	1	0	0	12	6
(c) Awareness of entitlement	71	15	62	5	46	24
(d) Bandwagon effect	0	0	0	0	4	2
(e) Other thoughts	19	4	13	1	20	10
Total families applying	100	21	100	8	100	51
Area O						
(a) Stigma awareness	25	3	9	1	11	7
(b) Uncertainty about eligibility	0	0	9	1	14	9
(c) Awareness of entitlement	58	7	64	7	62	41
(d) Bandwagon effect	0	0	9	1	1	1
(e) Other thoughts	17	2	9	1	12	8
Total families applying	100	12	100	11	100	66

applied more than once stated that they had thought about it for less than a month on the last occasion. Both the experience and the area effects are interesting—the former because it implies that on balance experience did not reinforce any reluctance to apply.

(ii) Thoughts when Considering Applying

Table 3.3 is based on answers to an open-ended question. These answers were coded in such a way that the number of respondents making different types of reply could be distinguished and counted. The types distinguished were answers that indicated that the context had some potential for stigmatizing either parent or child; uncertainty about eligibility; replies which implied an awareness of entitlement. The last we called a 'bandwagon effect', and included replies like 'other people are claiming—why shouldn't I?'

A number of mothers made statements that implied a concern with stigma, but it was a minority. An analysis of proportions quoting stigma factors by standardized income groups within meals and area groups showed that those eligible on income grounds tended to be no more likely to quote 'stigma factors' than others of their group; indeed they seemed to be less likely to do so. Awareness of entitlement was the main factor named by mothers.

Much the same proportions of those who had had experience of applying before stated that stigma factors were on their mind in thinking about applying on the last occasion. These are by no means easy results to interpret. Could it be that even by this midway stage of the interview, our interviewers had failed to establish adequate rapport, and were therefore likely to have understated the importance of stigma? This seems unlikely, since by that stage of the interview, parents had answered questions *inter alia* about their attitudes to the school, and had given information about their families, consumption of school meals in general, and free meals in particular. They had done so in a manner that was frank and full, judging from the consistency of the results, and the relative extensiveness of claims to have applied for free meals among the payers and non-takers. It is also unlikely, given our effort to recruit good interviewers and brief them carefully. Indeed, we had expected from the characteristics of our interviewers that any bias arising from interactions with them would be in the opposite direction. Again, the high response rate to difficult questions and a long interview also throws doubt on the argument that the rapport was inadequate.

Alternatively, was it that it is of the nature of stigma not to admit an awareness of your 'spoiled identity', even though you openly declare that you possess the attributes which spoil the identity? If the possession of an attribute which is not discernible unless information about it is volunteered by the possessor was held to be stigmatizing, would not at least some people have preferred not to volunteer the information that they possessed the attribute?

> When his differentness is not immediately apparent and is not known beforehand (or at least not known by him to be known to the others), when he is in fact a discreditable, not a discredited, person, then the second main possibility in his life is to be found. The issue is not that of managing tension created during social contact, but rather that of managing information about his failing. To display or not to display; to tell or not to tell; to let or not to let on; to lie or not to lie; and, in each case, to whom, how, when and where.[6]

One would have thought that in the once and for all encounter of the interview between strangers in circumstances of relative anonymity where confidentiality had been guaranteed, persons who thought about stigma aspects in considering school meals would have said so if such thoughts had been uppermost in their mind. Of course this is not to argue that stigma is not of importance to the decision maker. In the current state of the literature, it is not necessary to establish its existence. What is of importance is to establish whether or not it is of primary importance to the decision-taking of many, and whether it colours their perception of the school and society in general.

(iii) Factors Influencing the Decision to Apply

Additionally respondents were asked whether they could point to anything which made them apply for free meals for the first or only time. The results are shown in Table 3.4.

A fall in household income. A fall in household income was the most frequently mentioned factor in all groups. The proportions varied little between the groups. Loss of income due to the sickness of a wage earner was clearly important. It was named as the cause of loss of income in approximately one half of the free meals receivers in each area, and was quoted as the reason for their loss in income in 42 of the 102 families whose mothers claimed that their loss of income was the factor which made them decide to apply. Unemployment, short-

[6] E. Goffman, *Stigma*, Penguin, Harmondsworth, 1968, p. 57.

time working, redundancy, retirement was the second most important set of reasons quoted; appearing in 30 out of 102 answers. It was particularly important among the free meals receivers' sample for the under-achieving authority where it was named by two-fifths of respondents. The area effect is compatible with the under-achievement argument, since claiming free meals by the family of the unemployed creates circumstances which give rise to fewer problems to the applicant than claiming them in most other contexts. Also important for free meals receivers' families in the over-achieving authority was the drop in income caused by the absence of the wage earner due to death or other reasons. In this group it was named in 11 out of the 40 answers quoting a drop in income.

Table 3.4   Families by what factors were stated to make them decide to apply for free meals for the first (or only) time

	Non-takers' families		Payers' families		Free meals receivers' families	
	U %	O %	U %	O %	U %	O %
Drop in incomes expenditure	59	50	59	44	59	54
Publicity	12	7	8	11	7	8
Influenced by others	24	43	17	22	19	22
Other answers	5	0	16	23	15	16
Total per cent	100	100	100	100	100	100
number	(17	(14)	(12)	(9)	(58)	(74)

The influence of others. The second most frequent category consisted of answers which specified the influence of others. This was named more frequently among the samples in the over-achieving authority, particularly among the non-takers' families where the difference was significant at the $2\frac{1}{2}$ per cent level. The employees of the education department—teachers and education welfare officers—were important, accounting for more than one half of replies in each of the samples. That the proportions were higher in the over-achieving authority is therefore important to our argument. Ministry of Social Security officers were mentioned less than half as many times. Only four respondents mentioned the influence of friends or acquaintances, relatives or neighbours; two from the free meals sample for the over-achieving authority, and the same number from the equivalent sample for the under-achieving authority.

Asked specifically about the help of others, most mothers stated that other people were important in advising, assisting, or encouraging the respondent to apply for free meals. The proportion was lowest in non-takers' families in the under-achieving authority (53 per cent), and highest for the same meals group in the over-achieving authority. The proportion was higher in the over-achieving authority for free meals receivers also. Both these area differences are significant at the $2\frac{1}{2}$ per cent level. The differences exist irrespective of the degree of importance on which the comparison is based. The theory of over- and under-achievement must clearly be important to the explanation of the area differences in uptake rates.

Table 3.5   Analysis of respondents' statements about which persons were important in advising, assisting or encouraging them to apply for free meals for the first (or only) time[1]

Sample and area[2]	Non-takers' families		Payers' families		Free meals receivers' families	
Classification of person	U %	O %	U %	O %	U %	O %
(a) Persons employed by the L.E.A.						
(i) working within the school	30	40	62	50	47	38
(ii) education welfare officer	10	13	38	13	21	31
(b) Other social workers or public officials[3]	20	13	25	13	18	19
(c) Relatives, friends, neighbours	30	27	0	38	13	14
(d) Children of the family attending school	0	0	13	0	0	0
Number of families %	100	100	100	100	100	100
N	10	15	8	8	38	58

Notes: [1] The count was based on those considering other people 'very important', 'quite important', and 'not very important'.
    [2] U denotes the 'under-achieving' authority and O denotes the 'over-achieving'.
    [3] Includes the parish priest.

Table 3.5 summarizes respondents' statements about which persons were important. Clearly, they are the employees of the L.E.A.s themselves; particularly those working inside the schools—head teachers, teachers, and school secretaries. This applies notably to the head teacher. Two-thirds of those quoting someone in the school specified him. The degree to which head teachers took seriously their responsibilities for seeing that the needy children obtained welfare benefits was clearly of great importance to the process of getting potentially eligible families to apply for free meals for their children. 'Social workers' appeared unimportant.

Respondents were asked how much people were of help. The results showed that their contribution was not merely to mention the existence of free meals, or indeed to encourage and to persuade mothers to apply. Their importance was that they advised, gave help, or actually assumed responsibility for the application. This was the case for more than three-quarters of first applicants in each of the six groups. Again the proportions of mothers who were helped to this degree was consistently higher in the over-achieving authority. What was described as 'advice' was the most frequent form of service in all groups, the giving of help being next in frequency. It is clear that people obtained such services even when they had made at least one application previously.

Other publicity. Other forms of publicity were named relatively infrequently. In most of these answers, the 'personal circular' from the Ministry of Education explaining the existence of educational welfare benefits was referred to. This leaflet had been issued too recently before the survey to have influenced a high proportion of applicants. Most respondents could recall having received the D.E.S. publicity pamphlet some seven months before the survey was conducted. However, as high a proportion as one-half of non-takers in the under-achieving authority could not recall this leaflet. High proportions of respondents who had recalled having received the D.E.S. leaflet thought it helped them to understand how the scheme worked. Of those who could not recall it, low proportions could remember having received any information at all from the school about free meals prior to the time of the leaflet. Where mothers recalled that such information had been given, its principal means of distribution was verbal—mainly through the teacher or the head teacher telling the respondents. Other than the school, the most important sources of information were the mass media; radio, television, and newspapers. The proportions of mothers quoting the mass media were higher in the over-achieving authority, as were the proportions stating that local authority personnel provided direct information. No doubt the media themselves reflect authorities' attitudes towards and success in promoting services as well as having an independent influence.

(c) Predisposing and Other Events during the Year before the Application was Made

Mothers were asked what events during the twelve months preceding the application might have caused a need, created an awareness of need, or triggered off a procedure which had led to an application for free meals. The answers implied that a decrease in family income occurred in most of the families which had subsequently applied for the first time. The frequency of a positive response for each of the groups is shown in Table 3.6. The proportions did not differ greatly between the groups, save between non-takers in the over-achieving authority where it was lower than in the under-achieving authority. In the under-achieving authority, perhaps it took a drastic fall in income to make a higher proportion of families apply from the group who were most likely to contain families eligible for free meals. A decrease in family income also occurred in the twelve months preceding the last application. This was so for five of the six families who answered the question in the non-takers' samples, two of the three in

Table 3.6 Families applying for free meals for the first (or only) time by whether named events had occurred during the twelve months preceding the application

	Non-takers' families		Payers' families		Free meals receivers' families	
	%	No	%	No	%	No
'Under-achieving' authority						
(a) a new baby to take care of	42	19	27	11	45	67
(b) an illness, injury or death in the family	56	18	42	12	46	67
(c) a decrease in family income	78	18	75	12	75	65
(d) an increase in family income	0	17	9	11	6	65
(e) a change in employment for anyone in the family	31	16	50	12	46	63
Number of families applying	—	19	—	16	—	68
'Over-achieving' authority						
(a) a new baby to take care of	58	12	55	11	43	69
(b) an illness, injury or death in the family	44	16	58	12	56	71
(c) a decrease in family income	50	14	73	11	68	78
(d) an increase in family income	10	10	10	10	2	56
(e) a change in employment for	50	8	50	10	25	59
Number of families applying	—	13	—	12	—	81

Note: This table summarizes the replies to five independent questions, the answers which were counted separately. The number of persons answering the questions are shown in the column headed N. The proportions stated are the proportions of those answering the specific question answering in the affirmative.

the payers samples, and twenty-two of the thirty-one in the free meals receivers samples.

A new baby was also a frequent occurrence during the twelve months preceding the first application. It was of equal frequency in the two areas in the free meals receivers samples. It was more frequent among the payers in the over-achieving authority. This was partly due to the higher proportion of large families among payers in the over-achieving authority (which had a large Irish-Catholic component in its population). On the last occasion when payers sample mothers who had applied more than once made an application, only one of the seven stated that a baby had been born within the preceding twelve months. The corresponding proportions for the non-takers and free meals receivers samples respectively were one out of five, and eleven out of thirty-nine. Additions to the family may have been less frequent in the twelve months preceding the application among those who had applied before than among those applying for the first time.

An illness, injury, or death in the family, too, was an event which happened in a high proportion of families during the twelve months before their first application. The proportions were not greatly different in the samples. It would seem from Table 3.6 that in several of the households both injury, illness, or death, and the arrival of a new baby had occurred. For a high proportion of the households in which there had been injury, illness, or death, the victim had been the father. The relative unimportance of the mother as a victim compared with the father is noticeable. The same pattern of relative importance of father and relative unimportance of the mother was evident in the figures for the twelve months preceding the last application.

A change in employment of a member of the family occurred among a substantial proportion of families. Among free meals receivers, the proportions were lower in the over-achieving authority sample. These differences are significant at the 5 per cent level. Again, a change in the father's employment was more probable than in the mother's. Similarly the corresponding figures, relating to the period preceding the last application of those who had made more than one application, yielded a similar pattern.

II   Stage 2: Experiences of Applying

(a) Whether Making the Application was Considered Difficult

High proportions of those who had applied claimed to find the procedure simple rather than difficult. They were particularly high (more than 90 per cent) among free meals samples. They are reconcilable with what is known about the prevalence of inadequate degrees of literacy only when interpreted in the light of the proportions of families receiving help of the kind described earlier in this chapter. However, the desire not to admit to a stigmatizing degree of illiteracy may well have affected the answers. Illiteracy may well have been more stigmatizing than receiving free meals. Only one person in our sample quoted problems with understanding the form as a difficulty in making an application.

Respondents who found the procedures for applying difficult were asked to specify at what stage the difficulties occurred. The principal difficulty was in completing the form, this being experienced by fourteen of the twenty-two cases who admitted to difficulties. Difficulty in providing evidence of income was admitted by seven respondents, and in finding out whom to contact by five.

(b) Whether the Application Procedures had Unpleasant or Objectionable Aspects

Respondents were asked whether any particular aspects of making the application were found unpleasant or objectionable. One mother in five did so among groups other than payers and free meals receivers in the under-achieving authority, where the proportions were much lower.

(c) Who was Contacted First when Applicants had Decided that they Wanted to Apply

Between one-half and two-thirds of mothers in each group (except free meals receivers in the over-achieving authority) made their first contact with persons working at the school. Among free meals receivers in the over-achieving authority, contact was more frequently made with the education welfare officer. Perhaps this is partially explained by his greater accessibility (described in Section I(a) above). The teacher (rather than the head teacher or school secretary) was the first contact for most of the families in each group who specified exactly who was approached first. School secretaries were the least important, being quoted in all by only three respondents. The head teachers were less important than one would have anticipated. There was no clear difference between samples whose 'named child' was from primary schools and those whose 'named child' was from secondary schools, so that there is no clear evidence that the head teacher or secretary was more or less important as a first contact in primary than secondary schools. Among those who had applied on more than one occasion, the teacher was also the person most frequently contacted the last time an application was made. Thus in this aspect of applying for free meals also, the employees of education departments themselves played the crucial roles. The attitudes of teachers could well have had a large effect on which children took up their entitlement.

III   Stage 3: The Results of the Application

(a) Proportion of Applications Successful

That there were high proportions of first (or only) applications being successful implies that most applications were made only when the need was clear. This is entirely compatible with our earlier assertions that many who were eligible had refrained from applying.[7] There is also a suggestion that the proportions accepted may have been higher in the over-achieving authority. Perhaps that authority (if anything) may have erred more on the side of generosity in the discretionary components of its assessments. It is also possible that the population of the over-achieving authority contained a greater number of poorer families.

Among families who had applied more than once, the comparable figures relating to their last application also yielded high proportions of applicants granted free meals. All twenty-six applicants in the over-achieving authority were successful, and this was also so for sixteen of the seventeen in the under-achieving authority. High proportions of families whose applications were successful were granted free meals for all their children; the proportions exceeded 75 per cent in all groups. The proportions were similar among those in the most recent application. There was also a tendency for the proportions to have been higher in the over-achieving authority.

(b) Reasons for rejecting unsuccessful applicants

Two-thirds of those stating whether they had been told why they had been rejected answered in the affirmative in the under-achieving authority. All did so in the over-achieving authority.

[7] Bleddyn Davies and Mike Reddin, 'School meals and Plowden', *New Society*, 11 May 1967, pp. 690–2; and Hilary Land, *Large Families in London*, Bell, London, 1970.

IV Respondents' Opinions about the Reasons for the Widespread Non-Uptake of Free Meals by those Eligible

It was suggested in the discussion of the results of Table 3.3 that respondents may have been unwilling to admit the fact that they thought receiving free school meals spoiled their identity (or that of their children); although they were willing to admit to receiving free meals. There are other problems. People may not have been fully aware of the degree to which they felt that taking school meals stigmatized their children or themselves; they may have been unwilling to admit it to themselves. Their actions may have been substantially constrained by the feeling of stigma at the unconscious level. Further, they may have felt that it was irrational to have a personal feeling of spoiled identity when they claimed free meals as a right. Society admires rational behaviour and to some degree deprecates irrational behaviour, especially when it is at the expense of other members of society, particularly children. Thus respondents may have felt a strong need to rationalize their behaviour to the interviewer, and thus not to admit that the irrational stigma arising when free meals were claimed affected their attitudes towards applying for them, although receiving free meals would have benefited their children. Indeed admitting this would have been tantamount to a failure to bear one of the responsibilities of parenthood, just as admitting that the family qualified for free meals might have been taken by the wage-earner as an admission of failure to bear his or her responsibilities. Such admissions might have been very damaging to the self-esteem of both parents. It is therefore quite likely that stigma feelings were kept at a subconscious level; or that, if respondents were conscious of them, they would not have been admitted openly to an interviewer.

Faced with such problems, social psychologists use 'projection techniques'. In the time available it would not have been feasible to develop a way of using them with any rigour in our research. But asking people's opinions about what motivates people in general allowed us to make use of an important finding that underlies much work in the sociology and psychology of political behaviour—that deep-seated attitudes which, for the type of reason we have discussed, are not stated openly in an interview situation, are 'projected' on to people in general. However, the replies to such questions remain ambiguous. Studies of political socialization show us that we learn sets of political stereotypes and myths. These relate only crudely to the complex real situations, and are much influenced by past circumstances which are no longer relevant. People's opinions about the attitudes of others to means-tested services may have provided an example of this. Thus people may themselves no longer (even subconsciously) have felt that receiving a means-tested service was stigmatizing, but may have continued to feel that other people in the same circumstances would have thought it stigmatizing to a degree which would have affected their behaviour. If, therefore, we find that people thought that stigma was an important determinant of the behaviour of others, it was possible that one or other or both of the following propositions might have held: first, that stigma remained of relevance to individual's behaviour; and second, that there was a widespread belief that stigma did affect behaviour with respect to means-tested service.

The question was asked in two ways. First, all parents were asked

Table 3.7   *Proportions of respondents giving various explanations of why eligible families did not apply for free school meals*

	Non-takers' families		Payers' families		Free meals receivers' families	
	U %	O %	U %	O %	U %	O %
(a) Stigma (including parents' pride or shame, or the dislike of the invasion of privacy involved)	39	43	48	55	40	39
(b) Ignorance (including not realizing that they are eligible, not knowing about free meals, not understanding the system	35	24	40	22	18	20
(c) Dislike of food	12	18	5	7	19	17
(d) Parents can afford to pay	6	0	2	7	2	1
(e) Parents apathetic	0	4	7	6	12	10
(f) Prefer to eat at home	4	11	0	3	5	10
(g) Others	6	2	2	0	4	1
Total number of persons giving codable explanation %	100	100	100	100	100	100
Number	66	56	61	71	67	69
Total number of respondents to the survey Number	77	68	79	79	68	81

Note: U denotes 'under-achieving' area, O denotes 'over-achieving' area.

why some children eligible for free meals did not take them. They were allowed to answer this in their own words, and their answers were recorded as fully as possible. Second, they were asked whether they agreed with a specific set of propositions. The question was asked in the first manner so that the relative priority of reasons in respondents' minds should show through, so that the actual wording could be analysed, and so that the danger of not obtaining information about reasons that people considered to be important would be lessened. The question was asked in the second manner so that we could ensure a more complete coverage of reasons which our knowledge of the field suggested are important, and so that we could factor analyse scores.

Table 3.7 shows an analysis of replies to the open-ended question. Feelings of pride, shame, or the invasion of privacy formed the most important type of reply in each sample group. Not unexpectedly, this feeling was strongest among the paying samples in each area, and low among free meals recipients. (The paying sample contained a higher proportion of small better-off families, the free meals samples the highest proportion of large low-income families.) However, the proportions quoting stigma factors were rather similar. Second in overall importance to stigma were statements to the effect that parents did not know about the service or understand its working. These were particularly important among the non-takers and payers samples in the under-achieving authority. The differences between the proportions in the two authorities in each of the two samples was large enough to reject the null hypothesis of no association between the populations at the one per cent level of significance. This also is a result of great interest to our argument of Chapter 1.

Other results are of interest. One is the gradient between the three groups in each area in the proportions stating that they disliked the food served in schools. It supports the argument that social class and income gradient in food consumption patterns was a not unimportant factor in determining uptake. (This argument has been put, for instance, by Hilary Land.)[8]

Table 3.8 shows proportions of parents who agreed with various propositions about what were the important reasons why eligible children did not receive free meals. These results confirm and elaborate some of the conclusions drawn from the analysis of the replies to the open-ended question. The first is that aspects of stigma other than teachers' inverse favouritism were thought by most to be important. Stigmatiza-

[8] Hilary Land, 'Provisions for Large Families', *New Society*, 23 November 1966; and *Large Families in London*, op. cit.

Table 3.8   Proportions of respondents agreeing with propositions as important explanations of why eligible children did not receive free school meals

	Non-takers' families		Payers' families		Free meals receivers' families	
	%	N[1]	%	N[1]	%	N[1]
'Under-achieving' authority						
(a) Do not need them	32	76	27	79	53	68
(b) Other children stigmatize receivers	58	77	61	79	56	68
(c) Teachers pick on receivers	30	77	15	79	10	68
(d) Thought to be charity	70	76	70	79	78	68
(e) Application too complicated	51	76	56	79	34	68
(f) Don't like stating incomes	44	77	70	79	76	68
(g) Don't like employer to know that applying	57	77	54	79	50	68
(h) Don't know about the service	74	77	70	79	60	68
'Over-achieving' authority						
(a) Do not need them	40	67	27	78	19	81
(b) Other children stigmatize receivers	68	68	65	79	62	81
(c) Teachers pick on receivers	12	68	15	79	12	81
(d) Thought to be charity	82	68	75	79	78	81
(e) Application too complicated	43	68	52	79	25	81
(f) Don't like stating incomes	65	68	63	79	74	81
(g) Don't like employer to know that applying	57	68	52	79	63	81
(h) Don't know about the service	63	68	47	79	46	81

Note: [1] Number of persons giving an answer referring to the proposition. The percentages are proportions of this number.

tion by other children was thought to be important—less important than the parents' own dislike of receiving charity, and in some samples less important than the dislike of stating incomes, but more important than not liking the employer to know; and more important than the fear of teachers 'picking on' free meals children. A second feature is that the proportions tended to be higher in the answers to the stigma-related questions for the over-achieving authority's samples, particularly among the crucial free meals receivers' and non-takers' groups. This is at least indirect evidence implying that one should not attribute all the over-achievement of the authority to a perception by the population that the service had less potential for stigmatization. However, completely compatible with the authority argument of Chapter 1 was the result that a much higher proportion of the non-takers' group in the under-achieving than over-achieving group thought that teachers were expected to 'pick on' free meals recipients more.

A third feature was that the two ignorance statements in general obtained less support than some of the stigma propositions. More interesting, perhaps, was the difference in proportions between the under-achieving and over-achieving authority for the two 'ignorance' propositions. In both cases, the proportions of the under-achieving area were higher. Also, the differences were greater for the second statement—involving complete ignorance of the existence of the service —than the first. This cannot be accounted for by the differences in the proportions of the samples which were from the newer Commonwealth countries, although it may to some extent have been accounted for by the characteristics of Irish-born populations which were more prevalent in the over-achieving authority. In part, it may have been due to better promotion of the service by the over-achieving authority.

Part B Beliefs about the Causes of Poverty and Appropriate Policy Interventions

This part describes the beliefs of mothers about the causes of poverty, and the values which interact with these beliefs, and assumptions about the costs and consequences of intervention, to produce a judgement about what action would be appropriate. The beliefs and the proposals for action partly resulting from them are important for two reasons. First, they influence mothers' responses to their own problems and opportunities. Secondly, they provide further information useful for assessing what policies would have been acceptable.

Respondents were asked whose fault it was that people were in poverty. The replies are tabulated in Table 3.9. The most frequent reply among the non-takers' and payers' strata was that it was the fault of the poor themselves, the second most frequent being the attribution of blame to a combination of factors. The order of importance of the two categories was reversed in the free meals receivers' strata; but even among free meals receivers, more than 35 per cent of respondents attributed the blame to the poor themselves.[9] The mothers had also

[9] This phenomenon is general. In 'Policies towards the unemployed' in *Dear David Donnison*, Michael Hill quoted from F. Herron's *Labour Market in Crisis*, Macmillan, London, 1975, p. 142: 'Many of the men expressing contempt for the "regulars" had experienced considerable difficulty in getting back into work and were often again unemployed when interviewed. This, one might have thought, would have persuaded them to see other unemployed men in a different light ... (but) it was their concern with "layabouts" which they chose to emphasise.'

Table 3.9   *Proportions of respondents attributing the blame for poverty on various factors*

	Non-payers' sample		Payers' sample		Free meals receivers' sample	
	U %	O %	U %	O %	U %	O %
'If people are in poverty it's mainly':						
(a) 'their own fault'	44	47	48	42	38	35
(b) 'the Government's fault'	3	3	8	3	2	12
(c) 'the fault of their education'	4	5	1	4	4	4
(d) 'the fault of industry (for) not paying better wages'	3	8	3	4	12	6
(e) 'a combination of some of these'	34	36	30	43	43	48
(f) 'none of these'	4	0	5	0	0	0
(g) 'anything else'	4	0	1	1	0	3
(h) 'don't know'	5	15	4	4	2	4
Number of respondents replying	77	66	79	79	68	80

been asked whether 'there was such a thing as *real* poverty these days'. Surprisingly, less than one half of the mothers agreed, the proportions among the mothers of free receivers being little different from others. That an appreciation of the extent of poverty was not widespread is an inadequate explanation, since proportions were not higher among poorer groups. It has been suggested that the word 'poverty', particularly the expression 'real poverty', conveyed stigma to some persons. Perhaps an admission of the existence of 'real poverty' may have made it more difficult, rather than easier, for people to claim free meals. Perhaps if some people could have kept their realization that their children were in need of (and eligible for) free meals separate from an idea that they were in 'real poverty', they may have been more likely to apply. If this were so, it would have been of considerable importance for the debate about the tools of universal or selective provision, since it might be predicted that the more widespread and automatic the range of provision accompanying eligibility, the greater the association of eligibility with poverty, and thus the greater the stigma felt in receiving the services.

Mothers' responses to the question about whether real poverty existed were strongly correlated with the answers to the question of what could be done about poverty. Most of the persons who did not agree that 'real poverty' existed did not make a codable statement. Answers were coded so as to record the number of persons making positive suggestions for collective action, those predominantly stressing that people should do more to help themselves (for instance, by better household management), and those who implied that little or nothing could be done. Table 3.10 shows the proportions whose answers fell into each category. One half of the respondents answering the question suggested some form of collective or State action. Some suggested that the Government should raise the level of employment. Others suggested the redistribution of income, the cutting of prices, the raising of wages, pensions, and benefits. (Few—nineteen from all groups in both areas—suggested more benefits in kind or vouchers rather than cash.) A number (larger in the over- than under-achieving authority) suggested the increased detection and investigation of poverty. A few suggested increased education, for instance in home management and child care. Answers suggesting that poor people might do more to help themselves (for instance, by working harder or by better management) were less frequent among the free meals receivers and non-takers' mothers in the over-achieving authority than among others; but the minority remained substantial.

Table 3.10 *Proportions of respondents whose suggestions about action about poverty could be categorized as collective action, self-help by the poor and fatalistic*

	Non-takers' families %	Payers' families %	Free meals receivers' families %
'Under-achieving' authority			
(a) Collective and Government action	50	54	55
(b) Self-help	35	32	19
(c) Fatalistic[2]	12	7	10
Number of respondents[1]	34	41	42
'Over-achieving' authority			
(a) Collective and Government action	67	48	47
(b) Self-help	15	33	27
(c) Fatalistic[2]	0	2	7
Number of respondents[1]	27	42	45

Notes: [1] Number of respondents giving codable replies.
[2] For instance, 'very little, or nothing can be done'.

Conclusions

This chapter presents the survey evidence about the perceptions of mothers of the free meals service. The following are the principal results:

1. Actually making the decision to apply appeared to be crucially important, since high proportions of those who did apply were successful, particularly among mothers from the over-achieving area. In general, applications were made only when the need for meals was clear.

2. Stigma did not appear to be a primary reason for non-application among mothers who did not apply; though it was clearly important for a minority of mothers. The result suggested that the lack of knowledge was more important in the under-achieving area—a result that was not surprising in view of the greater effort made to promote the service by the over-achieving authority.

3. Most mothers claimed to have thought about applying for a month or less. Mothers from the under-achieving area appeared to have hesitated about applying for a longer period than mothers from the over-achieving area.

4. A fall in household *per capita* income was named by most applicants as the factor which caused them to apply. However, the influence of others (particularly employees of the Education Department) was also mentioned frequently, particularly by mothers from the over-achieving area. The help given by these employees was often substantial. Applicants received more than encouragement to apply: in a substantial proportion of cases, the employees advised, gave help, or actually assumed responsibility for the application. Not only was the influence of others mentioned more often by mothers from the over-achieving area, but also the help given by the employees of the L.E.A. appeared to be greater in that area.

5. High proportions of mothers claimed that they did not find the procedure difficult.

6. Most respondents thought that feelings of pride, shame, or the invasion of privacy were the most important reason why some parents did not take up their children's entitlement.

7. Large minorities of mothers, even mothers of receivers, tended to attribute the blame for poverty on the poor themselves. Only a minority thought that real poverty still existed. Although of those who made suggestions about action about poverty, a majority sug-

gested State intervention, substantial minorities reacted to the question by saying that the poor should do more to help themselves.

The opening paragraphs of this chapter postulated two models of mothers' perceptions. On balance, the results of this survey suggest that the second is more generally applicable than the first. On the whole mothers did not appear to think that people were powerless to prevent themselves from being in poverty. Of those who did not apply, most did not quote the stigma of applying for or receiving free meals to be the most important reason for not claiming their entitlement, and the potential for stigmatization did not appear to weigh heavily on the minds of most mothers who did apply during the period when they were considering whether or not to do so. The employees of the Education Department were not so much seen as 'gatekeepers' applying explicit and implicit criteria, based on ideologies antipathetic to claimants to prevent some from obtaining their entitlement, but as 'brokers' who actively helped mothers and encouraged potential recipients to claim. Of course some of these data are imprecise, and survey data on perceptions of complex issues must always be fragile. More important, we are not here discussing the reasons for the mothers' perceptions. All that we infer is that it would have been incorrect to argue that more than a minority of mothers saw the application for and receipt of this means-tested benefit as a battle against hostile agents of society, a battle whose outcome was arbitrarily determined by the caprice of these agents. The perceptions of most mothers provide little support for those who would make the abolition of means tests itself an ultimate objective in the war against social injustice. On the contrary, they provide support for those that argue that to do so might in some circumstances needlessly hamper the conduct of the campaign. We defer until Chapters 4 and 5 our attempt to understand better the reasons for these perceptions.

Except in contrasting the perceptions of mothers from the two areas and those of mothers whose named children were in different meal groups, this chapter has presented evidence about the perceptions of mothers as a group. No attempt was made to describe differences among mothers classified by causally important characteristics. Before we can undertake such an analysis, we must develop our theoretical argument. This is the subject of Chapter 4.

PART II: THE CAUSAL ANALYSIS

4 The Explanation of the Non-Uptake of Free Meals: A Theoretical Framework

Our task in Chapters 4 and 5 is to explain non-uptake. In the first of these chapters, a theoretical link is established between the non-uptake of means-tested services, broad structural factors, and the relationship between perceptions about the structure of society and the normative bases for social policy. In it, we attempt to show how the narrower contextual factors which this literature has suggested to be of influence fits into the broader context. Our analysis is therefore of factors operating at two levels of generality. One level is that of relationships between selectivity and alienation in the context of a general theory of motivation. The other is that of contextual factors, much of whose true importance lies in their relationship with the more general causes.

Three main types of contextual factors specific to the uptake of means-tested services in general (and free meals in particular) are emphasized in the political and academic discussions: the stigmatization of those that apply for and receive the services; the lack of precise information about the services; and difficulties in handling the procedures by which the services are obtained. Although the implicit assessments of the relative importance of these factors differed, all three reasons were quoted by commentators when it first became clear that there were at least as many eligible children not taking free meals as were receiving them. For instance, a document prepared by the social policy sub-committee of the National Executive Committee of the Labour Party stated: 'where tests of means are involved, those in greatest need often fail to apply, either through ignorance of their rights, dislike of the means-testing procedure, or the difficulty found by the less educated and articulate in coming forward to establish their entitlement'.[1] Similar sets of factors have been listed by other studies

[1] Quoted by Alfred Morris, M.P. (*H.C. DEB., 1967/8, 759*, Col. 608). Molly Meacher lists more reasons, but we treat some that she distinguishes as cases of our broader types. (See Molly Meacher, *Rate Rebates: A Study of the Effectiveness of Means Tests*, London, Child Poverty Action Group, 1973.)

of means-tested services. The factors are proximate not ultimate causes: indeed, they are causal factors immediately prior to behaviour in the causal sequence. We shall not understand their operation unless they are seen in the context of more general theory which maps them as points of intersection in a causal network.

How the evidence of the survey should be handled depends upon what we expect to be the main features of the network. An examination of the literature suggests that the three proximate causes are in turn influenced by substantially different sets of factors. Therefore it would seem reasonable to analyse the causes of variations in each of them separately. What part contextual factors play in the network is also important for how we should handle the evidence. Their presence may enhance the impact of such general causes as alienation and anomie: the contextual factors may operate indirectly through their influence on the general causes; or they may have a direct as well as this indirect effect. It is with such considerations in mind that we must discuss the contribution of the literature to the task of delineating the causal network.

The Literature and the Causal Network

It is one of the main predictions from the causal theory implicit in the argument of the universalists that means testing causes alienation and anomie. The importance of alienation and anomie to the theory clearly relates the debate to the main-stream of sociological writing and to

---

[2] By the late 1950s it was clear that the meaning the concept had acquired and the various uses to which it was being put required clarification. In particular the concept was being used in middle-range studies based on social survey data in a way that quite substantially changed its nature—indeed in some studies the meaning was very imprecise and the researchers cavalier in their methods of devising indicators. It is therefore not surprising that sociologists like Horton attacked the use of the concept by the 'middle range sociologist ... who ... re-packages classical theories into workable hypotheses which can be used by any number of non-theoretically inclined specialists in the many substantive areas of sociology'. (J. Horton, 'The Dehumanisation of Anomie and Alienation', *British Journal of Sociology, 15*, 4, December 1961, 294.)

Although the method of collecting evidence in this way limited the meaning of the indicators used to operationalize the concept, the focus and individual attitudes and characteristics gave the concept and their operationalizations new depth since it became easier to relate them to the work of the social and individual psychologists. For instance psychologists' theories about the conditions for action and inhibitions to learning can now be used to make more precise the specification and interpretation of models, and so allow finer differentiation of meanings in causal argument, since the larger body of literature that can be drawn on had made great progress in distinguishing rival theories from one another and testing them against evidence. Again the operationalization of the

the development of middle-range theories using versions of these concepts. Clearly an analysis of the demand for free school meals would
be the poorer if it made no attempt to draw upon the insights yielded
by the connections with alienation and anomie. Using them enables
all the intellectual processes required in the research to be enriched by
bodies of theory, methodologies, and evidence whose relevance would
not otherwise be seen.

However, the concepts 'alienation' and 'anomie' have been accorded
very different meanings in the sociological literature.[2] An influential
paper by Seeman[3] published in 1959 gave precise expression to the
rather different meanings observable in the attempts to operationalize
the concept, and it provided a set of definitions which made it possible
to develop more elaborate measuring instruments. The meanings distinguished by Seeman were operationalized by others in ways appropriate to the focus of their analysis. For instance alienation from the
work situation was measured in a different way from political alienation[4] and was more narrowly focussed. As inevitable as the influence
of the context, and the meaning of the concept, is the influence of the
unit of analysis, the person. There is no escaping the risk of making
wrong inferences about the existence or strength of structural relationships when the data is for individuals whose insight into structural
relationships is likely to be limited.

Seeman distinguished five meanings of alienation: powerlessness,
meaninglessness, social isolation, normlessness, and a sense of self-
estrangement. Of these, powerlessness, normlessness, and (to a lesser

---

concepts could make use of the techniques of attitude scaling developed by the psychologists and psychometricians. The implicit relevance of these techniques demanded of the
sociological research worker a greater degree of professional competence. It is therefore
not surprising that during the period when the survey was growing fastest in popularity,
the methodology textbooks increasingly dealt with the measurements of attitudes and
related statistical techniques. Psychometrics was as important a source of technical
sophistication for a survey analyst during this period as econometrics has become for
the sociological model builders of the later 1960s and early 1970s.

Nevertheless the literature of the period developed indicators that were crude if not
slipshod. No doubt this failure to develop strong indicators was one cause of the reaction
against the literature as a whole. It is unfortunate that this reaction has made respectable
a philistine rejection of the approach and provides an easy argument for those seeking
an excuse for their methodological naïveté.

[3] Melvin Seeman, 'On the meaning of alienation', *American Sociological Review*, 24,
6, December 1959, pp. 783–91.

[4] See for instance, W. R. Thompson and J. E. Horton, 'Political alienation as a force
in political action', *Social Forces, 38*, 3, March 1960, pp. 190–5. W. Kornhauser, *The
Politics of Mass Society*, The Free Press, Glencoe, Ill., 1959. A. Campbell, *The American
Voter*, Wiley, New York, 1960.

degree) self-estrangement seem to be the most salient to our research problem. They illuminate most clearly the essence of the nature of explaining variations in the probability of taking up a means-tested service when analysed in the context of Atkinson's theory of motivated action.[5] This postulates that the probability of motivated action is a function of three types of factor: the strength of motives or intra-psychic predispositions to behave; the expectancies (subjective probabilities) of achieving the goals by the prescribed means; and the relative incentive provided by the external environment to attain the goals. The propositions of this theory are compatible with many forms of relationship between the probability of action and the three causal factors. Atkinson himself did no more than specify the general form $A = f(M, I, E)$, but his argument is incompatible with some forms. Perhaps the simplest form compatible with it is:

$$A = \alpha M^{\beta_1} I^{\beta_2} E^{\beta_3}$$

where M is the strength of motivation, the internal force creating the disposition to act; E is the expectancy that the goal can be achieved by the given means; I is the incentive, the relative attractiveness of the goal; and A is the probability of action.

Implicit in this theoretical statement is that each of the three factors are necessary conditions—that action would not take place in the absence of any of them. The consequence for the probability of action of an infinitesimally small difference (or increase) in one of the factors (say M) is given by the partial derivative $\delta A / \delta M$, which for the form of equation stated above is $\beta_1 \cdot A/M$. For both theoretical argument and policy discussion, it is potentially interesting to be able to estimate what additional 'quantum' of one factor would compensate for the loss of a unit of another in the sense of leaving the probability of action unchanged. For instance, it would be valuable to be able to estimate what additional Incentive would be necessary in order to tempt mothers whose Motivation levels were low to have the same probability of entitlement as mothers in general. If there were only the two factors I and M to consider, one measure of that would be $\beta_1 I / \beta_2 M$

[5] J. W. Atkinson, 'Motivational determinants of risk-taking behaviour', *Psychological Review*, *64*, November 1967, pp. 359–72. See also J. W. Atkinson's *An Introduction to Motivation*, Princeton, van Nostrand, 1964. Atkinson's theory is sufficiently close to other areas of study by psychologists to make other evidence relevant. Among these are the theories enunciated in J. B. Rotter, *Social Learning and Clinical Psychology*, Englewood Cliffs, Prentice Hall, 1954, which is frequently referred to in the sociological literature.

This ratio is of theoretical as well as of practical significance: it expresses the relative importance of the response to the environment postulated by the selectivists, and the culture-determined inertia postulated by the universalists. This ease with which I would compensate for M could be expressed as an elasticity coefficient, as a measure of the rate of change of $\beta_1 I/\beta_2 M$. However, with this form of basic equation, such an elasticity coefficient would be unity. There is no good reason why this should be so. We have not discovered any writing by theoretical psychologists which discusses forms with less implausibly restrictive properties than this. However, a useful characteristic of the form is that if $(\beta_1 + \beta_2 + \beta_3)$ exceeds unity, successive increases in E, M, and I will raise A more and more; whereas if $(\beta_1 + \beta_2 + \beta_3)$ is less than unity, the opposite will be the case. But it is another weakness of the model that the effects on it of increases in E, M, and I are assumed to be the same for mothers whose scores on all these variables are high as for mothers whose scores are low.

The remainder of this section discusses the possible causes of variations in the uptake of free meals using the Atkinson theory and the theory of alienation.

(i) Powerlessness and the Expectancy of Goal Achievement (E)

The third term (E) in Atkinson's formula is the expectancy of powerlessness—or, more precisely, its mathematical complement. Much of the literature treats powerlessness as the most central of the Seeman dimensions,[6] and there is some evidence that suggests that powerlessness may be the dimension most highly correlated with other dimensions.[7] Seeman defined powerlessness as the expectancy or probability held by the person that his own behaviour cannot determine the occurrence of the outcome or reinforcement he seeks.[8] This is the dimension stressed by political sociologists like Thompson and Horton, Kornhauser and Campbell. Similarly this aspect is stressed in the writings of some of the universalists. It is possible that a sense of

[6] Particularly R. Blauner, *Alienation and Freedom*, University of Chicago Press, Chicago, 1964. In contrast, Cotgrove stresses self-estrangement. (See S. Cotgrove *et al.*, *The Nylon Spinners*, Allen and Unwin, London, 1971.) See D. G. Dean, 'Alienation: its meaning and measurement', *American Sociological Review*, 26, 5, October 1961, pp. 753–8.

[7] D. G. Dean, 'Alienation: its meaning and measurement', *American Sociological Review*, 26, 5, October 1961, pp. 753–8.

[8] Seeman, op. cit., p. 785.

powerlessness has salience to the claiming of a means-tested benefit in a number of ways.

First, a sense of powerlessness may inhibit the potential applicant from taking the steps necessary to establish his entitlement and then to claim the benefit. As we have seen, Atkinson's theory predicts that no action will be undertaken if the person feels completely powerless. With a high expectancy of powerlessness, action is very unlikely. Whatever the relative incentives to obtain free meals as against, say, risking stigmatization, and whatever the mother's degree of internal motivation (reflected in her attitudes to the child's education perhaps) the mother is unlikely to make a sustained effort to obtain the service unless the perceived probability of success is substantially greater than zero. There is evidence that an expectancy of powerlessness inhibits action in related areas. For instance, Bullough found that an expectancy of powerlessness (as well as anomie) deterred people from making the sustained effort necessary to overcome the barriers to moving from ghettoes. He found that their expectancy of powerlessness not so much distinguished those willing to make a single attempt as it distinguished those who were willing to make a sustained effort.[9] As Atkinson's theory predicts, an expectancy of achieving the goals with the means available was a pre-condition of effective action, rather than merely a contributory factor whose presence increased a non-zero probability of effective action.

Learning about the existence of the service, the eligibility rules, and the procedures for obtaining it involves as much motivated behaviour as actions involved in following these procedures. The sociological literature provides evidence in support of the theory that an expectancy of powerlessness inhibits learning. Seeman showed that hospital patients scoring highly on powerlessness acquired less knowledge about their condition.[10] It was not possible in this study to eliminate the possibility that learning affected the expectancy of powerlessness, or that learning and powerlessness were both caused by an uncontrolled third factor. In a later study which did collect evidence for which there could be little doubt about the direction of causation, Seeman showed that prisoners who felt powerless to avoid retreating to a criminal career on discharge less successfully learned parole information.[11] Both

[9] R. Bullough, 'Alienation in the ghetto', *American Journal of Sociology*, 72, 5, March 1967, pp. 469–78.

[10] M. Seeman and J. W. Evans, 'Alienation and learning in a hospital setting', *American Sociological Review*, 27, December 1962, pp. 772–82.

[11] M. Seeman, 'Alienation and social learning in a reformatory', *American Journal of Sociology*, 64, 3, November 1963, pp. 270–84.

Seeman studies showed that a sense of powerlessness affected other forms of behaviour than learning. Similarly, Bullough's study showed that a sense of powerlessness inhibited people's learning of their rights in the housing market. Thus a sense of powerlessness is likely to affect people's acquisition both of information and of the skills needed to handle welfare systems. Therefore the expectancy of powerlessness might well affect two forms of behaviour which crucially influence the probability that an eligible child would receive a free meal.

High level theory is useful to the analyst of a low level policy issue to the degree that concepts based on the theory but related to the issue can be developed and operationalized. No British attempt has been made to use statistical techniques to study perceptions of powerlessness in relation to poverty. Indeed, the theoretical literature on poverty is not such as to allow a concept specification precise enough to be useful in statistical analysis. Therefore, we had both to develop a concept and indicators of it in the course of a small piece of research which took too little time to allow anything but the most superficial preliminary theoretical analysis, or even the piloting (far less the development of components) of the questionnaire and its analysis.

The concept of powerlessness was designed to be general enough to allow our evidence to be seen in the context of the broader literature (especially that on political science and political sociology), and general enough to give credibility to a 'funnel of causality' argument—an argument that a general and pervasive belief about the nature of society is logically prior to more specific attitudes, the recognition of and interpretation put on pieces of evidence about that nature, and behaviour itself. The concept was also intended to be specific enough to make obvious its causal relevance to a theory of the behaviour of persons with low income. That concept was the expectancy about the success of steps taken to avoid poverty. The principal indicator of this poverty-related concept of powerlessness was a variable based on statements that the main responsibility for being in poverty lay with the poor themselves—or, more precisely, that if people were in poverty, it was their own fault. This perception we described as an individualized responsibility for poverty. The indicator was based on answers to questions about what could be done about poverty, what would be described as poverty, and the reasons for people being poor. Answers which were coded as self-help solutions to poverty, which blamed poverty on those who were poor, or which attributed it to some form of personal inadequacy were treated as reflecting an attitude of individualized responsibility for poverty. A composite *Individualized*

Responsibility for Poverty (*IRPS*) score was computed by summing the number of questions answered thus.[12] Of course, by operationalizing powerlessness at a higher level of theoretical generality than the decision to apply for a benefit, we have departed in one respect from the conditions for which Atkinson's theory is relevant, except to the extent that we can treat IRPSD as an indicator of the expectancy of the successful outcome of the procedures of application.

(ii) Anomie, stigma, and the internal drive to apply (M)

What Seeman discusses as one dimension of alienation, anomie, is as relevant as powerlessness to the reasons for the non-uptake of means-tested free school meals. Seeman defines anomie as a high expectancy that socially unapproved behaviour is required to achieve socially approved goals.[13] Like powerlessness, anomie can be related to important features of the free meals context that may be causally important for uptake. Claimants are stigmatized for seeking to obtain a benefit provided by society for a purpose which society approves. If the stigmatization itself and the sense of shame that it reinforces cause anomie, they might lower the motivation of the subject to attain the goal by reducing his capacity for satisfaction in its attainment.

Anomie has been widely used in theories explaining related phenomena so that precise explanations can be postulated and tested, based on analogies with other contexts, and so that the relevance to free meals of evidence marshalled for these other contexts can be seen.

Like powerlessness, anomie has been extensively analysed by the urbanists. In 1938, Wirth's classic essay described the way of life of the city as anomic; and it retains an element of truth although his description has been challenged as an overstatement for the inner city and untrue for the outer city and suburbs, and even though the relationship may be weaker than was thought.[14] Although the argu-

---

[12] In a unidimensional Likert scale, the score on the general factor is equal to the sum of scores on the items. The specification of the variable was not entirely based on deductive criteria. Answers to salient questions were factor-analysed, and the results taken into account in defining and specifying the indicator. This was also the case for the other composite indicators.

[13] Seeman, *On the meaning of alienation*, op. cit. This is clearly related to Durkheim's concept in *Suicide*, and is the concept developed by Merton. It is less related to the concept in *The Division of Labour in Society*.

[14] See, for instance, H. J. Gans, 'Urbanism and suburbanism as ways of life', in A. M. Rose, ed., *Human Behaviour and Social Processes*, Routledge & Kegan Paul, London, 1962, pp. 625–48; C. S. Fischer, 'On urban alienation and anomie: powerlessness and social isolation', *American Sociological Review*, June 1973, pp. 285–301.

ment that the nature of cities causes these characteristics has been challenged, and the theories made more complex so as to allow for the interaction in causal processes of the essentially city characteristics with other factors, the association of anomie with urbanism has not been questioned.[15] In particular, anomie has proved an important explanatory variable in studies of the ghetto, and the theory has been used to account for the modes of social interaction associated with higher degrees of anomie, to draw attention to and explain low anomie in ghettoes in some circumstances,[16] and the inhibiting effects of anomie on participation in voluntary organizations.[17] However, in many of these studies, the way anomie is measured makes it indistinguishable from powerlessness and other dimensions of alienation.

The universalists also argue that anomie undermines the legitimacy of society's norms.[18] This argument was explored in the literature on delinquency, where its importance in some contexts was confirmed. For instance, Cloward and Ohlin wrote: 'It is our view that the most significant step in the withdrawal of sentiments supporting the legitimacy of conventional norms is the attribution of the cause of failure to the social order rather than to oneself.'[19] Its importance is also clear in British work, such as that of Lockwood and Goldthorpe. The perception of norms as illegitimate makes it acceptable 'to get one over on them', as Sheila Kay put it in a discussion of means-tested services.[20] Attitudes to society in general are made more instrumental, a consequence of self-estrangement that Cotgrove has emphasized in relation to employment. More important for the study, this perception may protect the individual from a loss of self-esteem if he applies for free meals for his children.

The importance of anomie theory lies in the reasons why it is potentially stigmatizing to apply for and receive a means-tested service like

[15] See, for instance, Ruth Glass, 'Conflict in Cities' in A. de Reuck and J. Knight, eds, *Conflict in Society*, Churchill, London, 1966, pp. 141–62; or John Rex, 'The Sociology of a zone of transition' in R. E. Pahl, ed., *Readings in Urban Sociology*, Pergamon, London, 1968, pp. 211–31.

[16] See, for instance, R. A. Wilson, 'Anomie in the ghetto; a study of neighbourhood type, race, and anomie', *American Journal of Sociology*, 77, 1. July 1971, pp. 66–78.

[17] For instance, W. Bell, 'Anomie, Social Isolation, and the Class Structure', *Sociometry*, 20, June 1957, pp. 105–16; E. M. Mizrouchi, 'Social Structure and Anomie in a Small City', *American Sociological Review*, 25, December 1960, pp. 645–54.

[18] R. K. Merton, *Social Theory and Social Structure*, Free Press of Glencoe, Illinois, 1957.

[19] R. A. Cloward and L. E. Ohlin, *Delinquency and Opportunity*, Free Press of Glencoe, Illinois, 1960.

[20] S. Kay, 'Problems of accepting means-tested benefits', in D. Bull, ed., *Family Poverty*, Duckworth, London, 1971, p. 29.

school meals. In order to maintain and legitimate their institutional order, societies ensure that their children are taught 'virtues' that help societies meet their aims. By this process of learning, society is made meaningful and acceptable to its members. Members of society are reminded in various (frequently unpleasant) ways of the importance of these virtues which pervade their thoughts and actions. A special emphasis is put on work, self-help, and independence—the economic virtues—and lesser emphasis on virtues like mutual aid, which do not assist in attaining economic goals. Mutual aid is based on unilateral transfers rather than on equal exchange implicit in self-help and independence. Therefore the receiver of a unilateral transfer inevitably suffers from some loss of esteem and self-respect.[21]

As Pinker writes: 'It is always (thought to be) less prestigious to receive than to give. It is postulated that a sharp distinction exists in the consciousness of ordinary people between "givers" and "receivers" of social services whose respective statuses are elevated or debased by virtue of the exchange relationship.'[22] This has two consequences. The first is an ambivalence among many potential applicants amounting to a sense of guilt about seeking a service. It is this subjectively-perceived potential for stigma that has the most inevitable effect on his behaviour. Two persons facing precisely the same context, and presenting the same characteristics to other actors in that context, can perceive quite different degrees of stigma potential. Because the evaluation of the stigma potential of a context is highly subjective, it is unnecessary for actors in this context to transmit stigmatizing messages to potential recipients consciously or even unconsciously for the context to have stigma potential. '"Affective neutrality", which is the desired norm for a good bureaucrat, provides interesting opportunities for projection. The derogatory term "faceless bureaucrat" indicates the fear that many people have of just that impersonal style to which civil servants aspire. Certainly, it is easy to read into such behaviour indications of feeling; the complexities of the kind of interaction are such that it would often be impossible to sort out projection from an accurately received unspoken communication'.[23]

[21] P. Berger and T. Luckman, *The Social Construction of Reality*, Penguin, Harmondsworth, 1967. Piven and Cloward argue that market values and market incentives are both weakest at the bottom of the social order, and that the creation of an outcast class treated with contempt by the agents of welfare bureaucracies celebrates the virtue of work and deters actual and potential workers from seeking aid. (See F. F. Piven and R. A. Cloward, *Regulating the Poor*, Pantheon, New York, 1971, p. 165.)

[22] R. A. Pinker, *Social Theory and Social Policy*, Heinemann, London, 1970, p. 170.

[23] Olive Stevenson, *Claimant or Client*, Allen and Unwin, London, 1973, p. 23.

Indeed, actors need never have done so in this context. The context may have stigma-potential merely because it has attributes which class it with other situations which have stigma potential; for instance, because it is associated with recipients who are thought by the possible recipient to receive more from society than they contribute to it. Examples abound of contexts in which the receipt of services has become more or less stigmatizing as changes have occurred in the proportions of their clienteles thought deserving.[24] But it is a second consequence of the inequality of exchange that actors tend to have

[24] Glazer found that the stigma associated with the receipt of AFDC increased as the proportion of recipients who were white widows fell. (See N. Glazer, 'Beyond income maintenance: a note on welfare in New York City', *The Public Interest, 16,* Summer 1969, pp. 102–40. Similarly Matza found that the father's imprisonment and desertion increased the stigma of illegitimacy. (See D. Matza, 'Poverty and Disrepute' in R. K. Merton and R. Nisbet, eds, *Contemporary Social Problems,* Harcourt Brace, New York, 1971, pp. 616–17.) See also J. B. Williamson, 'The stigma of public dependency', *Social Problems, 22,* 2, December 1974, pp. 213–28.

The changing composition of a service clientèle is not the only factor causing changes in stigmatization. The emergent theory of the tax-welfare backlash suggests factors which would cause the tide of stigmatization to ebb and flow. (Harold L. Wilensky, *The 'New Corporatism', Centralisation, and the Welfare State,* Sage, London, 1977.) Wilensky argues that the tax-welfare backlash is an inevitable consequence of the incompatibility between the rise in expectation generated during a period of growing prosperity with a declining capacity of governments to meet demands for benefits and services without sacrifices by others. The tax-welfare backlash is based on the discontent of the upper working and the lower middle classes mobilized by such politicians as Reagan and Nixon in the United States, Glistrup in Denmark, Powell and latterly Sproat in the United Kingdom. Wilensky argues that the strength of these political pressures is least in societies whose political structures are most corporatist, since 'new corporatism' makes possible policies which make more effective the containment of the pressures towards backlash. What is important to the ebb and flow of stigmatization in society as a whole is not the outcome of the Wilensky models, the ratio of social services expenditure to the national income, but the degree to which the political arguments supporting welfare backlash are articulated and held. This is particularly the case since many of the gate-keepers of the social services belong to the social classes most likely to espouse the arguments. Wilensky's argument helps to explain the increasingly neurotic public reaction to many groups of welfare recipients. Although he alludes to it, Wilensky does not make either growth itself, or changes in growth, central to his argument, since he does not incorporate indicators of them into his modelling. Growth may well help to create the conditions in which corporatism can develop and survive, just as it may directly influence the probability of the discontent exploited by the Powells and Sproats. In this, the Wilensky argument is slightly different from that of commentators who ascribe the disappointed expectations to the deceleration of growth itself. In this Wilensky's argument is plausible. Certainly, recent British history suggests that explicit attempts to reinforce the emergent corporatism of the British political system have been weakened by the strains caused by a declining economy; for instance, the corporate steamroller visibly juddered when it encountered the resistance of British Leyland tool-makers. Many argue that the corporatist argument has been over-simplified. See for instance, Brian Barry, 'The consociational model and its dangers', *European Journal of Political Research, 3,* 4, 1975, pp. 393–413.

punitive attitudes towards applicants. This is based partly on prejudice and the need for the ideology of a culture to provide scapegoats. The theories of prejudice and labelling have much to contribute to the theory of stigmatization. We do not develop the argument here because our primary concern is to augment the theoretical framework for handling evidence about the perceptions of the stigma potential of a context among those who may be the object of the stigmatization. We must distinguish clearly between a subjective sense of stigma and the stigmatization of the subject by others.[25] The specific structural context that gives rise to the stigmatization may reinforce anomie: but since very specific experiences do not generally have a powerful effect on

[25] Some American writers have recognized the salience of labelling theory to stigma. (See, for instance, P. M. Horan and P. L. Austin, 'The social bases of welfare stigma', *Social Problems*, *21*, 4, 1974, pp. 643–57.) The theory postulates that the stigmatization, caused by being labelled a deviant, causes the subject to be perceived and interacted with as if he were a deviant, and to be treated as a deviant in other ways. Membership of a deviant group reinforces or creates a sense of 'deviant identity' and a rationalization by subjects of their position. Whether membership of the deviant group leads to a sense of identity with other members of the group and to a rationalization by the subject are important tests of the salience of the theory.

Horan and Austin reserve the term 'stigma' for the feelings of shame and degradation that their argument predicts will follow the labelling. They argue that these indicate a more serious penetration of the deviant label, an internalization of the negative evaluation of significant others; and that this is an effect of a different order from an expectation by the subject of stigmatization of discrimination.

A list of cases between which it is important to distinguish would include the following: (a) the expectation of stigmatization by others—that is, the expectation of systematic attempts by others to confer a lower status; (b) the subjective loss of self-esteem irrespective of the recognition of a lower status by an external world, and without any expectation that streams of external disbenefits will follow from it; (c) the subjective perception that to receive 'gifts' is to entail obligations which demand the surrender of autonomy—a dis-welfare in the form of what Blau has called a 'compliance cost' (in P. M. Blau, *Exchange and power in social life*, Wiley, New York, 1964); and (d) the expectation of a generalized re-labelling by others; for instance, the unconscious reassessment of a child's home background as a result of claiming a means-tested benefit, with consequences for expectations about the child's educational success. The distinction between cases (a) and (d) is important during periods in which stigmatization is least powerful, and in which therefore it is the second effect that may often have most influence. The distinction between (b) and (c) is similarly of importance both for the evaluation of a context and for assessment of alternative ways of changing it. Perhaps it was this lack of conceptual clarity which caused Rudolph Klein to call stigma 'the phlogiston of social theory'. Like phlogiston, stigma might well become a redundant concept when we gain a better understanding of the causal structures of which these four kinds of disbenefits are outcomes. Like phlogiston, stigma is not a homogeneous entity; and like phlogiston, it is not an elemental phenomenon directly observed, but merely a concept convenient at a primitive stage of theoretical argument. (Rudolph Klein, 'Priorities in the Age of Inflation', in Rudolph Klein, ed., *Inflation and Priorities*, Centre for Studies and Social Policy, London, 1975.)

more global attitudes, it is probable that the subjective sense of stigma is usually effect, not cause.

The messages transmitted by an actor to a potential recipient, like the subjective assessment of a context as potentially stigmatizing prior to any direct evidence about behaviour in the context, can be the result of applying a general and relatively pervasive value to a specific situation. 'If men and women feel they are inferior, subordinated persons, they in part stigmatise themselves and in part mirror what others think of them'.[26] Since potential recipients and other actors can be influenced by the same cultural values, and since the subjective assessments of contexts by potential recipients and attitudes to recipients among other actors depend on a wide variety of factors and vary greatly, it is very difficult to unravel the web of causal relations. However, it is important to attempt to distinguish between factors whose influence bears directly upon the assessments of the stigma-potential of a context among possible recipients, and those whose influence on these is indirect, operating through the attitudes of other actors.

The inequality of exchange stressed by Berger and Luckman is a powerful agent, but it would be to stretch the concept too far to make it a complete explanation of stigma.[27]

There are a wide variety of criteria for success in our society ... It happens that, by virtue of its function, the Supplementary Benefits Commission brings together in one place—the local office—a number of people whose sense of failure derives not only from poverty but from other failures to achieve the normal "goods" in society. Thus the unemployed, the handicapped, the separated wife, and the mother of the illegitimate child queue together for money. Each in his own way feels the guilt and anger associated with failure in a role deemed to be of significance in our society. It can readily

[26] Richard Titmuss, *Social Policy*, Allen and Unwin, London, 1973.

[27] Boulding and others have argued that the unilateral transfer is the hallmark of the market. One might therefore conclude, as some sociologists appear to come close to doing, that receiving social services is always to some degree stigmatizing, and secondly, that the theory of exchange provides a theory of stigma. Neither conclusion is valid. As the economists have pointed out, much social service provision can be justified as a form of investment in human capital where the rates of return to society may not be less from that to the individual. Indeed, some have externalities which make the rate of return to society much greater. Others redistribute income over the life-time of the individual more than they redistribute between individuals. It is therefore not surprising that there is no evidence that receiving some services is not stigmatizing. Secondly, although stigma is predicted in some circumstances from the theory of exchange, the theory of exchange does not predict all kinds of stigma. For instance, moral behaviour that has no exchange consequences can be the object of stigma.

be seen, therefore, that the SBC is likely to be the focal point of emotion, not all of which is to do with the stigma of poverty alone.[28]

There is evidence that the community in general applies values which are intolerant of many of those who would be potential recipients of free meals;[29] and also evidence that many recipients subscribe to the same values.[30] Earlier chapters of this book have shown that high proportions of mothers from low income families ascribed the blame for poverty to the poor themselves, and in other ways displayed symptoms of a low degree of self-esteem.

There is not one but many reasons why the school meals context might be perceived as potentially stigmatizing. Whether or not each of the ways the context might evoke a sense of stigma is so perceived depends upon a multeity of contextual factors as well as some of pervasive causal importance. The application form demands a statement of household income. In households in which the mother is not able to present evidence about the total family income, it is necessary to seek the active help of the husband. Whether or not he will co-operate will depend, in part, on his perception of how it might affect his own reputation and self-respect. The father's involvement in the family, the degree of conjugal role segregation between man and wife is likely to be of importance to the outcome. Being the father of a large family and therefore paying lower marginal rates of tax sometimes causes resentments among work-mates, Hilary Land found. But more important than this is that it can be damaging to the identity of a father to admit to having such a low earning capacity that he and his family are counted among those whose incomes require supplementation from the State because his esteem in a society which values economic contributions highly depends upon relative income, and, more relevant in many cases, his position in his own family may often owe itself to being the bread-winner. With the seeking of help must come the danger to the respectable man that he will be mis-classified as someone of lesser social status, and inferior character and standards in the mind of the official and of a wider society. Being a welfare claimant can lead to a re-classification with what Matza calls 'the disreputable poor'. Klein argues that 'the disreputable poor' are a powerful negative reference

---

[28] Olive Stevenson, *Claimant or Client*, op. cit., p. 16.

[29] For instance, Bryan Glastonbury, 'Community perceptions of social work', *Policy and Politics*, *1*, 3, March 1972, pp. 191–211; and D. Clifford, 'Stigma and the perception of social security services', *Policy and Politics*, *3*, 3, March 1975, pp. 29–60.

[30] See in particular, Clifford, op. cit., and Scott Briar, 'Welfare from Below: recipient views of the welfare system', *California Law Review*, *54*, 1966, pp. 370–85.

group, and that much in the 'respectable' working-class life is intended to differentiate them from what she calls the 'roughs'. For instance, housekeeping standards are set not so much to emulate those with higher standards as not to resemble those with lower standards.[31] The environmental factors that might influence behaviour are often little different, she argues.[32] Klein's argument is important.

> The respectables are at pains to attain or maintain standards of domestic behaviour and social intercourse which distinguish them from the roughs in the neighbourhood. They are different from them, but not in economic situation. A period of *illness* or *unemployment*, or some other misfortune, could, until recently, push a whole family below the poverty line. Then help from others would be needed. When this happens, it is very bitter to be mis-classified by an outer world which does not appreciate that one is managing as best one can, handicapped only by misfortune, not by a failure of character. The outer world, 'they', may think someone a cadger who asks for help, because 'they' can not distinguish between those who are cadgers-by-misfortune and those who are cadgers-in-character. The patronising, contemptuous or bullying attitudes of 'them' are felt by the respectable and self-respecting working class working man to be more appropriately directed to a lower stratum than his own. At the other end, the traditional rough is more likely to react to 'their' exercise of authority with violence, subterfuge, exploitation or indifference, and in any case without much psychic pain. In a respectable man, the resentment created when he finds himself mis-classified evokes rather a reaction of stoic independence, a determination to stay clear of 'them' as long as possible.[33]

To the respectable working class, the 'disreputable poor' are visible. As Matza says, 'they are part of what is seen and commented on through the lace curtain'.[34] The respectable working class—or, at any rate, some sections of it—owe much of their self-respect to the fact that they are part of the 'proletariat' rather than the 'lumpen-proletariat'.

This is the case in stable working-class areas where the degree of respectability of a family is partially ascribed and partially won over a long period of time. It is even more the case in loose-knit communities where the status of a family depends more on current symbols

---

[31] J. Klein, *Samples from English Culture*, Routledge, London, 1965, I, p. 99.
[32] Ibid., p. 200.
[33] Ibid., p. 204.
[34] D. Matza, 'Poverty and Disrepute' in R. K. Merton and R. Nisbet, *Contemporary Social Problems*, Harcourt, Brace, and World, New York, 1961, p. 625.

of relative affluence. Response rates to questions about incomes are nearly always relatively low among the working-class people in loose-knit communities where most incomes are thought to be higher than that of the working class. (On the other hand, the perceived need for help—because of the absence of family and community support—may be greater in the newer loose-knit areas; and the lower degree of community solidarity can result in a smaller degree of reluctance to accept help from 'them'.)

The determination to be independent, to preserve privacy about this delicate area which can be closely associated with status differentiation within the working class, makes a decision to apply for assistance a major one. Applying for free meals implies a surrender of privacy. As Coser has argued, privacy in certain areas sensitive to the individual is almost a right of citizenship. 'The protective veil that is available to other members of society is explicitly denied to the welfare claimant.'[35] This could be particularly so where the education welfare officer visits the applicant's home. Coser writes that 'such an invasion of home territory, because it prevents the usual stage management for the visiting outsider, is necessarily experienced as humiliating and degrading.'[36] To many people, the visit of the education welfare officer can be doubly embarrassing since his main task, judging from the statements of the officers themselves, is to perform the social control function of securing attendance by truants. To the disreputable poor, writes Matza, the scrutiny is a reminder of their undeserving character: 'their disrepute is noted, commented on, and filed away'.[37]

The children themselves may be stigmatized when receiving free meals. In 1968, schools were not in general sensitive to the need to prevent free meals children from being identified by their class-mates. Although most L.E.A.s had reviewed their systems for collecting dinner money in the months preceding February 1968, this did not result in the universal use of systems in which confidentiality was ensured. There were also cases in which free meals receivers served paying children, and in which paying children were allowed second helpings while the free meals receivers were not. A Scottish Education Department circular in the autumn of 1967 specifically expressed displeasure at free meals and paying children entering the dining room by separate entrances, sitting at separate tables, and being served different meals. The probability of stigma may vary with the age and sex of the child.

[35] L. Coser, 'The Sociology of Poverty', *Social Problems*, *13*, 2, Fall, 1965, p. 145.
[36] Coser, loc. cit.
[37] D. Matza, 'Poverty and Disrepute', op. cit.

Older children, particularly girls, may be particularly sensitive. The type of school may also be important. Less stigmatization is likely in non-selective schools in poor areas than in selective schools or schools in more prosperous areas.

The attitudes and actions of social service personnel clearly influence the applicant's perception. Among others, Marsden has described how the visit to the office of the Ministry of Social Security (M.S.S.) can influence recipients.[38] This is due partly to the mixing of different client groups in contexts in which privacy is denied, particularly of groups more and less conscious of their self-respect. This teaches or reinforces a perception that receiving the services concerned is stigmatizing because their recipients contribute less than their share to society. This is less likely to be a problem in making an independent application for free meals. For this reason, among those who are referred for free meals by the M.S.S., there may be many who have a high tolerance of stigmatizing situations. But the attitudes of many local officers of the M.S.S. also contribute to the client's feeling of disrepute. This is particularly the case among those who may have additional stigmatizing characteristics. Stigmatizing characteristics affect the likely reaction of applicants to potentially stigmatizing situations. Marsden's unmarried mothers (and his younger widows) were made to perceive receiving social security and not being in employment as more stigmatizing because of the officers' suspicions of co-habitation. Therefore they were less willing to seek assistance. Officers' behaviour is difficult to control, and the causes of their resentment against many recipients are well known—earnings not much higher than benefit, acute staff shortages, membership of social and occupational groups whom Runciman has shown have felt a particular sense of relative deprivation in the post-war world, and which is either near enough to the respectable working class in origins to need to distinguish themselves from it, or to feel that their differences from the disreputable poor are clear. Coser has also argued that the nature of the relationship, which prevents a flow of affect, prevents the officer from thinking of the applicant as anything but a recipient of aid, and so increases the consciousness of social distance and unilateral exchange.[39]

Such factors are also likely to influence education welfare officers and teachers, particularly the former. Certainly there is evidence that education welfare officers understate the degree to which child poverty is due to the less avoidable accidents of economic and social life, and

[38] D. Marsden, *Mothers Alone*, Allen Lane, London, 1969.
[39] L. Coser, 'The Sociology of Poverty', op. cit., p. 146.

overstate the degree to which it is due to parental apathy and incompetence.[40] A low proportion of education welfare officers have a social work qualification. Indeed, in 1964 only $2\frac{1}{2}$ per cent had a social welfare qualification, the proportion having a modest welfare qualification in 1971 being 12.0 per cent. However, the proportion with a social work qualification in 1971 was only $1\frac{1}{2}$ per cent.[41] Education welfare officers' perceptions must be much influenced by their social control function of securing school attendance. At one time, well within the careers of a high proportion of persons now in the profession, this was their only major task. It seems to remain their most time-consuming activity.[42] Therefore association with the education welfare officer, still called in some working-class areas, 'the attendance man', is likely to be stigmatizing to the respectable because of his role in dealing with truants; and is difficult for those less worried by stigma because he is likely to be a symbol of authority, against which an overt reaction is likely.

Teachers' attitudes may be even more important if teachers can inform parents about free meals and encourage them to claim them, and

[40] *Poverty*, Winter 1967, drew attention to a report of the Chief Welfare Officer of Liverpool which ascribed this opinion to the school welfare service. The rate of unemployment in Liverpool in the November of 1967 was 3–9 per cent. It is an area with a low proportion of women in employment. Our own interviews with education welfare officers also provided some support for the allegation of, at least, occasional prejudice against recipients.

[41] *Children and their Primary Schools*, op. cit., para. 220; Local Government Training Board, *Report of the Working Party on the Role and Training of Education Welfare Officers*, Local Government Training Board, Luton, 1975.

[42] The Ralphs Report, op. cit., did not present estimates of the use of time, but see *Children and their Primary Schools*, op. cit., I, para 215. It is also what they regard as their most important function. The Presidential Address of the Society of Chief Education Welfare Officers for 1972 was largely devoted to a discussion of attendance. Its argument stressed the advantages of compulsion in school attendance. It also discussed the costliness of truancy, and presented an estimate of the value of the resources not utilized because of truancy. It discussed the subsequent 'delinquencies, the lack of earning ability and all the other things which can follow in its train', quoting the song for the Ragged School:

> Better build school-rooms for 'the boy'
> Than cells and gibbets for 'the man'.

In the context of discussing the effects of raising the school leaving age on attendance, the speaker wondered whether young people 'should be brought to understand that present obligations (to attend school) are equally important' as thinking about life after leaving. (See *Journal of the Education Welfare Officers' National Association*, 150, May/June 1972, pp. 5–8.) Whatever the conclusion for the division of labour between the education and social service departments of the fact that truancy is now widely recognized as a symptom of personal behavioural problems, family disturbance, or other misfortunes, the education welfare officers prefer not to become a part of local authorities' social service departments.

so help parents to unlearn their association of means-tested services with stigma; but they can also reinforce the association of the service with stigma. The teachers can guide parents in the use of the free meals scheme. More than guidance may be needed, since the form to be completed is substantial and complex, and since there is evidence that a substantial minority of the adult population have a level of competence at reading which makes it necessary for them to have such assistance. But even sufficient information for a potential applicant to recognize that he may be eligible can allow him to avoid such stigmatizing enquiries that might lead to nothing. The manner in which it is provided may help to reduce the degree to which contexts are perceived as stigmatizing. Publicity which stresses the legal right to services consumed by a wide range of families can have an effect on stigma factors themselves. Such publicity may well affect not only the potential recipients but others involved in running the service. The Ministerial circular issued in the autumn of 1967, though not ideal, gave clear information, stressed entitlement, but related the services to people 'in poverty'. It is therefore possible that situations were perceived differently by persons who had received the services before the circular, and before the other approximately contemporaneous attempts made by some L.E.A.s, including our 'over-achiever' authority, to publicize the service.

The time when mothers had had experience of applying or receiving the service might be important for other reasons. The more recent the experience, the more likely the mother is to be young; and the less likely she is to have her perception of means-tested services dominated by the inter-war experience. Also, the more recent the experience, the more likely is it to have been caused by the rising unemployment of the late 1960s. The children of those put out of work at a time of deepening recession are more likely to receive free meals without taking special initiatives—and with less personal confession of failure. Head teachers enjoy considerable discretion in granting free meals pending an investigation of parents' income, and this is used with varying generosity. And the school is one of the most recognizable and powerful of the social institutions that transmit accepted codes of conduct. As purveyors of morality over a wide range of issues, the 'meaning' that the teachers attach to receiving a service may be of particular importance, particularly to those with positive instrumental (and perhaps affective) attitudes towards education and the school, who are most likely to relearn the 'meaning' of the service since these are often families poised for social mobility. The substance of the teaching affects its acceptability. Teachers' attitudes are variable. Kerr mentions that in Ship Street, many teachers had been children from poor Catholic families in the neighbourhood and therefore tended to be sensitive and sympathetic.[43] The Irish Catholic cultures, in spite of their strong tendency to matrilocality and strict marital role segregation, may be receptive to the values of the (Catholic) school. But Hilary Land's example of the insensitivity of a teaching nun to a boy without a proper uniform shows how uncertain such generalizations can be.[44] Regional —indeed local—cultures may well have a strong influence in a profession which has been an important ladder to social mobility for working-class children whose reference groups are sometimes only slightly less localized than that of their parents. Corresponding to variations in working-class cultures between (and within) North and South are variations in what 'meanings' the schools try to teach. Similarly, there must be corresponding variations in the body of L.E.A. policies and traditions which help to define objectives for the teachers, and attach weights to their relative importance. These policies and traditions are probably sensitive both to the style of leading officers and to the local political climate which reflect some aspects of local culture. But it is not obvious that the pattern of variation is such as to make what the schools teach more acceptable to all potential recipients of means-tested services. And since it seems unlikely that the culture of the schools varies as much as the local sub-cultures that they serve, parents' and children's perceptions of the legitimacy of school values, their perception of the role of education in general and the school in particular, and their personal and cultural resources for making use of the school, may well be the crucial variables.

It is not easy to catch even important nuances in a social survey without a substantial number of indicators. Whatever may be argued about such variations, some teachers, particularly in secondary-modern schools, are concerned to maintain social distance for reasons similar to those that apply to education welfare officers, and because of the type of frustrations involved in dealing with the most culturally deprived child that Klein describes for teachers in Branch Street. In selective schools, or schools where few children are in poverty, teachers may frequently not recognize that it is part of their function to spot children whose educational progress and welfare is hampered by

---

[43] M. Kerr, *The People of Ship Street*, Routledge, London, 1958. See for more general evidence M. Steinman, 'The class correlates of head teachers attitudes', *Policy and Politics*, 1, 4, June 1973, esp. Table 6.

[44] Hilary Land, *Large Families in London*, Bell, London, 1969, p. 86.

poverty. Indeed, some may almost see the abrogation of their entitlements as a test of whether a child or parent has relinquished its sub-cultural reference group in favour of the normative reference groups to which the school encourages adherence. This discussion of the way in which similar cultural factors can influence teachers and welfare officers as well as potential recipients shows the extraordinary difficulty of separating out the causes.

The ethnicity of the family is likely to be one factor determining outcome. West Indian families differ among themselves substantially. Particularly among those who come to this country early, there are many with a way of life that has an almost Victorian bourgeois respectability, since the immigrants were a self-selected group who aspired to what they perceive as middle-class forms of behaviour.[45] Such families may subscribe to the doctrine that poverty is caused by individual and cultural factors, and feel the stigma of poverty keenly. However, many maintain in this country features of the family systems of the Caribbean.[46] The instability of marital unions has consequences for child-rearing and therefore the formation of personality that may interact with structural (as distinct from 'cultural') factors. The children who are already of school age tended to be badly taught in the Caribbean. West Indians tended to come to this country with higher expectations than other immigrant groups. Rose has shown that their achievement has been relatively worse than other groups.[47] This, in the context of race prejudice, has caused much antagonism[48] For these reasons and others (including ineffective school organization and sometimes teacher prejudice, and the prejudice of the wider society

[45] J. Rex and R. Moore, *Race Community and Conflict*, Oxford University Press, London, 1967. See also E. J. B. Rose, *et al.*, *Colour and Citizenship*, Oxford University Press, London, 1969, pp. 429–32.

[46] An anthropologist wrote of these: 'Their domestic units vary widely in size and constitution. Many adults live entirely by themselves; many women live with their children and grandchildren; materterine kinship provides an important basis for the domestic placement of illegitimate offspring of kinswoman. Males generally head units based on their co-habitation, and many of these units include the kin as well as the children of their mates by former unions ... Marriage generally occurs in or near middle age, and female widowhood is quite common. In all our samples, there are substantial numbers of single women of mature age, most of whom are mothers and heads of households also. In all our samples, legitimate offspring tend to live with both parents in homes of which their fathers are head, and the majority of the children living apart from their fathers or apart from both parents are illegitimate.' (See M. G. Smith, *West Indian Family Structure*, University of Washington Press, Seattle, 1962, p. 244.) Therefore, the stigma of poverty is likely to be compounded with the stigma of illegitimacy, and that of anticipated race prejudice.

[47] *Colour and Citizenship*, op. cit., pp. 196–7.

[48] Ibid., p. 434.

operating at the school level), children of West Indian parents have often rebelled against schooling. Rose writes that they have been 'a source of bafflement, embarrassment, and despair, in the educational system'.[49] The negative relationships make it less likely that teachers would inform West Indians about free meals and encourage them to apply.

The attitudes of Indians and Pakistanis are likely to be different, and to be affected in a different way by teachers. The purdah of the Pakistani women (particularly among West Pakistanis), their inability to speak English, their desire to maintain themselves as a group apart, and their role as custodians of Pakistani culture and religion, makes it difficult to inform them of rights directly. On the other hand, like the Sikhs, who comprise four-fifths of Indian immigrants, some communities have their own efficient networks of communication and throw up their own leadership. Problems of diet may well arise for religious reasons. The Indians and Pakistanis, like the West Indians, may well contain high proportions of eligible children. Rose notes that in the West Midlands, the Pakistanis are employed in jobs of the lowest socio-economic status, and he demonstrated that the number of children per family tended to be higher among immigrants.[50]

Other 'structural' factors are important to the role of teachers. The high rates of turnover, often leaving a permanent caucus of older, unqualified staff who have opted out (and who rationalize their attitude by recourse to prejudice) to determine the ethos of the institution, reduces the chance of personal contact which, as Bernstein stresses, might help the school perform its functions better. The wider the culture gap, Rex argues in his Parsonian analysis of the functions of the school, the greater the emphasis it places on social training in middle-class (Christian) values and behaviour, and aspirations.[51] Thus if the middle-class work ethic is transmitted effectively to the immigrant child in the schools, there is a special danger that the teachers and the

---

[49] Ibid., p. 281.

[50] *Colour and Citizenship*, op. cit., pp. 172–7, and Table 11.5, p. 117.

[51] J. Rex and R. Moore, *Race Community and Conflict*, op. cit., p. 237.

[52] An unsavoury episode in British political history illustrates the argument. Peter Griffiths was a former headmaster. This status may have helped to give legitimacy to his prejudiced statements and he was shrewd in using the school as an agent for fostering prejudice. He was, for instance, quoted as stating about race prejudice in schools, 'We cannot stop children reflecting the views of their parents'; and after some allegations of vice among immigrants had been made, he had urged headmistresses to warn pupils not to enter houses occupied by immigrants for they would be 'in grave moral danger'. (See N. Deakin, *Colour and the British Electorate*, 1964, Pall Mall Press, London, 1965, p. 78.) However, the Smethwick campaign was exceptional. Deakin *et al.* showed how

schools may teach stigma both with respect to poverty and the aspects of the immigrant's culture that conform least to middle-class English norms.[52]

The disjunction between socially approved ends and means, that is the core of Mertonian anomie, must affect attitudes to education as a whole, the school in particular, and so the nature of parental contacts with the school. It has been argued that anomie can either result in apathy and retreatism (low levels of internally-determined motivation) or activism and innovation.[53] Whether it leads to the one or the other is vital to the probability of applying for free meals. It is therefore necessary to distinguish between those dimensions underlying attitudes to school and education that discriminate between retreatist and activist reactions to anomie, as well as high and low degrees of anomie itself. This is potentially of importance for the probability of uptake since we have shown the school to be a major source of information and assistance in managing procedures. Our discussion has suggested that the nature of the effect must be complicated by the type of area of the town, the characteristics of parents and children, and the school, and other factors. A single dimension therefore seems inadequate to reflect nuances of importance. The questionnaire contained a range of questions reflecting attitudes to education and the school, and the nature of contacts with the school.[54] After factoranalysing the answers to these questions, we allocated most of them to one of three domains. The first domain consisted of correlates of *positive instrumental attitudes to education in general*, and the second of correlates of *participatory instrumental attitudes to the particular schools attended*. Two variables, EDID and EDIIID were computed from them. Low scores on these variables would imply a probability of more than typical anomie, but would not indicate whether the consequence was retreatist or activist. The second domain comprised variables that reflected *negative contacts with the school*. The com-

variable was the degree to which race had been exploited for political ends as between apparently similar constituencies. One could expect a similar variation in the impact of ethnic characteristics on the perception of a potentially stigmatizing context.

[53] See, for instance, the operationalizations in Dean, 'Alienation: its meaning and measurement', op. cit.; G. Nettler, 'A measure of alienation'. *American Sociological Review, 22*, 6, December 1957, p. 672; L. Srole and A. G. Neal, 'On the multidimensionality of alienation', *American Sociological Review, 32*, 1, February 1967, p. 54–61.

[54] The face validity of many of these had been enhanced because their covariation in a national sample had been examined. Central Advisory Council on Education (England), *Children and their Primary Schools*, H.M.S.O., London, 1968, II, Appendix 3.

posite variable based on it was called NEGCOND. High scores on this variable would imply both a probability of anomie and a retreatist response to it. Among the high scores, therefore, anomie might inhibit the application for free meals. Low scores on variables in the first two domains who were also low scorers on variables in the third would have a high probability of being atypically anomic but to have reacted by playing the system—by 'trying to get one over on them'. Among these, anomie might have a positive effect on the probability of uptake. Scores for each of these dimensions were separately computed by aggregating responses in the hypothesized direction to form indicators EDID, EDIIID, and NEGCOND (see Appendix A, p. 257 for short definitions). In this way we hoped to distinguish the effects of a commitment to socially approved goals (the correlates and rewards of social mobility) and an acceptance of socially approved means (education) from practical participation in the education system and therefore close and positive contacts with it, and from a mutual rejection by the school and parents reflected in negative contacts.[55]

This discussion of anomie and stigma suggests the following conclusions:

1. Each of the contexts created by the free meals scheme which might be perceived by recipients as potentially stigmatizing implies a causal process that is significantly different. The relative importance of these processes is not just of theoretical interest but also has policy implications.
2. The perceptions are likely to be influenced by a wide range of causal factors, some of which are of pervasive theoretical importance for the perception of stigma potential and for the acquisition of information and a capacity to handle complex welfare systems.
3. The causal factors are likely to have direct effects on perceptions of stigma potential, and indirect effects through their influence on anomie.
4. The measures of anomie are indicators, indices of correlates of the concept, not of the concept itself. The correlation between the indicators and the concept may well vary between groups; for instance, the relationship between NEGCOND and anomie could well differ among ethnic groups.

[55] Unlike the index of powerlessness (IRPSD), the indicators of anomie are therefore indicators of some of the more salient consequences of the causal factor, not of that factor itself. These outcomes may be influenced by other factors also—including IRPSD. We are therefore using one set of consequences of anomie as an indicator of another consequence, the perception of certain norms as illegitimate.

5. Contextual factors may influence the effects of the main causal variables: for instance, the effect of anomie might be enhanced by such factors as being an unmarried mother, so that being an unmarried mother *and* having a high level of anomie might cause a difference in expectancy of being stigmatized much greater than the sum of the two effects observed in isolation from one another.

(iii) Super-subsistence income, relative deprivation and the incentive to apply (I)

Such British literature on the uptake of means-tested benefits as *The Financial Circumstances of Retirement Pensioners*[56] and *Welfare Rights: Project 2*[57] shows that the amount of benefit that would be gained is among the factors that influence uptake. The benefit of a meal is indivisible. Other factors are therefore more important in determining incentive. For instance, the relative incentive necessary for applying must depend *inter alia* upon the perception of what are the eligibility levels. Even after the Ministerial circular to all parents (and the similar circular issued to all parents in one of the authorities some time earlier) which gave some evidence about income levels which qualified children for meals, our informants were vague about the income levels at which people were eligible.[58] However, it is certainly arguable that the lower the family income (allowing for family composition), the greater the incentive to apply. The questionnaire collected all the income and expenditure data required to perform the free meals test of income. The data was used to means-test each family. Means-testing consists of making a variety of deductions from household income and making an allowance for capital resources and the number of dependents to arrive at an estimate of net income. The dif-

[56] Ministry of Pensions and National Insurance, *The Financial Circumstances of Retirement Pensioners*, H.M.S.O., London, 1966.

[57] Peter Moss, *Welfare Rights: Project 2*, Merseyside Child Poverty Action Group, Liverpool, 1970.

[58] Molly Meacher found the same for rate rebates. See M. Meacher, *Rate Rebates*, op. cit., 12. That people were expected to be uncertain about eligibility levels was one reason why we did not develop variables which would indicate the perceptions of the general population of short-falls in the welfare of the poor of different degrees of poverty. Like the 'dollar poverty gap' used in the United States Census, such variables would have been of direct theoretical importance, measuring immediate influences on the social demand for interventions to maintain the levels of living of others—the social demand which gives the distribution of levels of living its 'public good' character—and so providing data of great value for the derivation of indicators of the effectiveness of interventions.

ference between a family's 'net income' and the eligibility level of income of a family with the same number of children as the family in question was treated as an indicator of the low income incentive to apply. In this context we conceived of it as though it is the same concept as the 'standardized income' of Chapters 2 and 3, where it was classified into four levels, as is indicated in Table 2.3.

However, it is subjective perceptions not objective status that affect behaviour. It is therefore likely that feelings of deprivation in relation to key reference groups are as likely to influence the probability of uptake among the eligible as the size of the gap between net income and the eligibility level. Runciman's classic analysis discussed relative deprivation in relation to Weber's three categories: class, status, and power. In our analysis, relative deprivation with respect to income and wealth appear to be the most relevant. The survey therefore asked how well off the respondents felt compared with four reference groups: other people of a similar age in the area, the average in the country, the rest of the respondent's family, and the respondent herself in the past—a reference group which Runciman's results implied were the most important. The answers formed the basis of five variables of which four distinguished respondents who felt worse off than a specific reference group, and the fifth distinguished respondents who felt worse off than three or more reference groups. The last of these is an indicator of the pervasiveness of the feeling of being worse off than members of the reference group—an indicator of the generality of the feeling of being relatively badly off. No attempt has been made to assess for each subject the two necessary conditions for relative deprivation—that the subject wants equality with (or superiority to) the reference group, and that he sees such equality (or superiority) as feasible.[59]

Lee Rainwater computed functions yielding variables of this kind. Surprisingly, perhaps, he seemed to establish good fits for functions predicting social status and 'magnitude of poorness' from income. Possibly, this aspect of his results is partly an artifact of his selection of a measure of 'goodness of fit', the coefficient of determination. The coefficient of determination may leave the reader with a false impression of 'goodness of fit' in this case because it reflects the large variance and skewed distribution of income. A more appropriate basis for judging the goodness of fit would be variances of estimates of the dependent variable at different levels of income deficit compared with median income. Since it is likely that Rainwater's fits are heteroscedastic, one could not accept without question the ratio of the standard error of the regression estimate to the mean of the dependent variable as an adequate measure of goodness of fit. Unfortunately, Rainwater does not present results which would allow an assessment of the validity of his functions by these criteria. (See Lee Rainwater, *What Money Buys: Inequality and the Social Meanings of Income*, Basic Books, New York, 1974, chapter 7.)

[59] *Relative Deprivation and Social Justice*, Penguin, Harmondsworth, 1965, p. 10.

Therefore, our data could not measure the Runciman concept itself, and neither could they distinguish between the effects of the magnitude and degree of relative deprivation.[60] Whether the combined effects of magnitude and intensity of deprivation are usually great enough to have general influence on behaviour was taken to be the limit of the concern of this study; and *prima facie* evidence of that could be established if one or more of the reference group poverty indicators had an effect on other variables in appropriate multivariate models. In particular, it would show whether or not a feeling of poverty in relation to any one reference group was a precondition for attitudes or action; or whether a sense of being pervasively worse off than others is necessary; or whether when treated as an incentive it is much affected by the negative incentive of a perception of one or more aspects of the free meals context as potentially stigmatizing.[61]

It could be argued that relative deprivation was unlikely to play an important part in the causal processes we are investigating, since Runciman found that in general people did not feel acutely deprived. But since 1962, the last year for which Runciman had empirical data, events have been such as to cause one to predict an increase in the importance of feelings of relative deprivation. Higher rates of unemployment than were prevalent in the early 1960s have been accompanied by an acceleration in the rate of inflation. Both would contribute (possibly interactively) to an enhanced feeling of relative deprivation. Comparisons of standards of living with other groups might well have been encouraged by the preoccupation of political debate with rising prices (particularly of food and housing), with incomes policies and their implementation, with the Industrial Relations Act, the Housing Finance Act, and the raising of charges for social services. There has also been

---

[60] By the magnitude of relative deprivation, Runciman meant 'The extent of the difference between the desired situation and that of the person (as he sees it)'. By the degree of relative deprivation was meant the intensity with which deprivation was felt.

[61] Neither the concept nor its present operationalization are free of difficulties. Runciman's work was over simple because it implied that there is a small number of relevant reference groups, Burns arguing that 'few sociologists now credit the idea of the reference group with the structural rigidity and usefulness which Runciman seems to believe it has'. (T. Burns, 'Relative deprivation and social justice', *British Journal of Sociology, 17*, 4, December 1966, p. 431.) Certainly little progress has been made in mapping important reference groups for issues such as poverty even if the preconditions of such mapping exist. Also, much of the literature is unclear about the level of causal process implied in arguments using reference groups—whether they are sociological, social psychological, or psychological; and the observed phenomena seem to be explicable with equal plausibility using other concepts (like status dissent). Of course, this study has been unable to tackle such fundamental issues of basic social science, but must make the best it can of the problems on which it focusses with the tools available.

widespread discussion of our slow rates of economic growth and low real wages by international standards, and (judging from opinion polls and emigration statistics) these may now have a strong effect on public perceptions. Wilkinson and Turner imply that the incomes of manual workers have suffered disproportionately from the effects of taxation and rising prices, as Townsend argued for the poor in *Labour and Inequality*.[62] Increases in the frequency of strikes and the unwillingness of trade unions to co-operate with either party in voluntary wage restraint is additional evidence of a growth in feelings of relative deprivation.

The nature and impact of feelings of relative deprivation, like that of stigma, must depend upon a range of contextual factors. One such factor is the degree of close-knittedness of the area. In the close- knit area, the normative reference groups are more likely to be local than national. It may well be the opposite in the loose-knit area. Alternatively, in the loose-knit area, the local reference group may be replaced in importance by the individual's own experience as the basis of comparison which affects action. In a loose-knit community, a feeling of relative deprivation in relation to the individual's past experience may well cause him to consider afresh his attitudes to the free meals service. In the transition area can be found a greater variety of reactions, reflecting the variety of socialization and experience of its inhabitants.

The discussion of the influence of an expectancy of powerlessness (E) in Atkinson's equation, anomie (M), and the incentive to apply (I), suggests that the basic relationships of the model can only be estimated if they are distinguished from the effects of many contextual factors both structural and cultural—factors like low social class; ethnicity; incomplete family structures where households were without fathers; mothers' employment status; and whether there are children of under school age at home. Such factors include attitudes (like those towards poverty) which reflect personality characteristics, aculturation, broad life experience, and specific experience of the free meals system. Any analysis of the causes of non-uptake of free meals should attempt to take these into account.

Secondly, the discussion has shown that the strength of some factors

---

[62] F. Wilkinson and H. A. Turner, 'The Wage Tax Spiral and Labour Militancy' in D. Jackson, H. A. Turner and F. Wilkinson, *Do Trade Unions Cause Inflation?*, Cambridge University Press, London, 1972; and P. Townsend and N. Bosanquet eds, *'Labour and Inequality'*, Fabian Society, London, 1972.

depends upon the presence or strength of others, and the variables that measure them are indicators whose association with the factors may well vary between groups. Therefore what statisticians call interaction effects, the effects of the presence or level of one causal variable on the influence of another—are crucial to the argument. Indeed, the argument suggests that what is important is not to derive some average values over the whole population for the direct and indirect effects of the factors, but to examine how the factors influence relatively homogeneous groups of persons. This has important consequences for the form of our analysis. In particular, a model which assumed that the effects of the factors were additive would be inappropriate.

Our analysis has developed a general theoretical model from the causal assumptions of the universalists. However, the three causal factors—powerlessness, anomie, and incentive—have their significance for the policy analyst because of their impact on the three proximate causes of non-uptake—stigma, lack of knowledge, and difficulty in claiming—since it is these that he is most likely to be able to influence. Moreover, the discussion has made it clear that the causal pattern is complicated. The effects of many of the causal factors (pervasive as well as contextual) depend on the presence or absence of others, and our evidence about the pattern of causal relations is incomplete. It is important to explore the pattern of causation, and in particular to assess the compatibility with the arguments we have stated here, before undertaking our policy analysis.

5 The Reasons for Non-uptake: the Analysis of the Survey

Part I of this chapter outlines what we infer to be the principal implications of the detailed analysis of the survey data. Such a summary has been attempted so that readers need not lose the main thread of the argument of the book by devoting effort to the detailed analysis at their first reading. Nevertheless, a reading of Part II is indispensable. The inferences of Part I are at a far higher level of generality than those contained in Part II. Since it is one of our main themes that policy should be developed to take account of the variation in the impact of factors between groups of consumers, the more detailed evidence of Part II is an essential basis for the policy argument. Moreover, the causal processes examined are complex, and the data and theoretical framework which make them interpretable are insufficiently robust to allow sweeping but unambiguously correct conclusions. Only by examining the relationship between our argument and the evidence of the analyses is it feasible to judge what different causal inferences are compatible with the data, and so what different alternative policies would be viable. Inevitably, Part II includes only some of the written argument developed during the course of the research, and only a few of the results of the analyses on which that argument was based. Nevertheless, it is hoped that the publication of Part II will enable readers to exercise their own knowledge and imagination in extending the range of causal explanations and their implications for policy.

I The Principal Implications of the Analyses

It was argued at the end of Chapter 4 that a simple model built exclusively from the indicators of the three main causal factors distinguished there would be inappropriate for our purposes. Our interest was rather to seek for interactions between these factors with the contextual variables which in general have such a large influence on outcomes. We chose a technique which would do this. We have therefore not attempted to estimate the parameters of our general model in this chapter, although it would be feasible (though laborious) to do so in a way that allowed for the complexity of the interaction effects between these and the other variables. We have been content merely to seek the crude understanding needed before such modelling could be undertaken—to look for the more important of the effects of the variables and to assess whether the direction of causation is in general that predicted.

1. We examined whether alienation and anomie had positive effects on the probability of perceiving the free meals context as potentially stigmatizing, it being an essential argument of the universalists that alienation, anomie, and perceiving a context to be stigmatizing are mutually reinforcing and so positively correlated. In general, the results fail to support the argument. It would seem that retreatist anomie, as measured by NEGCOND (negative contacts with the school) lowers the probability that mothers see the school meals context as pervasively stigmatizing. It would seem that the perception reflected a general attitude acquired through a general socialization process rather than specific experience. It would seem from a comparison of the results for PDKD (an indicator of expectancy of unawareness of eligibility rules) and OSPSD (an indicator of the pervasiveness of the expectation of stigmatization and loss of self-esteem) and other stigma indicators that among those with high retreatist anomie and high alienation, stigma may have been a less important reason for not claiming their entitlement than a lack of knowledge about the service. There were, of course, groups of mothers in which alienation had the positive effect predicted by the universalists. Examples of this have been discussed in the text.

The theory predicted other relationships. The third causal factor specified in our theoretical model was Incentive. In general this was negatively associated with the probability of perceiving the free meals context as pervasively stigmatizing. An important feature of the general theory was that all three causal factors would interact. The analyses provide some evidence that such interactions were not powerful determinants of the stigma, lack of information, and the perception that 'applying' was complex, though such interactions were apparent among some groups of mothers.

It would therefore be mistaken to believe that our general model contributes the kind of understanding of causes of variations in the three factors (and so of uptake itself) needed for policy analysis. To my mind, this is not a surprising result. It is exactly analogous to the comparative failure of statistical models incorporating only resource and other instrumental variables (but omitting contextual factors) to explain variations in educational achievement or health status. The former were reviewed by Jencks,[1] who pessimistically concluded that such efforts are doomed to failure. No doubt he is right if modellers are unwilling to complicate their analyses from their very inception by attempting to control for the contextual factors whose influences are powerful. Analyses such as those undertaken in this chapter are a necessary preliminary to the modelling process.

The interactive relationships, both among the contextual factors and between contextual factors and others, yielded some interesting insights. A feature of the results was the interaction between characteristics which have stigmatizing properties quite independent of the free meals contexts, and the perception of the stigma potential of that context. The free meals context was a catalyst. It presented others with the opportunity, an arena in which to stigmatize on such grounds as race, colour, or being an unmarried mother.

2. The Area argument presented in Chapter 1 received support from the analysis. The causal processes operated more through stigma than through the availability of information or perceptions about complexity of obtaining the service. For instance, mothers were more likely to think that teachers would stigmatize in the under-achieving authority, but that other children would stigmatize in the over-achieving authority; and higher proportions in the under-achieving authority accepted the proposition that non-uptake occurred because free meals were thought to be 'a charity'. Thus stigmatization by agents of the authority was considered more likely in the under-achieving authority. Moreover, in the under-achieving authority, closeness of contact with the school increased the probability that mothers would think teachers would stigmatize, whereas the opposite was the case in the over-achieving authority; and the declaration of income was accepted as a cause of non-uptake by mothers of fatherless families more in the under-achieving authority. Again the effects of the higher level of publicity in the over-achieving authority seemed to have been particularly powerful among groups who were likely to have been exposed to it longest.

3. Low income itself did not appear to make much difference to the pattern of associations of causal factors with a perception that the free meals context was pervasively stigmatizing. The analysis of STATINCD suggested that low income was not in itself a stigmatizing charac-

[1] Christopher Jencks *et al.*, *Inequality*, Allen Lane, London, 1973.

teristic. However there was support for the argument that mothers of families with low incomes were more likely to think that applying would be complicated.

4. Whether or not mothers had had experience of free meals seemed more of an outcome than a cause of the perception that the meals context was stigmatizing. Publicity might have been successful in reducing the probability that the context would be seen to be stigmatizing, but the evidence was compatible with the argument that some mothers had probably been deterred from applying because they perceived the context as stigmatizing. Those with recent experience tended to have lower probabilities of accepting the proposition that the context was stigmatizing. This result can be explained in a number of ways. First, the probability of being stigmatized might well have been diminishing in the 1960s with the rediscovery of child poverty, the publicization of policies to mitigate it, and the recruitment of teachers from a generation whose social values and assumptions reflected a new compassion and optimism. Similarly, successive cohorts of mothers might also have applied to the context these changing values and assumptions, ideas which would make them less likely to feel ashamed about revealing their need. Our results confirm that the perceptions of the stigma potential of the service by the poor was similar to those of mothers in general.

Had the results implied that experience of the free meals scheme was generally such as to cause mothers to perceive the context to be stigmatizing, it could have been argued that stigma was important in the causal process which Rodman described as 'value stretch'.[2] That this was not so may have been due to the more extensive adoption of an ideology that could be expected to diminish value stretch.

The Supporting Evidence

The results of this chapter are not the only ones yielded by the survey to contribute to our assessment of the importance of the influence of local authorities and the three proximate causes listed in the second paragraph of Chapter 4. It is appropriate to summarize here other results of relevance to the assessment. Section (i) does so for the proximate causes; section (ii) for local authority influence.

---

[2] H. L. Rodman, 'The lower class value stretch', *Social Forces, 42*, December 1963, pp. 205–15.

(i) The Impact of the Three Proximate Causes

Stigma. Stigma and lack of knowledge are among the causal factors whose influence is most complex. Our findings, which throw light on the importance of the former, include the fact that stigma appeared to have been absent among the thoughts of mothers who were thinking about applying and who subsequently applied for the first and only time; that once families had applied, there was little delay in first thinking of and actually applying on subsequent occasions; that only two out of fifty respondents, one of whose families had not been granted free meals as a result of their applications, said that they would not apply again for reasons which might be connected with stigma; that a minority, varying in size between less than a tenth and a fifth, of those mothers whose families had not received free meals and who had not considered applying for them, quoted stigma factors as reasons for not considering applying (in particular, their unwillingness to reveal personal information, their pride as parents, and the possibility of embarrassment to the child); that a low proportion of respondents said that they had thought about stigma factors before applying for the second or subsequent time; that between 39 and 55 per cent of respondents to an open-ended question gave stigma factors as reasons why parents of eligible children do not apply for free meals; that high proportions of respondents agreed with specific proportions implying forms of stigma as explanations of non-uptake by those eligible to apply. Not unexpected was the fact that 44 and 48 per cent of free meals receivers were from social class III families—eminently among the 'respectable' working class.

When respondents were asked about their own considerations and actions, they did not rate stigma factors highly; but when they were asked to account for other people's behaviour, they did so as much in terms of stigma as of any other factor. There are many possible explanations for this. One is that respondents were unwilling to be completely honest with the interviewers, and avoided stigma factors when talking about themselves, but were quite willing to talk about it in relation to other people. However this hardly seems compatible with their honesty and frankness in other parts of this questionnaire —including the 45 questions which preceded some of the stigma questions. (Some of these were likely to be untruthfully answered if a sense of stigma was felt, but were not.) A second is that people may not have been willing to admit to themselves that receiving something, whose benefit to the family is clear, was stigmatizing; because the stigmatized behaviour was very attractive, they were unwilling to face a dilemma consciously by admitting to themselves that the behaviour was stigmatizing. This does not seem, on the face of it, to be compatible with attributing stigmatizing qualities to the behaviour of other people. A third explanation might be that respondents' ideas about what influences other people's behaviour might have been more a reflection of political mythology and stereotypes than of knowledge or projection of their own experience and feelings. In the context of the inherited hostility towards the means-tested services which was learned from parents and older members of the family who had experienced them before the war, this was not an implausible hypothesis. In our view, the last is the most probable explanation; the second is less probable; and the first is much less probable. It seems to us likely that stigma was not the main cause of non-uptake for as many mothers as was believed in the late 1960s. In retrospect, this conclusion may seem less surprising than it was at the time. Indeed, we ourselves greeted our results with incredulity. (See for instance my discussion in the Seth Lecture for 1971.)[3] When expectations have been aroused by theoretical or ideological argument backed by many examples reliably reported by politicians and the media, even the most clear-cut findings are difficult to accept.

This analysis gives less support than expected to the universalists' argument that alienation, anomie, and a perception that the free meals context is potentially stigmatizing, mutually reinforce one another. Perhaps this was a more surprising result than that stigma was not overwhelmingly the most important reason for non-uptake. Indeed, the general model of Chapter 4 proved an inadequate basis of understanding for a policy argument. This was so although an attempt was made to enhance its intellectual coherence and broaden the range of evidence on which its plausibility depends by linking the arguments of the (mainly) British social policy writers with sociological argument that had been extensively tested and developed in other contexts. Perhaps a broad causal theory is generally an insufficient basis for policy argument about the desirability of policy alternatives without the analysis of detailed evidence about their costs and consequences. The reason is often that the propositions of causal theory must be combined with other propositions if they are to be used for predictions about consequences needed for policy analysis; and all of the propositions are probability statements, based on relatively weak statistical relation-

[3] Bleddyn Davies, *Planning Resources for Personal Social Services, The James Seth Memorial Lecture*, University of Edinburgh, 1972.

ships. Therefore the derived predictions about consequences are inevitably weaker than the causal propositions on which they draw.

The effectiveness of publicity had been evident from the reaction of parents to the 'personal circular' issued by the Minister of Education for all parents of school children in November 1967. This letter contained information about the levels of income at which children were eligible for the benefit. Not all of the subsequent increase was attributable to the chain reaction set up by the Minister's letter, since the September count for 1967 had yielded a free meals uptake rate well above the value one would have predicted from the rates for the previous decade. It is clear that the discussion provoked by the rediscovery of child poverty (confirmed by the Plowden Report's emphasis on the problems of the deprived pupil) had been having some effect before the November circular was issued. But the doubling of the free meals uptake rate, although to a large extent due to the inclusion of all fourth and subsequent children among those eligible, provided dramatic evidence that lack of information was a major cause of non-uptake.[4] Our survey provided further evidence of this. Substantial proportions applying for free meals for the first or only time named uncertainty about their eligibility as something they had thought about during the period (often of considerable length) when they were considering applying. It is probable that the proportion would have been higher among those (two-thirds of respondents) who had first applied before November 1967. Substantial proportions of those with no experience of free meals and who had not considered applying for them gave as reasons either that they did not know much about the free meals scheme or that they were ineligible because they were at work. The proportion was more than a quarter among the non-takers' group in the under-achieving authority—a group with a relatively high probability of being eligible. Between a fifth and two-fifths of all respondents gave ignorance as the main reason why eligible children were not receiving free meals. The proportions were particularly high among non-takers and payers in the under-achieving authority. Between a half and four-fifths of respondents in the receiving groups agreed with the proposition that not knowing about the service was an important reason why children were not receiving free meals though eligible for them. Again there is evidence that this might have been felt particularly in the under-achieving authority. High proportions of those respon-

[4] It is also possible that the November letter and the fourth child rule had reduced the feeling that to claim free meals would have stigmatizing consequences.

dents who did recall the leaflet did not recall having any information from the school before November 1967.

But the survey also suggested that it is likely that ignorance interacted with other factors to cause shortfall. Among these was the complexity of the procedure. Between a tenth and two-fifths of those who had applied stated that they had found applying a difficult rather than a simple procedure. This, given that a substantial minority of mothers was as nearly enough illiterate as to make the filling in of forms a difficult task, and that illiteracy is very stigmatizing, was likely to have been an understatement.[5] Most respondents admitting to difficulty stated that this arose principally in filling in the form. A second factor was the high proportion of persons in the sample who had not been born in this country. Roughly one-quarter of mothers in each group had not been born in the British Isles. A third factor is that between a third and two-fifths of mothers of non-taking children in the two areas worked, and this added to the pressure on their time and ability to chase up opportunities. It is therefore not surprising that respondents depended to a considerable extent on help they received. Particularly interesting is how much they depended on employees of the local education authorities (particularly teachers) and how little on relatives, neighbours, or friends. Thus there is no shortage of evidence to suggest that the absence of information, taken with mothers' inability to devote time and energy to coping with a complex system, was probably the most important factor causing the shortfall in uptake. However, the survey results also show that occasional publicity, even of the directness of the leaflet, may have had less impact than might have been expected, since high proportions of respondents did not recall receiving the leaflet, and low proportions had a poor recollection of what it contained. Respondents did, however, agree that it was an important factor in making people decide to apply for free meals for the first time. And of those who returned a completed application form as a result of the leaflet, 70 per cent proved eligible. High proportions of respondents, particularly among the non-taker and free meals groups, thought that parents ought to receive information which would enable them to work out whether or not they were eligible.

(ii) The Influence of the Local Authority

Without doubt, these results confirmed our earlier findings about the

[5] Department of Education and Science, *A Language for Life*, H.M.S.O., London, 1975.

importance of variation in the performance of individual authorities. Perhaps the residuals of the Davies and Williamson models exaggerated the under- and over-achievement of authorities to some degree. But there can be no doubting that the phenomenon of local authority variation in shortfall was a real one. The statistical analyses showed not only that most of the variation in the free meals uptake rates could not have been explained in terms of need correlates in 1966 (under assumptions about the relative importance of different aspects of need, that are likely to maximize its explanatory power), but also that changes in the free meals uptake rates through time could not have been explained to any significant degree by changes in the incidence of need. Variation in free meals uptake rates paralleled large unexplained (and unjustified) variations in paid meals uptake in all the years looked at and (more justifiable perhaps, but widely differing) rates of growth in uptake.

The survey provided evidence throwing more light on the apparent under- and over-achievement of authorities. There was evidence that a wider cross-section of society had had experience of the scheme in the over-achieving authority. This might have reflected the degree of social organization in an area, and other factors, but it was also likely to reflect attitudes to the services influenced by supply conditions, and might itself have reduced the danger that receiving the service might cause stigma. A higher proportion of non-takers and payers in the under-achieving authority were from incomplete families. The proportion of families receiving free meals for a short time was greater in the over-achieving authority. This is in some ways a crucial index, since it suggested a pattern in which those of marginal eligibility might have had a higher probability of receiving meals, and a pattern in which the uptake rate was sensitive to the fluctuations in incomes which caused considerable numbers to become eligible for relatively short periods of time. Unemployment was a more important factor causing people to apply for free meals in the under-achieving authority. It was the group whose head of household was in low-paid employment who was most likely not to obtain free meals. For instance, the Ministry of Social Security survey showed that 37 per cent of non-taking children from families with more than two children whose family resources would have made the children eligible were from families where the father was in full-time work.[6] Non-takers' mothers were more likely not to have considered applying for reasons of ignorance in the under-achieving authority. A fall in family income was a more frequent event occurring

[6] Ministry of Social Security, *The Circumstances of Families*, op. cit., Table II.

in the twelve months preceding the making of an application in the under-achieving authority. It is possible that such a fall was necessary before people there would consider applying for free meals. The mean number of children granted meals per application was greater in the under-achieving authority, implying that the relative need of the families was greater, and the relative increase in the number of children receiving free meals as a result of the leaflet was greater. In the under-achieving authority, higher proportions of non-takers' mothers claimed that there were times when their children could not afford meals. Higher proportions of respondents in the under-achieving authority in each group could not recall having received any information from the school before the D.E.S. leaflet was issued. The proportion in the non-takers' group who thought that the D.E.S. leaflet had helped them to understand how the scheme worked was higher in the under-achieving authority. The proportions of mothers from the non-takers and free meals receivers groups who stated that advice from a third person was of at least some importance in helping them to apply were lower in the under-achieving authority, and the principal sources of this help were employees of the local education authority.

The interviews provided further evidence. The over-achieving authority appeared to be more promotional than the under-achieving authority in several respects. An education welfare officer was available to parents for advice at one of the schools in each area on one day a week. The under-achieving authority had a lower ratio of education welfare officers to children than the over-achiever, and the three under-achieving authorities had a lower average ratio (1 : 3,300) than the three over-achievers (1 : 2,900). One of the over-achievers had issued leaflets containing comprehensive information about the free meals scheme and other means-tested benefits to all parents through the schools. There appeared to be a tendency for the over-achieving authorities to provide better facilities for training welfare officers. The analyses discussed in Chapter 5 confirmed that the area effect on uptake was felt more through stigma than through the other proximate causes.

All this is circumstantial evidence, results which, taken individually, might have alternative explanations. It would have been possible to collect at least some equally ambiguous evidence which would have implied that the under-achieving authority was in fact doing better than the over-achieving authority. Therefore the concepts of under- and over-achievement must be used very carefully. Our data was not such that we could unambiguously assess the relative importance of the consequences of authorities' actions (and the attitudes and behaviour of their employees) from attributes of the respondents. For such reasons, one cannot take the results of the survey presented in the body of our report as being entirely due to varying local provision just because there was a difference in the attitudes or behaviour of respondents and their families, any more than one can accept the size of the residual in the Davies and Williamson model as being an exact indicator of the relative performance of the authorities. It is of the nature of the research process in a complex situation where one cannot use laboratory experiments that analyses cannot eliminate the ambiguity of the evidence collected. Moreover, that part of the differences in shortfall that were in some way due to the authority's own provision was not to be explained in terms of current provision. Studies of voting behaviour remind us yet again that the family is the most powerful as well as the most fundamental unit for socialization and the determination of behaviour. Family attitudes to means-tested services, to education, to the use of leisure, are acquired over a long period. The kind of service being offered in the mid-fifties was probably of great importance in determining shortfall in uptake during the late 1960s. New attitudes and behaviour are not learnt quickly. They take a long time to spread through society in the absence of dramatic events which force issues into the open and compel a re-evaluation of circumstances. What help an authority provides, and how it provides that help, interacts with external environmental forces to determine what is expected of it, and thus the demand for its services. In this servo-mechanistic recursive process, provision in the quite distant past is of great influence.

The analysis of causes of short-fall was the principal focus of our enquiry. Some of the other results—particularly those showing how respondents felt the service to be of use and those giving clues about the possible losers and gainers from the various changes—yielded evidence relevant to a judgement about the constraints on political action. The service was popular. Respondents would, it appears, have preferred to see more spending on the general school meals subsidy than on making more children eligible for free meals, but, rather inconsistently, the most popular basis for school meals pricing was one which implied a means-tested service for all receivers. Most people approved of collective action to tackle poverty problems. Mothers were, in general, satisfied with the quantity and quality of the meals served, and thought the accommodation and supervision to be adequate. The meals were particularly liked by the mothers of free meals receivers. Few mothers seemed to see any disadvantages either for themselves or their child in taking meals. Groups other than free meals receivers' mothers placed considerable emphasis on the saving in travel, fatigue, and other non-nutritional advantages to the child. Most of the payers' mothers saw the main advantage to themselves as allowing them to work, a result which confirms one of the Davies and Williamson findings,[7] and which is quite compatible with the results described in Davies et al.[8] Other mothers saw the main advantage to themselves as being a reduction in their work, although a substantial minority of free meals receivers' mothers quoted cheapness as the main one. A surprisingly heavy emphasis was placed on the non-nutritional advantages.

(iii) Conclusion

Our main conclusion is that our general theoretical argument, though it would seem plausible and well supported by salient evidence from the contexts, would have been a misleading basis for policy-making, since in practice it does not predict with any reliability how the benefits and disbenefits of alternative policy options would have been felt by different groups of mothers and children. Perhaps this is generally true. A general causal theory usually explains too little of the variance of the principal outcomes to be more than an inadequate basis for assessing policy proposals, even when its most important predictions are in general compatible with the evidence, though of course the analysis of the causal processes can contribute to the basis of understanding acquired for developing alternative policies. It is clear that other kinds of models must also be employed, models whose purpose is to describe the consequences of alternatives and the incidence of these consequences. An attempt to develop such models is made in the next chapter.

II The Elaboration of the Analysis of the Survey Data

Section 1 explains why the analysis focusses not on mothers' statements about their own experience, but on their judgements about the importance to others of the proximate causes of non-uptake. It also outlines the main dependent variables used. The second section discusses the analyses of the main stigma indicator, OSPSD, and a second indicator

---

[7] Bleddyn Davies and Valerie Williamson, 'School meals: short-fall and poverty', op. cit.

[8] Bleddyn Davies et al., 'Some constraints on school meals policy', op. cit.

of the perceived pervasiveness of stigma, OSD. The third section contains the discussions of mothers' views about the importance of specific forms of stigma. Section 4 is based on the analyses of our indicators of how complex mothers think claiming entitlement to be, and their views on whether lack of knowledge was an important reason for non-uptake.

1. Dependent Variables

(i) Mothers' Statements about Factors which Affected their own Decisions to Apply

The questionnaire contained a large number of questions whose analysis could throw light on the importance of stigma, difficulties in handling the mechanics of applying, and ignorance of the service and the conditions under which it is provided. It is unnecessary to re-state the results of our analyses of the answers to these questions here, the results having been described in Chapter 3. Some analyses are particularly important and revealing. Among these are the analyses of the statements by mothers applying for the first and only time about what factors they had in mind at this time, and of the reasons for not applying given by people who did not do so.

(a) It will be remembered that the analysis of mothers' statements about their thoughts when considering applying revealed four features: first, stigma-related factors were mentioned by a substantial minority of respondents; second, uncertainty about eligibility was also mentioned by a substantial minority of mothers; third, the most frequently mentioned thought was an awareness of their entitlement and therefore that they should claim the service; and fourth, no mothers mentioned difficulties in handling the service. It is interesting that such a high proportion of mothers claimed to be aware that they were entitled, and yet, as the answers to another question showed, waited for a long time before applying. Is this evidence of rather stronger feelings of stigma than the respondents were willing to admit? Did the process of applying seem to be more complicated at the time than it appeared with the benefit of hindsight, and did respondents tend to forget this? The same features were as apparent among mothers from low income groups as among mothers in general.

(b) Another question, asking specifically whether the procedure of applying had difficult aspects, yielded answers confirming the apparent unimportance of difficulties. Again, the same feature was apparent among mothers with low standardized incomes. Is this evidence compatible with what is known about the large minority of adults who have limited skills in using the written word? Newcomers from the West Indies, India, and Pakistan were well represented in the sample.

It is possible that those who applied are in some ways less vulnerable to stigma and the other factors than others. Among mothers who had never considered applying—as much among those of the mothers who were from households whose incomes were low at the time of the survey as among others—a minority claimed stigma factors to be an important reason for not doing so. Another substantial minority either made statements which admitted that they did not know about the service, or made such statements as their children were not eligible because they (the mothers) were in paid employment, so implying that they did not know about the criteria of eligibility. Also it is likely that some of the respondents who thought themselves ineligible may have considered applying if they had known the criteria for eligibility.[9]

Our analysis cannot be based on these results alone. They are based on small numbers of respondents. It is also difficult to interpret what respondents mean by some of the categories used, such as 'simple', 'difficult', and 'consider'. What degree of difficulty had they in mind? How deeply did they consider applying before they stated that they did? Did the mother, for instance, always discuss it with her husband at this stage? More important, one suspects that some of the figures may understate the true importance of the factors. It is clear that the mothers' statements about factors which affected their own decisions to apply were an inadequate basis for the analysis required to unravel the causal processes discussed in Chapter 4.

(ii) Dependent Variables Analysed

We have shown that a substantial minority of persons with experience of applying for and receiving free meals felt stigma in connection with doing so. These results are what one would expect from other evidence.[10] Are the statements of mothers in the survey likely to under or

---

[9] It is important that stigma appeared to be more important in the over-achieving area, and lack of knowledge to be more important in the under-achieving area. We have independent evidence that the Education Department of the over-achieving area had devoted more attention to publicizing the service than the Education Department of the under-achieving area.

[10] See, for instance, Hilary Land, *Large Families in London*, op. cit.; Peter Moss, *Welfare Rights Project, '68*, Merseyside CPAG, Liverpool, 1969; and Peter Moss, *Welfare Rights Project Two*, Merseyside CPAG, Liverpool, 1970.

overstate the scale of stigmatized response? A number of factors might cause some biases. Replies to questions, particularly open-ended questions asking for generalizations about services, can sometimes have some of the characteristics of a conversation whose function is, at least, partly affective, and therefore may err towards the statement of whatever is expected. The result might, in many cases, be an overstatement of stigma. Any anxiety in discussing issues with an interviewer might also bias responses towards the conventional. The conventional response would be the one which was compatible with the general 'meaning' of the service learnt by the respondents. Past experience would have a substantial effect on the meaning perceived. As a means-tested service this would bias the results towards an overstatement of the impact of stigma. Also we believe it more likely that any interview bias would lead to the overstatement rather than understatement of this impact.

However, it is also plausible to argue that understatement may occur. For instance, if someone possesses a potentially stigmatizing characteristic, he may choose not to admit it.[11] If a person conceals the stigmatizing characteristics of taking free meals, it may well be the case that he would not be prepared to divulge a sense of stigma in applying for free meals. However, this argument seems incompatible with our evidence. First, applying is probably more stigmatizing than receiving the service. Therefore if the mother does not confess that she receives the service, she is unlikely to confess that she applied for it; and, if this is so, she would not be asked the questions about stigma. Secondly, there are few cases in which people in our free meals sample concealed the fact of receiving free meals. Neither respondents nor interviewers knew we had independent evidence that one of the respondent's children received free meals.

A more likely cause of understatement might be that mothers see the considerable benefit of the service to their children, and would not admit to themselves that receiving such a benefit might be stigmatizing. People may not be (consciously) aware of the degree to which they feel that taking school meals stigmatizes their children or themselves. Nevertheless, their actions may be subconsciously affected by the

[11] 'When his differentness is not immediately apparent and is not known beforehand (or at least not known to him to be known to the others), when, in fact, he is a discreditable, not a discredited person, then the second main possibility ... is to be found. The issue is ... that of managing information about his failing. To display or not to display, to tell or not to tell, to let on or not let on, to lie or not to lie, and, in each case, to whom, how, when and where.' Erving Goffman, *Stigma, Notes on the Management of a Spoiled Identity*, Englewood Cliffs, N.J., 1963, p. 57.

feeling of stigma at the unconscious level. Moreover, some mothers may feel that it is irrational to have a personal feeling of spoiled identity when they are eligible for free meals as a right. Society admires rational behaviour and to some degree deprecates irrational behaviour, especially when it is at the expense of dependent members of society. This is particularly so when the other members of society are dependents for whose care the persons are responsible. Thus respondents may feel a strong need to rationalize their behaviour to the interviewer, and thus not to admit that the irrational stigma that arises when free meals are claimed affects their attitudes towards applying for them, although receiving free meals would benefit their children. Indeed, admitting to such an irrational fear of stigma could be tantamount to showing a disregard for one of the responsibilities of parenthood if the form of stigma feared was one that affected the parent rather than the child, and if the fear was suspected to be irrational; just as admitting that the family qualifies for free meals might be taken by the wage-earner as an admission of failure to bear his responsibilities. It is therefore likely that stigma feelings are suppressed; or that if respondents are conscious of them, they are reluctant to confess them to the interviewer. On balance, therefore, we suspect that stigma might be understated in our results, although we cannot provide anything more than circumstantial evidence to support this suspicion.

Respondents who might be unwilling to confess feelings of stigma, or who are not willing to admit to themselves their own feelings of stigma, may, nevertheless, attribute such feelings to others. Thus the answers to our general questions about the reasons for non-uptake of free meals among those eligible are probably our most reliable indicators of our respondents' perceptions of the forms of stigma that may accompany taking free meals. Taken individually, they do not reflect the relative intensities of the stigmatizing possibilities of claiming free meals among those who feel stigma strongly enough to call it an important reason for non-uptake. However, it is likely that those who feel the potential for stigmatization most strongly would also feel that it would have stigmatizing consequences in most situations. Such people would tend to claim that a relatively large number of stigmatizing consequences would flow from claiming free meals. They would feel that the stigmatizing consequences would be pervasive. In the next section we analyse indicators of this as if they measured respondents' own sensitivity to stigma. However, we would not argue that they measure this alone. They must certainly also reflect respondents' views of how people in general are influenced by the images resulting from social-

ization (particularly political socialization) as well as their own acceptance of this image.

Since the objective of the analysis is to explore the processes by which
scores are determined, and in particular to examine the interactive as
well as the additive effects of predictors in their determination, the technique used in Chapter 2 has been chosen, since it does not assume
additivity. It will be remembered that the technique uses predictors to
explain a dependent variable by scanning all possible binary splits of
each and every predictor, and then chooses the one which minimizes
the ratio of between category sum of squares to total sum of squares.
Having done so, it repeats the process for the new groups created in the
previous stage.[12] At each stage, important parameters are printed, as
is information about alternative splits that might have been made.
Among other things that can be assessed from the values of the parameters are whether or not the relationships are additive or interactive.

The analyses of the result of each principal model that follow use
the abbreviated names for variables described in Appendix A, p. 253
and in Table 5.A on p. 139. Some of the variables have been con-
structed from the answers to groups of questions. OSD, OSPS and OSPSD
are based on answers to questions about the reasons why children (in
general) do not have free meals when eligible for them. OSD is a
dummy variable whose value is unity for respondents who did not
quote any stigma-related reason (or agreed with any stigma-related
proposition about the reasons) for non-uptake. OSPS and OSPSD indicate
the number of types of stigma which the respondents agreed were
important, OSPSD being the probability of agreeing with less than a
typical number, and therefore a negative indicator of stigma. We have
already discussed the importance of respondents' perceptions about the
pervasiveness of stigma. A respondent was allotted the higher value for
OSPSD (Others' Stigma Pervasiveness Score Dummy) when her OSPS
value was three or less. DIFFHLPD is a dummy based upon respondents'
statements that they found the processes of obtaining free meals difficult, or that they received help in obtaining meals. The other dependent
variables—PDKD, COMPD, OCHLDD, TCHERSD, CHARD, EMPLD—are
dummy variables based on the answers to only single questions. Whereas OSPSD is an inverse stigma indicator, PDKD and similar variables are
direct indicators.

---

[12] Various constraints are imposed by the analyst which determine the number of splits
the operation of the program on a set of data will yield.

Table 5.A   *The analysis of reasons for the non-uptake of Free School Meals of variables used in Chapter 5 and their abbreviations*[1]

Variable	Abbreviation

DEPENDENT VARIABLES

Others Stigma Dummy	OSD
Others Stigma Pervasiveness Score (Scored 1 = low, to 5 high)	OSPS
Others Stigma Pervasiveness Score Dummy	OSPSD
Found Difficulty or Received Help Dummy	DIFFHLPD
Other Children make Receivers feel Small Dummy	OCHLDD
Picked on more by Teachers Dummy	TCHERSD
Parents think Free Meals Charity Dummy	CHARD
Applying too Complicated Dummy	COMPD
Don't like Stating Incomes Dummy	STATINGD
Don't like Employers to Know Dummy	EMPLD
Parents Don't Know about Free Meals Dummy	PDKD

INDEPENDENT VARIABLES

(a) Alienation (E)

Individualized Responsibility for Poverty Score Dummy	IRPSD

(b) Anomie (M)

Indicator of Positive attitudes towards and interest in Education	EDID
Negative personal contacts with the schools (Retreatist anomie)	NEGCOND
Positive Opinion of Teachers	EDIIID

(c) Incentive (I)

Reference Group Poverty Pervasiveness Score Dummy	RGPPSD
Family Reference Group Poverty Dummy—Worse off than 'the rest of the family'	FAMRGPD
Locality Reference Group Poverty Dummy—Worse off than 'other people round here of similar age'	LOCRGPD
Country Reference Group Poverty Dummy—Worse off than 'the average in the country'	COUNRGPD
Self Reference Group Poverty Dummy—'Worse off than Ever'	SELFRGPD
Standardized Income Group—the difference between assessed income and eligibility level, using Codes:	SIG

1. less than eligibility level
2. the eligibility level and less than £2 per week above category 1 maximum
3. the eligibility level + £2 p.w. and less than £3 per week above category 2 maximum
4. above the category 3 max.

SIG is based on SUPERI, super-subsistence income, a continuous variable used in Chapter 6

(d) Contextual factors and other causes

Occupation of Husband classified as RG Class V	LSCD
Marital Role Segregation Dummy	MRSD
Mother in paid Employment	MOTHEM

Table 5.A—cont.

Variable	Abbreviation
Code 0. Not in employment	
1. in part time paid employment (not exceeding 5 hours a day)	
2. in full time paid employment (exceeding 5 hours a day)	
Area: Over-achieving	OVERACH
Under-achieving	UNDERACH
Fatherless Family	MOTHALD[2]
Mother's country of birth	MCOB
Code 1. Great Britain	
2. Ireland	
3. West Indies	
4. India or Pakistan	
Experience of applying for free meals for the first or only time	EXP
Code 0. no experience	
1. within last year	
2. more than a year ago	
(e) Cost	
Potential cost of providing free school meals to a group, assuming 100 per cent uptake. (Used in Chapter 6.)	CUMPFMCOST

Notes: [1] The diagrams code 1 the possession of a characteristic or high scores on a dummy variable.
[2] MOTHALs in the text denotes fatherless family.

2. Others' Stigma Pervasiveness

A. OSPSD (Others' stigma pervasiveness score)

OSPSD is an inverse, not a direct indicator of the degree of pervasiveness of the perceived importance of stigma as an explanation of the non-uptake of free meals. Therefore high OSPSD scores indicate a low probability of perceiving pervasive stigma as a cause of others' non-uptake.

(i) The whole sample and the twelve predictors (Tables 5.1, 5.2 and Diagram 5.1)

The predictors used were: Area, IRPSD, LSCD, SIG, MCOB, EDID, NEGCOND, EDIIID, MRSD, MOTHEM, RGPPSD, and EXP. Diagram 5.1 shows the tree diagram which illustrates the stepwise binary splitting of the sample by the analysis of variance criterion of the highest ratio of between category sum of squares to total sum of squares. The cells of the diagram show the predictor and the classes of the predictor which are included in that cell, the cell mean, and the number of observations. The patterns of variation shown in the diagrams are not described. Instead, their possible implications are discussed.

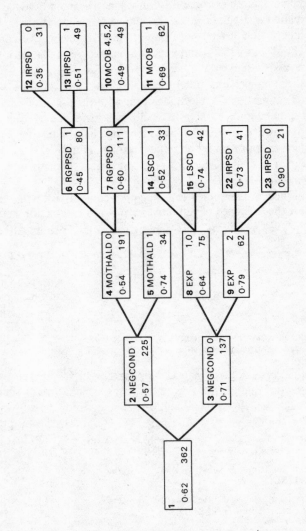

Diagram 5.1 Others' stigma pervasiveness score dummy (OSPSD) twelve predictors (including RGPPSD)

(a) Alienation, Socialization, and Experience of Applying

The analysis shows that NEGCOND (Negative Contacts with the School) was the best single predictor of OSPSD. Those with negative contacts with the school were more likely to have high OSP scores, although high proportions scored highly in each NEGCOND group. One would have predicted that the probability of stigmatization would be positively correlated with NEGCOND—for instance, the teachers are far more likely to pick on children whose parents have had negative contacts with the school than others, and negative contacts with the school may tend to be associated with other characteristics which may amplify stigmatization by persons other than teachers. The answers to the question reflect mothers' subjective appraisal of the potential of a context for stigmatization rather than the real incidence of such stigmatization. However important the latter may be for many purposes, it is the subjective appraisal by potential recipients that is the important determinant of demand. The two may not always be associated, but here it seems they are.

It was argued in Chapter 4 that negative contacts with the school could reflect the existence of retreatist anomie—a disjunction between socially approved means and ends leading to low motivation. Although

Table 5.1   *The means for NEGCOND groups of the constituent variables of OSPS*

Variable	NEGCOND Group	
	Low	High
Mothers thought that the factor named in the proposition was an important explanation of non-uptake of free meals by those eligible		
That other children make receiving children feel small (OCHLD)	.604	.664
That the children who take free meals are picked on more by teachers (TCHERSD)	.160	.175
That the parents of the children don't apply because they think that taking them is receiving charity (CHARD)	.716	.810
That the parents don't apply because they don't like stating their incomes (STATINCD)	.684	.744
That parents don't apply because they don't like their employer to know that they are applying (EMPLD)	.538	.584

(Proportions of 1)

someone might have a high score on NEGCOND for quite different reasons, the school would be marked as a particularly alien institution of a broader society whose main influences on the person were perceived as repressive and exploitative. If the school itself were perceived with particular distrust and antipathy, the impact of NEGCOND on those of the components of OSPSD which most clearly reflect the mother's perception of the school—the propensity of teachers to stigmatize children, or of other school children to stigmatize them—would be greater than on the other components. Table 5.1 shows that this is not so, although NEGCOND has an effect in the same direction as it has on OSPSD in each case. If anything, the form of stigma, the perception of which appears to be most enhanced by NEGCOND, is parents' perception of meals as a charity, and the effect on this is smaller than that on OSPSD. The results described in Table 5.1 therefore seem to be more compatible with the view that low NEGCOND scores are a reflection of a disposition that is not specific to the school but is pervasive. This disposition—reflected to some degree in NEGCOND—is not mainly a low social class phenomenon. Not only is NEGCOND a superior predictor of OSPSD than is LSCD, but the proportion of mothers of low social class is similar among the high and low NEGCOND groups. Similarly it is not mainly a reflection of mothers' perceptions of the causes of poverty, since the proportions of mothers in the two groups with high IRPSD scores is no different. Perhaps therefore it is a general and pervasive sense of retreatist anomie that is indicated by NEGCOND, and which tends to create an expectation of stigma—as again is implicit in the argument of Chapter 4. And perhaps the retreatist anomie that is causally important was learnt as part of the process of aculturation rather than as a reaction to specific experience. That NEGCOND has an influence on the pervasiveness of feelings of stigma more than on individual types of stigma supports this argument.

The Atkinson theory postulated that Alienation, Anomie and Incentive indicators would interact—without the presence of all the factors, no action would be taken. Evidence of such interaction would be interesting, especially if it were a global feeling of anomie that was important. In particular, other component variables of the global concept of anomie should also contribute to the explanation of OSPSD in the same way as NEGCOND. IRPSD (Individualized Responsibility for Poverty) is an inverse indicator of alienation. Diagram 5.1 shows that in group 9, IRPSD has the predicted positive effect on the pervasiveness of stigma's importance. An individualized perception of the responsibility for poverty taken with the early exposure to the processes of applying for free meals, but with fewer than typical negative contacts with the school, seems to have a considerable effect on mothers' perceptions of the pervasiveness of stigma. It is not that IRPSD in this context distinguishes Matza's 'welfare poor' from the 'disreputable poor'—Klein's 'respectable' working class from the 'roughs'. One would expect the respectable to be more sensitive to stigma potential than the 'roughs' when they have had a similar exposure to poverty; indeed that the respectable believe more strongly that poverty is due to individual failure is probably one of the principal discriminants between the two groups. However, one would expect the 'roughs' to have high NEGCOND scores. IRPSD may also generate OSP among foreign-born mothers, the difference in means being particularly great in group 10,[13] and the residuals of group 13 also have a gradient compatible with the argument. However, IRPSD appears to have the converse effect on group 6.

RGPPSD, an incentive factor, had an effect in the predicted direction on group 4. LSCD (Low Social Class) is also an alienation correlate. Low class has a positive impact on OSPS among low NEGCOND scorers with only recent or no experience of applying for free meals. There also appears to be a LSCD effect on group 13 in the same direction. That the LSCD tend to perceive the context as pervasively stigmatizing is compatible with the above arguments, but is not compatible with those arguments about lower class sub-cultures which imply that since the system itself is not perceived to be legitimate, it is acceptable 'to get one over on "them"', and that taking advantage of services would involve little sense of stigma. The argument that mothers socialized in alienated subcultures are more sensitive to stigma seems the more convincing. But it is impossible to distinguish the global alienation from the more specific LSC effect with the crude indicators used here, since nothing is known about the characteristics of the error terms of the indicators. The evidence suggests that both global alienation and specific components and correlates of it have an influence, general political socialization being reinforced by specific aspects of alienation.

[13] One half of group 10 mothers were Irish.

[14] One might argue that LSCD is anterior to some aspects of alienation. In that case, it should be correlated with the component variables of alienation to a higher degree than OSPSD, and its correlation with OSPSD should be substantially reduced when either IRPSD or RGPPSD is controlled. Neither condition is satisfied—neither for RGPPSD among high NEGCOND non-MOTHALD mothers nor high NEGCOND non-MOTHALD. high RGPSD mothers. So among these high OSPSD mothers, at any rate, LSC is not so much a cause of alienation as a correlate of it. That alienation is one feature of lower social class people, rather than caused by being lower class, is implicit in the American theory of lower class subcultures.

One of the effects of the Minister's leaflet and its associated publicity might have been to make teachers and others less likely to see applicants and recipients as undeserving. If this were so one might expect that pre-leaflet EXP (experience of applying for free meals) would be associated with a perception of the free meals context as pervasively stigmatizing, because recent applicants or non-applicants would not personally have suffered the higher level of prejudice to which those with early EXP were exposed. One would expect this effect to have been particularly powerful among those who had few negative contacts with the school, since they would have a lower probability of expecting prejudice in the schools, or from other such institutions either, if NEGCOND is an indicator of one aspect of alienation. One would therefore anticipate pre-leaflet EXP to cause a perception of free meals as being pervasively stigmatizing among the non-alienated; and perhaps also to reinforce the effects of NEGCOND (Retreatist Anomie), and indicators of Incentive and Alienation (like RGPSD and IRPSD). However, the evidence is quite incompatible with this argument. Although EXP splits the low NEGCOND group, it is those with recent or no EXP who are more likely to perceive the service as pervasively stigmatizing, not those who had suffered early EXP. Is it therefore that OSPSD influences EXP rather than EXP influencing OSPSD? Certainly substantial proportions (30 and 73 per cent) of groups 8 and 9 are eligible on income grounds, and may have been eligible a year or more before the survey. And on *a priori* grounds, it seems as likely that a general disposition should influence specific decisions of a kind to which the disposition is very likely to be relevant, as it is for the disposition to be influenced by historical experience. But if the stigma-insensitive mothers applied before the others, and the Ministerial leaflet did not reduce the perception of the service as being pervasively stigmatizing, one would expect the early EXP mothers to have higher OSPSD proportions—lower probabilities of perceiving pervasive stigma—than non EXP mothers, unless the intensity of the expectation of stigma was related to EXP in a highly complex manner. If anything the opposite is the case. Of the 17 recently EXP mothers, 59 per cent (10) had high OSPSD scores, while of the 58 non-EXP mothers, 66 per cent (38) did so. It is therefore not obvious that EXP is an outcome of OSPSD though the evidence seems more compatible with this than the other causal sequences.

The argument that pre-leaflet EXP involved exposure to prejudice and stigmatization that was subsequently reduced, also suggested the prediction that pre-leaflet EXP would reinforce the effect of NEGCOND and other alienation and anomie indicators. In fact the timing or possession of EXP made little difference to the OSPSD scores of high NEGCOND mothers; though what variation in proportions existed was in a direction contrary to that predicted, the non-EXP being most likely to perceive the context as pervasively stigmatizing and the early EXP being the least likely to do so. The residuals for final groups 10 and 12 also imply that the non-EXP have the highest probability of perceiving pervasive stigma; although SIG (standardized income) might have as powerful an effect on variation in group 12 as EXP, and one would expect EXP and SIG to be associated. Similarly, Area might have as much influence on group 10 as EXP and might be associated with it. There is therefore no sign that early EXP reinforces the effect of negative contacts. Indeed, those with EXP and negative contacts tend to have a lower probability of feeling stigma to be pervasive. Again, the evidence suggests that EXP is more likely to be an effect than a cause of OSPS. One must therefore conclude that the importance attributed to pervasive stigma reflects broad patterns of socialization rather than experience of the service.

(b) The Importance of Low Social Class (LSC) and Area

Some of the theoretically interesting predictors prove unimportant. First, LSCD is weak relatively to specific historical experience (such as negative contact with the school, experience of applying for school meals), whether or not the mother lives with a husband, and—particularly interesting—the perceptions of the mother about her relative poverty, and the reasons why people are poor. The mean for low social class mothers in the whole of the sample on which this analysis is based is only 6 percentage points different from the mean for other mothers; and LSCD does not rival the predictors entering the model at each stage. It is true that LSCD is based on an occupational classification that can only imperfectly reflect some of the more complex concepts of social class reflected in the literature, supplemented with low terminal education age for those for whom occupation is not classifiable. However, it would be difficult to argue from such results as these that the failure of LSCD to have the importance accorded to a lower class concept in some American writing is due entirely to random measurement errors if only because it has a consistent impact on OSPSD in several groups.

Secondly, the mean score for each area in the whole sample differs little. It would seem from the tabulations of residuals that Area is likely to have an effect only on groups 10, 11 and 5. In two of these, groups 10 and 5, the direction of the effect is that predicted from the arguments about the way under- and over-achieving authorities determine the levels of demand for free meals within their area by means of their indirect influence on stigma through the human agents it is necessary for applicants to have contact with in the process of obtaining and receiving free school meals, and through their influence over other factors in the environment in which free meals are consumed. Groups 10 and 5 are likely to reflect the consequences for uptake of supply conditions in the recent past. Group 10 consists entirely of mothers born abroad, mostly in Ireland, and therefore likely to be long resident in the authority. Group 5 consists entirely of mothers from fatherless households, twenty-seven of them having an income that makes them eligible for free meals, and twenty-eight having had their first experience of applying for free meals more than a year before the survey. Therefore the tabulations of residuals support rather than weaken the general argument that authorities influence the demand for free meals from the Area, although they suggest both that the authorities may influence demand from different groups to differing degrees, and, indeed, that the influence of authorities on different groups may differ in kind as well as degree. (Of course, these results do not in any way affect the plausibility of the argument that the way authorities influence demand is through the control of information rather than the generation of the perception of the service as stigmatizing.)

(c) Mother's Country of Birth (MCOB)

MCOB is in general unimportant, and the effects are not identical across all groups. The number of persons in each birth-place is too small for detailed analysis. The British-born mothers tend to have higher OSP scores—a lower probability of thinking the context to be pervasively stigmatizing—than those born abroad. In the whole sample, the OSPSD means for the Irish exceed those for West Indians. In general, therefore, the results support the argument that the context is feared to be one in which social actors can reveal prejudice against characteristics unrelated to the receipt of the means-tested free meals service.

(d) The Scores of Final Groups

The characteristics of those most likely to feel the most pervasive sensitivity to stigma is of some importance. These characteristics are conveniently described by the definition of the final groups of Diagram 5.1. Table 5.2 summarizes these in descending order of their probability of perceiving the importance of stigma to be pervasive.

Table 5.2   *The characteristics of those with the perception that the importance of stigma for non-uptake is pervasive*

Group Identification Number	Group Specification	Mean proportion with high OSPSD	Number in sample
23	Low IRPSD, Pre-circular EXP, low NEGCOND	0.90	21
15	Non-LSCD, Recent or no EXP, low NEGCOND	0.74	42
5	MOTHALD, High NEGCOND	0.74	34
22	High IRPSD, Pre-circular EXP, low NEGCOND	0.73	41
11	British MCOB, Low RGPPSD, Not MOTHALD, High NEGCOND	0.69	62
14	LSCD, Recent or No EXP, Low NEGCOND	0.52	33
13	High IRPSD, High RGPPSD, Not MOTHALD, High NEGCOND	0.51	49
10	Foreign MCOB, Low RGPPSD, Not MOTHALD High NEGCOND	0.49	49
12	Low IRPSD, High RGPPSD, Not MOTHALD	0.35	31

(e) The Pervasiveness of Interaction Effects

A feature of the results of general interest is the pervasiveness of interaction effects. Only IRPSD (Individualized Responsibility for Poverty) is an important enough predictor to split the sample in different branches of the tree in the stages shown in diagram 5.1; and in this case the direction of the IRPSD effect is different in the two branches. Table 5.3 shows that the same predictors in the branches would not have proved nearly as effective as the predictors chosen by the algorithm. For instance, the impact of MOTHALD (Mothers Alone) on group 3 would have been in the same direction as on group 2, but the difference in means would have been one half as great; and MOTHALD has a ratio of between category to total sums of squares of less than a third that of EXP (experience of applying for free meals). Similarly, the impact of EXP on group 2 would have been in the same direction as on group 3, but the difference in means is small and the ratio of between category sum of squared deviations to the total sum of squared deviations is less than one tenth of that of EXP. The interaction effects are more pronounced for variables entering later.

(ii) Families Eligible because of Low Incomes (Diagram 5.2)

Although the probability of any family which was dependent on the

Table 5.3 *Means yielded by alternative predictors at each step of the AID2 elaboration for OSPSD*

Step	Predictor	Group	Code	Mean	Number of Observations
2	MOTHALD	2	Not alone	0.54	191
			Alone	0.74	34
		3	Not alone	0.69	116
			Alone	0.81	21
4	EXP	3	None or recent	0.64	75
			More than year ago	0.79	62
		2	None or recent	0.56	154
			More than year before	0.59	71
3	RGPPSD	4	High	0.45	80
			Low	0.60	111
		5	High	0.76	25
			Low	0.67	9
		8	High	0.56	25
			Low	0.68	50
		9	High	0.76	41
			Low	0.80	21
3	LSCD	8	High	0.52	33
			Low	0.74	42
		9	High	0.76	42
			Low	0.85	20
		4	High	0.50	88
			Low	0.57	103
		5	High	0.71	31
			Low	1.00	3
3	MOTHALD	8	Not alone	0.64	74
			Alone	1.00	1
		9	Not alone	0.79	42
			Alone	0.80	20
2	EXP	4	None or recent	0.55	148
			Distant	0.51	43
		5	None or recent	0.83	6
			Distant	0.71	28

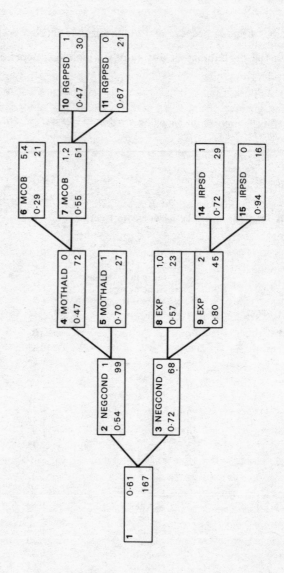

Diagram 5.2 Others' stigma pervasiveness score dummy (OSPSD) Mothers of families eligible because of low income

earnings of manual workers at some stage becoming eligible for free meals was high in the uncertain labour markets of the late 1960s, as in the early 1970s, it is the perceptions of those eligible on income grounds that are of most interest to policy-makers. We therefore analysed the data to see how the perceptions of mothers so eligible differ from those of the whole population. Perhaps the most striking feature of the AID results, summarized in Diagrams 5.2, is their similarity to those shown in Diagram 5.1: the factors that affect the stigma-perception (and probably therefore, sensitivity) of those eligible on income grounds seem to be like those of society as a whole. The same predictors have the most important effects, and the means for the groups are remarkably similar considering the small number of observations (and hence the large expected sampling variation) on which some of the means for the eligible are based.

The differences most worthy of comment are the apparently more general importance of MCOB among the poor with low scores in NEGCOND, and the unimportance of IRPSD for those among them with high RGPPSD scores. The more general importance of MCOB compared with RGPPSD is not surprising. The stigma potential of the school meals context in part depends upon the stigmatizing characteristics of the potential applicant. The school meals context could be catalytic, providing the opportunity for (but not causing) stigmatization. The Asians and West Indians might not have a long enough exposure to British society to have learnt the identity-spoiling meaning of a means-tested service, but could certainly see it as providing a context in which there may be inter-action between themselves and others where the others could exercise prejudice. However, RGPPSD has a considerable effect on NEGCOND British and Irish mothers: the low income, relatively deprived, who had more than the average number of negative contacts with the school were more likely to see stigma-potential. Some among them had at the same time positive attitudes to the school and had participated in its activities. Instead of having a lower probability of agreeing with three or more stigma propositions, such mothers had a higher probability of doing so. If the positive attitudes and involvement did diminish their expectations that a school service would in general have positive effects, this diminution was more than offset by one or more other factors. As seventeen of the thirty mothers had received early EXP, it is likely that one such factor was their own experience (and what they had observed in their contacts with the school).

The unimportance of IRPSD in group 10 is less easy to explain. An analysis of residuals showed that the difference between means for the two IRPSD groups is small. The difference between means is small also in the preceding groups; so that its unimportance is not to be explained by the collinearity with a better predictor that robbed it of its explanatory power. The situation is therefore not comparable to that of the low NEGCOND mothers with early experience, the importance of whose IRPSD for their perception of stigma appeared to be activated by the experience.[15] Although more than one half of group 10 mothers had had experience also, neither EXP nor IRPSD were in themselves important. These results therefore appear to provide further support for the interpretations suggested in the last section—particularly by those relating to the effects of anomie and alienation.

It may therefore be concluded that the causal factors were similar and operated in a like manner on those who were poor at the time of the survey and on the sample as a whole. It would be a mistake to analyse the poor as if their values and assumptions were markedly different from those of the population in general.

(iii) Whole Sample, Fifteen Predictors (Diagram 5.3)

The rationale of RGPPSD is rather different from that of IRPSD. The latter is not an indicator of the pervasiveness of the belief that poverty is due to the poor individual or family's own behaviour, but a composite indicator which is based on replies to closely-related questions, the consistency of the answers to which are reflected in high and low scores. The concept underlying IRPSD, like those underlying NEGCOND, EDID, EDIIID, and MRSD, is unidimensional. However, RGPPSD is a pervasiveness concept which is based on the perception of feeling worse off than four specific and different reference groups—the family, the locality, the country, and the respondent herself at an earlier period of time. It is not initially obvious that these are equally important to any of the groups, or indeed that they are equally important to all groups. One might postulate that for people living in those low income zones of cities in which a high proportion of the population are transient, the country reference group might be more relevant than the locality of reference group, since it has been shown that the area conceived by urban residents to be local is geographically small.[16] One

[15] The potential of IRSPD as a predictor was substantially better for group 9 than group 8. This was the case also for the model based on the whole sample. In the same way, RGPPSD activates the causal potential of IRPSD among the high NEGCOND mothers in the whole sample.

[16] Report of the Committee on the Management of Local Authorities, *The Management of Local Authorities, II, The Local Government Elector*, H.M.S.O., London, 1967.

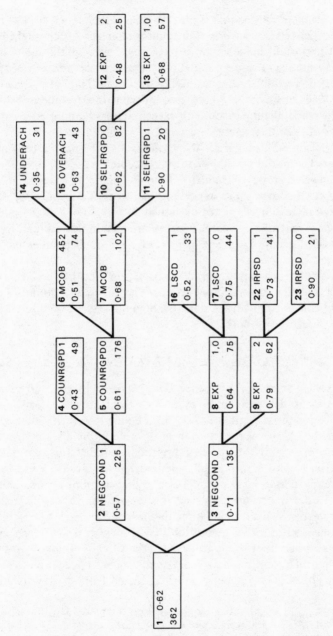

*Diagram 5.3 Others' stigma pervasiveness score dummy (OSPSD) Fifteen predictors
(including FAMRGPD, LOCRGPD, COUNRGPD, and SELFRGPD)*

might similarly argue that if the television is the main source of a perception of relative poverty, the country reference group might be the most important influence on perceptions. One might argue that in a close-knit area of stable population, the country reference group might be less powerful than the locality. In the changed labour market of the late 1960s, it might be argued that a decline in the standard of living might make a comparison with earlier standards more effective than either of the other reference groups.

Diagram 5.3 summarizes the main results. The main effects of predictors for mothers with low NEGCOND scores are identical to those in the twelve-variable model. Among high NEGCOND mothers COUNRGPD proved more important than MOTHALD at the third step.[17] The negative effect of COUNRGPD on OSPSD among high NEGCOND scorers is matched by a large negative gradient in the residuals for (low NEGCOND) group 17, albeit one based on a small number of observations.

The difference in means by COUNRGPD is in the same direction, but is small for other low NEGCOND groups. The impact of COUNRGPD therefore seems to be greatest among the high NEGCOND group, but is in the same direction for both.

(a) COUNRGPD, Alienation, and the Effects of the Leaflet on Stigma

COUNRGPD (Country Reference Group Poverty) may imply a set of social attitudes that might exacerbate the frustrations arising from relative material deprivation. Persons comparing their situation with what they know of the position in the country as a whole from television may tend to acquire powerful materialistic aspirations as a necessary concommittant of a desired life-style, and to pick up the values most associated with the work ethic, including a perception that receiving a means-tested service is stigmatizing. In this, a feeling of relative deprivation in relation to the country as a whole may be causally linked with a perception that applying for and receiving free meals is potentially stigmatizing. That the effect of COUNRGPD is greater on high NEGCOND mothers suggests that high NEGCOND mothers with high RGPPS may not be so much alienated from society as a whole

---

[17] The ratio of PSS to TSS for COUNRGPD was .0224, that for MOTHALD, its nearest rival, was .0201. Because the two predictors were substantially correlated, power of MOTHALD was considerably reduced by this split in both groups 4 and 5. Nevertheless, MOTHALD may be causally important, since mothers of fatherless families have higher mean OSP scores in every group.

as more acutely aware of their relative deprivation and more anxious that their children are successful in school—it confirms that NEGCOND is more an anomie than an alienation indicator. The negative contacts with the school might be due to a wider discrepancy between expectations about and experience of their children's schooling rather than to an attempt to defend their children against what is perceived to be the exploitation of an alien system.

One certainly cannot argue from these results as one might have done had the relationship between COUNRGPD and OSPSD been in the opposite direction. For instance, one might have argued that an orientation to a national reference group would allow an awareness of entitlement to the service after the leaflet had recently promoted its existence, and so reduce feelings of stigma. One might have argued that this might have its greatest effect among those whose alienation made them least likely to feel the receipt of a means-tested service to be damaging to their self-image and least likely to be worried about its effect on their image in the sight of others. That their reference group tended to be national would anyhow have made them less sensitive to the views of others in the locality. This argument would have predicted some such effect on all mothers. This effect of COUNRGPD (caused directly by national publicity) would be particularly great among the high NEGCOND mothers, among whom teachers might be less likely to promote the free meals scheme than among mothers with whom they had better relations (and for whom, perhaps, they felt more sympathy).

(b) COUNRGPD (Country Reference Group Poverty) and MCOB (Mothers' Country of Birth)

The grouping by COUNRGPD allows MCOB to create groups whose means are similar to those of groups 10 and 11 of the twelve-variable analysis at the third rather than the fourth step. The number of persons influenced by MCOB therefore appears to be much greater than would be inferred from the twelve-variable model. And unlike the gradient of means for the residuals of final group 13 of that analysis, for instance, the British-born mothers are less likely to perceive pervasive stigma potential. The residuals show that the British mothers have a higher OSPD mean than the Irish also in group 4, but a lower mean than the West Indians. The West Indians' scores are of particular interest in relation to the earlier discussion. Two-thirds (22) of the high NEGCOND West Indians have low COUNRGPD scores—they do not feel relatively deprived compared with the country as a whole. If our projection argument in Section 1 (b) is to be accepted, these are only more likely to be pervasively sensitive to stigma than the Irish, and are less sensitive to it than the British. However, it appears that the one third of high NEGCOND West Indians who feel relatively deprived may be less likely to be sensitive than the British and far less likely to be sensitive than the Irish. The high NEGCOND West Indians may well contain many of the less bourgeois recent immigrants whose expectations were probably lower, and who have had a shorter period of time in which to learn the meaning of the service. Perhaps, therefore, it is not (as one might have argued) the more bourgeois—who probably had greater expectations and therefore more acute sense of frustration disappointment, and relative deprivation—who are more likely to see the stigma potential of the service, but the more recent immigrants who feel the relative deprivation, and (particularly if they have negative contacts with the school) are sensitive to stigma. They are supported by the pattern of means yielded by the tabulations of residuals. The LSC West Indians with recent or no experience in group 16—probably the worse off, later immigrants—have a lower mean OSPSD than the British and Irish. Again it may not be the 'meaning' of the means-tested benefit that is influential, but the opportunity it provides for allowing others to reveal their prejudice. Of course such inferences must be very tentative, since they are based on two small area samples.

(c) Area, Supply, and Demand

Area appears to be important for foreign-born mothers, as can be seen from groups 14 and 15. As in the twelve-variable analysis, mothers in the under-achieving area have the lower mean. However this result (which strengthens our under-achieving argument) is untypical—it is not the pattern for groups 4 and 13 revealed by the residuals. But the evidence is far from unambiguous. The apparent support for the authority hypothesis is strengthened, since part of the explanation for the pattern is undoubtedly that a much higher proportion of group 15 than of group 14 consists of (high stigma) Irish mothers rather than lower stigma West Indian mothers.[18] Also, the Area effect is such that

[18] The proportion of Irish in group 14 is 36 per cent, and in group 15, 70 per cent. The predominance of West Indians in group 14 compared with the latter may account for the positive effect of LOCRGPD in group 14 but not group 15—perhaps the feeling of relative deprivation interacts with an expectation of prejudice. Similarly, the large effect evident in the residuals for group 16 may reflect the sensitivity to the stigma of poverty among LSC mothers in non-LSC areas.

mothers in group 16 in the under-achieving area are more sensitive to stigma, and the area difference in probabilities is large. Group 16 are LSC, mainly high IRSPD, with low NEGCOND scores, low EDID scorers, but low scorers on LOCRGPD, COUNRGPD, and SELFRGPD. Some of the evidence of this analysis therefore confirms that the way in which supply influences demand is through variables other than the perception of the receipt of free meals as pervasively stigmatizing in its potential.

However, some of the other results suggest that this conclusion is not valid for all recipients. First, high NEGCOND mothers with high COUNRGPD scores have a higher mean OSPD in the under-achieving authority and so a lower probability of perceiving the stigma potential of school meals to be pervasive. This is an interesting group since a high proportion are British, have had experience of applying at various times, have high FAMRGPD, and low income (76 per cent being in SIG 1 and 2). Again, it appears that a group of needy recipients has not acquired an expectation of pervasive stigma as a result of experience. Secondly, 80 per cent of a group (group 11), a low proportion of whom perceive stigma to be pervasively important and who have high NEGCOND scores, is drawn from the under-achieving area.[19] This group is interesting because most of the mothers are from low income groups, and had applied for free meals, and also because the mothers are British-born, not of low social class, feel their standard of living to have fallen, but do not feel their standard of living to be low relative to the country as a whole. That the over-achieving area appears to be associated with a higher (not lower) degree of sensitivity to stigma for mothers in these groups—and a very high degree of sensitivity in the latter group—is important, although the difference in Area means are not as great as they are (for instance) in group 16, because a fifth of the entire group have these characteristics, and because one would expect these characteristics to be far more prevalent in a national sample than in these area samples. Clearly, therefore, the Area effect on stigma is highly complex, the supply influences having effects that differ between groups.

---

[19] The number of mothers in group 11 possessing each of the characteristics are: living in UNDERACH, 16; low IRPSD scorers, 5; LSC, 9; SIG 1 and 2, 13; low EDID, 6; low EDIIID scorers, 6; low MRSD scorers, 1; non-employed, 14; MOTHALD, 15; applied before Circular, 10; FAMRGPD, 6; and LOCRGPD, 5. The preponderance of fatherless families gives the group a special character. SELRGPD had, if anything, a negative effect on group 16, residuals suggest. Although group 16 was mainly drawn from the under-achieving area, it contained no non-LSC mothers with pre-Circular EXP, and a minority were poor.

(iv) Analyses for Samples with EXP and Others (Diagrams 5.4 and 5.5)

Whether or not the determinants of OSPSD among persons experienced in applying for free meals is different from those not so experienced is of great importance to the exploration of the impact of the free meals scheme in 1968. EXP could possibly have altered the whole 'meaning' of the service. It could either have reinforced the stigmatizing meaning of the service, or it could have helped to counteract the historical association of stigma with means-testing. Similarly experience could have altered the importance of the predictors of stigma. The twelve-variable whole sample analysis in section (i) has shown that EXP is not the major influence on OSPSD. However, the nature of AID is such as to

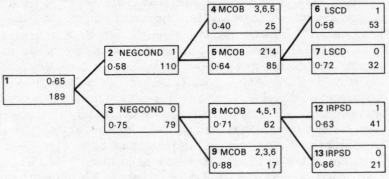

Diagram 5.4   Others' stigma pervasiveness score dummy (OSPSD)
Mothers with experience of applying. Twelve predictors

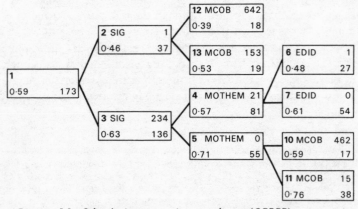

Diagram 5.5   Others' stigma pervasive score dummy (OSPSD).
Mothers without experience of applying. Twelve predictors.

make it easy to underestimate the importance of variables that are not of primary importance, since the variables that are correlated with the predictors that split groups lose their potential either for causing further division of the group or for causing difference between means in residual tabulations. For this reason analyses were run separately for those with and without EXP.[20] Diagrams 5.4 and 5.6 summarize the main results.

The diagrams illustrate that EXP has relatively little correlation with OSPSD, there being a difference in means of only 6 percentage points. The difference (such as it is) suggests that EXP diminishes rather than reinforces sensitivity to stigma. A superficial glance at the diagrams suggests that controlling for EXP has a marked effect on the patterns of correlation, since SIG is the best predictor for those without EXP while NEGCOND is the best predictor for the others. However, NEGCOND would have an effect on group 1 of Diagram 5.4 that is similar in direction—though not in degree—to that in Diagram 5.5. Indeed, the mean for mothers with high NEGCOND is similar for both EXP groups: the effect of low NEGCOND is therefore to make the effect of EXP 8 percentage points greater. NEGCOND predicts OSPSD better in Diagram 5.5 than SIG does in Diagram 5.4. Indeed, SIG has little or no influence on the group 1 mothers of Diagram 5.4. This could mean that the SIG effect among the non-EXP mothers is a reflection of a general attitude to means-tested services which specific experience negates. With EXP, it is the nature of contacts with the school that becomes important. This would imply that it is the attitudes of people who tend to have the lowest incomes—attitudes reflecting general influences in acculturation, not specific experience—which are the important causal factors, rather than poverty itself, or specific experiences associated with poverty. Alternatively, the causal paths may be in a different direction: EXP may be the outcome of the process, rather than primarily a cause. For instance, one might argue that those with high NEGCOND might see little danger to a relationship with the school that is already bad arising from applying for free meals, whereas those with low NEGCOND might see such a danger because their relationships with the school are good and therefore might not apply. However, this particular causal sequence is unlikely to be generally the most powerful, since the proportion of EXP mothers with high NEGCOND scores is lower than the proportion on non-EXP mothers with high NEGCOND scores. Therefore

[20] The models omitted the theoretically important variable MOTHALD. Secondly, they distinguish between EXP = 2 and Others. Other analyses suggest that the latter is the more important division. They are therefore inferior to those reported in sections (i) to (iii).

one draws much the same inferences from the results as from those of the twelve-variable whole-sample analysis in section (i) above. The argument stated in that section therefore gains support.

MCOB has an effect at the third stage in Diagram 5.5 as it has at the fourth stage of Diagram 5.3 and in Diagram 5.4. The British have a higher score than the Irish. However, the Irish with EXP clearly perceive the stigma potential of free meals to be less pervasive than the Irish without EXP. This result is incompatible with the argument that the Irish who had actually applied for free meals had thereby suffered more anti-Irish prejudice than was expected by the Irish mothers in general. Indeed, it suggests that EXP had actually lowered the degree to which they viewed applying for the service as pervasively stigmatizing. However, some Irish mothers may well fear that applying and receiving free meals puts people into a context in which they will tend to air their anti-Irish prejudice. Evidence for this is that the Irish have lower OSPSD proportions (and so lower proportions accepting three or less stigma propositions) than the British among ineligible non-EXP families, and lower proportions than the British among high NEGCOND mothers with EXP.[21] However, this does not appear to be a factor of importance among the economically important eligible non-EXP mothers in group 2 of Diagram 5.5, since the proportions for the 7 Irish and 12 British mothers are almost identical. The comparison between West Indian and British mothers implies similar conclusions. Much the same proportions have high OSPSD scores among the important non-EXP but eligible group 2 of Diagram 5.5, and among those with EXP and high NEGCOND scores (group 2 of Diagram 5.4).

B. OSD (Diagram 5.6)

This is another inverse indicator of stigma. We have seen that only a small minority of mothers (6 per cent) did not agree with any of the propositions that stigma was an important cause of non-uptake of free meals among those eligible for them. Because OSD proved to have little variance, it is a much inferior variable to OSPSD as a discriminant between those who had a general sensitivity to stigma and others. However, OSD picks out the minority who might be particularly insensitive to stigma.

Diagram 5.6 shows the AID tree for OSD. The under-achieving area contains a large number of persons relatively insensitive to stigma; and

[21] Of the 26 Irish in group 5, 58 per cent score unity on OSPSD; whereas of the 57 British, 65 per cent do so. Of the 11 Irish in group 9 of Diagram 5.6, 64 per cent do so, whereas of the 36 British mothers, 75 per cent do so.

these persons are particularly concentrated amongst those with low scores on EDIIID—indicating co-operative attitudes to, and activity-related contact with the school—who are born abroad. One third of such mothers did not have a positive score on OSD. That it was those with the fewest positive contacts with the school who had a low probability of feeling stigma to be important qualifies what would otherwise be clear counter-evidence to the under/over achieving hy-

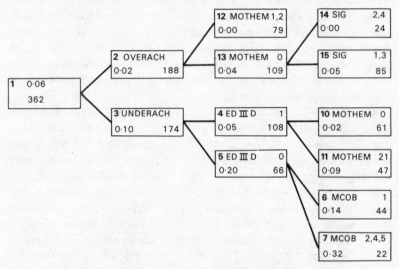

Diagram 5.6   Others' stigma dummy (OSD)

pothesis. There may well be cultural factors exogenous to the school that reduce the perceptions of the free meals service as potentially stigmatizing; but those who have the closest positive contact with the school have much the same probability of perceiving at least one aspect of the service to be stigmatizing as many mothers in the over-achieving area. Further, those in the over-achieving area with high EDIIID scores are actually *more* likely not to think any aspect important than those with low EDIIID scores—in the over-achieving authority close 'positive' contact with the school may actually reduce the perception of the dangers of stigma.[22] This evidence is therefore compatible with our arguments about under- and over-achievement. That it was mothers born abroad who had a high probability of not believing stigma of any type to be 'important' suggests that any expectation that

[22] The absolute difference between OSPSD scores for high and low EDIIID scorers in the over-achieving area is small, one percentage point.

the service provides a context in which prejudice could be overtly expressed is more than outweighed by the awareness that applying for and receiving free meals is widely regarded as stigmatizing. The ten Irish mothers were more like the other foreign-born in this context. The same is not so among those with positive attitudes for the school and positive contacts with it (the high EDID scorers). All of the thirteen Irish-born mothers in group 4 thought that stigmatization connected with at least one aspect of the service was an important cause of non-uptake, while 4 per cent of the British-born thought otherwise. However, 11½ per cent of the sixteen West Indians did not believe stigma of any form to be important. Therefore, in general, the evidence supports the argument that persons not fully socialized into the national cultures may be those who are the least aware of the stigma potential of receiving free meals.

The analysis did not distinguish other groups with a substantial proportion of mothers who did not believe stigma to be important. However, another analysis revealed a clear relationship for low EDIIID mothers in the under-achieving area, a group of eighteen mothers who did not perceive the main advantage to themselves (ADVMOTH) to be that the service provided child-minding, 50 per cent did not think that any form of stigma had an important effect. Most (ten) of these saw no particular advantage of the service to the mother. Thus nine of the twenty-two mothers in the entire sample who were non-believers in stigma were in this group. However, it is difficult to think that this relationship is other than a statistical freak. It is certainly difficult to provide a satisfactory explanation of it. The same models, run for mothers with and without EXP, yield results that are very similar to Diagram 5.6. Both show Area as the best predictor. Both imply that EDIIID is of importance in the over-achieving authority. Separate elaborations for EXP groups imply that EXP is unimportant.

3. Others' Stigma—Specific Forms

(i) 'Other children know who gets them free and make these children feel small' (OCHLDD) (Diagram 5.7)

Diagram 5.7 shows the AID tree. A majority of the mothers agreed with the propositions. EXP is the best predictor. It is not that EXP itself is positively or negatively associated with agreement with the proposition, but that those who had had EXP only recently had a lower probability of agreeing than either those whose first experience was distant or those with no experience. One could hardly argue that those who

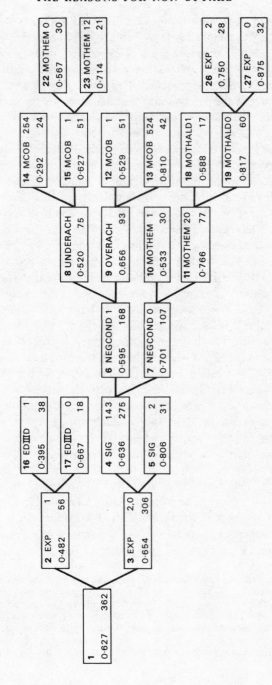

Diagram 5.7 *Why eligible children do not receive free meals*
Other children make receivers feel small
Agree = 1 Disagree = 0

least believed in it were those most likely to apply. If that were so why had they not applied before? Perhaps recent experience may have convinced many mothers—a tenth of the group—of the absence of this form of stigma. The publicity given to the service might well have caused them to have approached their application with different expectations about the perception of recipients among the community in general and other school children in particular from those of earlier applicants. Whether it caused them to have different expectations which caused them to interpret procedures and interactions with others in the process of application, or whether it caused them to have different expectations about the degree to which applicants would be labelled 'disreputable' is not ascertainable from this dependent variable. It is important in this context that it is the high EDIIID mothers who have a low probability of thinking that this form of stigma is important, because they are the mothers who are least likely to see the school as alien, and are therefore those whom one would most expect to be responsive to changes in perceptions in the schools—since they have a more than usual interest in (and positive contacts with) them, and because they are most likely to have positive support, help, and encouragement from the teachers. One might well have found that EDIIID had an effect in the opposite direction. A mother having positive participatory attitudes might well be very sensitive to any context that has potential for creating a stigmatizing situation for her child. Again, a mother with close positive contacts with the school would be in a better position than most to detect any stigmatization that took place.[23] An examination of the residuals for group 16 shows that among these recently-experienced high EDIIID mothers, low social class mothers had particularly low scores. It is known that such mothers often have a deferential attitude to teachers, and that this attitude may distort their perception of reality. However, non-LSC mothers with high EDIIID scores and recent EXP also have a relatively low probability of agreeing with the proposition. The evidence in favour of the argument is therefore impressive. Why did those with earlier experience believe in this form of stigma to a greater degree?[24]

[23] EDIIID has a strong negative association with the dependent variable among group 5 and 22 mothers, but not among group 12 mothers. However, there is a strong negative association with EDID in group 12, and EDID countervails EDIID (where they are negatively correlated); positive instrumental attitudes to education as a whole being linkable with the outcome in much the same way as positive attitudes to (and participation in) the school.

[24] The difference in means between the non-EXP and those with early EXP was one percentage point.

The reason for the apparent importance of SIG 2 at the second stage is not obvious. SIG has a ratio of BSS/TSS of 0.0116, whereas its nearest rival MCOB has a ratio of 0.0098 with the 63 Irish in group 3 having a higher score than others.[25] All but seven Irish mothers are in this group. There is no difficulty in explaining why Irish mothers might be sensitive to the stigma potential of receiving free meals. The free meals context is one in which other children could be expected to express the latent hostility that exists among working-class British against the Irish in many areas, Glasgow and Liverpool being only the most widely known of these. This may well be a good example of a context in which other recognizable characteristics of one or more of the family are the cause of potential stigmatization, but in which the application for free meals provides a circumstance which permits expression (or the intensity of its expression). The association of responses with SIG 2 remains unexplained. The analysis of residuals provides no obvious explanation, although it is perhaps not unlikely that those on the margins of poverty should be more sensitive than the poor or the better off if one of the major aims of social life is to distinguish oneself from the 'roughs'.[26] However it is possible that the correlation is spurious.

The influence of NEGCOND at the next step of the model is in the opposite direction to that in Diagram 5.1 (for OSPSD). However, an analysis of residuals implies that the effect may not be similar for all groups. The effect of Area in the under-achieving authority on high NEGCOND scorers is paralleled by the negative effect on the biggest final group of the low NEGCOND scores, although the proportions for the two areas in group 7 are almost identical. The British-born mothers have a far higher probability than other mothers of agreeing with the proposition in the under-achieving area but a far lower probability of doing so in the over-achieving area. Indeed, British-born mothers have a lower probability in the over-achieving than the under-achieving area —as would be predicted if our arguments about the role of the authority in suppressing and stimulating the demands for its own services were correct. The Area effect that distinguishes group 8 from group 9 is thus seen to be entirely the result of a large difference in the attitudes of immigrants in the two areas. Further analysis shows that 30 of the 42 mothers in group 13 are Irish, whereas 16 of the 24 mothers in group 14 are West Indian and Asian. It is therefore possible

[25] A score of .746.
[26] See the arguments based on Klein and Matza mentioned earlier. Of the 35 SIG 2 mothers in the sample, 31 are members of group 2.

that the Asians and West Indians are found in schools in which there are few white children and so do not fear stigmatization by other children as much as the Irish who are likely to be more dispersed.

The importance of MOTHEM for high NEGCOND mothers may be that mothers in part-time employment may have different types of NEGCOND —although we lack positive evidence of this. Those in full-time work may include many who are least child-orientated, and those not in employment may include many of the eligible with large families. It is these rather than the MOTHALDs who fear stigmatization by other children. Among some of the eight classified in SIG 1 and 2, the fear may have been so great that they had not applied, although most are relatively well-off and include a large number of high scorers on EDID, an indicator of the bourgeois virtues of *les familles éducogènes*. This interpretation is, of course, speculative. One must neither expect the relatively primitive statistical technique to yield a true picture of variations for the populations from this small sample, nor overstate the degree to which our indicators are robust enough to bear the weight of argument based on them.

Those without EXP have a higher probability of agreeing with the proposition than those with early EXP in group 19. This suggests that the experience of those with long memories of the service does not make them as likely to fear the stigmatization as much as those who have never had any contact with it. This is of great importance because eight of the 32 people in group 27 are eligible for free meals. They may well have chosen to forgo their right for fear of stigmatization. However the results provide little evidence that other groups reacted thus.

(ii) 'The children who take them are picked on more by the teachers—an important reason for non-uptake' (TCHERSD)—Diagram 5.8

A far smaller proportion agreed with this proposition than with the idea that other children stigmatized receivers. It is striking that none of the Asians in the sample agreed with the proposition that receivers being picked on more by teachers was an important reason for non-uptake. Results already discussed suggest that this would not be surprising if they were drawn predominantly from some groups. The impact of EXP is similar in form to that at the second stage of the model described in Diagram 5.7. The discussion of its effect there seems to be equally relevant in this context. The area effects at the third and fourth steps are, however, in the opposite direction to those

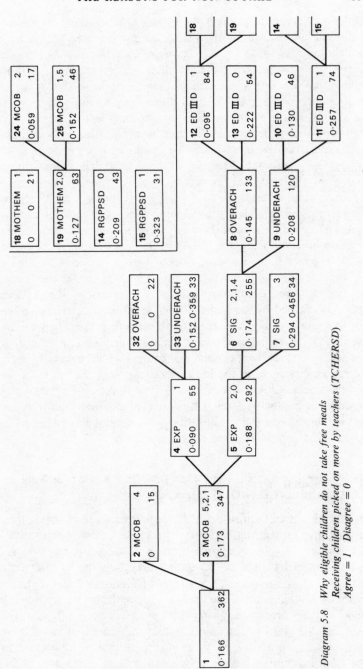

Diagram 5.8 Why eligible children do not take free meals
Receiving children picked on more by teachers (TCHERSD)
Agree = 1 Disagree = 0

shown in Diagram 5.7, as is the difference in residual means for group 7. Thus although fewer mothers from the under-achieving area believe that the stigmatization of receivers by older children is an important reason for non-uptake, more from the under-achieving authority believe that teachers stigmatize. Although we have shown that the result shown in Diagram 5.7 was due largely to the composition of the groups, this is an important set of findings in the context of our argument about the roles of teachers in the process by which authorities can stimulate or suppress the uptake of free meals, since they suggest that the source of stigma, which to some degree lies within the control of the authority, is perceived more strongly in the under-achieving area, whereas the source of stigma that is more likely to be community-generated is perceived more strongly in the over-achieving area. The area difference in this analysis exceeds the area difference for British mothers in Diagram 5.7. Although it is SIG that splits group 5, the area effect is in the same direction as in group 4, though the difference is only 6.6 percentage points. The difference in the residuals for mothers from the two areas in group 7 confirms the argument. This is confirmed by the fact that high EDIIID scorers are more sensitive to stigma in the over- than under-achieving area. However, the interaction between EDIIID and Area is of greater importance than this additive effect. That closeness of contact with the school *increases* the probability more in the under-achieving area that mothers think that the teachers stigmatize receivers, while in the over-achieving area closeness of contact *reduces* this possibility, providing powerful support for the argument that authorities' own employees can have a substantial effect on the demand for the service.

(iii) 'Taking free meals is charity' an Important Reason for Non-Application (CHARD) Diagram 5.9

This variable is an indicator of the internalized sense of shame that is an outcome of the stigmatization process. A high proportion of mothers agreed with the proposition. A lower proportion of West Indians and Irish than of British and Asians believe this to be an important cause of non-uptake. Thus whereas Diagram 5.8 shows that the Asians do not believe that the teachers' stigmatization is an important cause, a higher proportion than others probably believe that receiving free meals is a charity. The association of the dependent variable with MOTHEM in group 2 is not much stronger than that with NEGCOND and SIG. Low SIG mothers have high probabilities. Nevertheless high

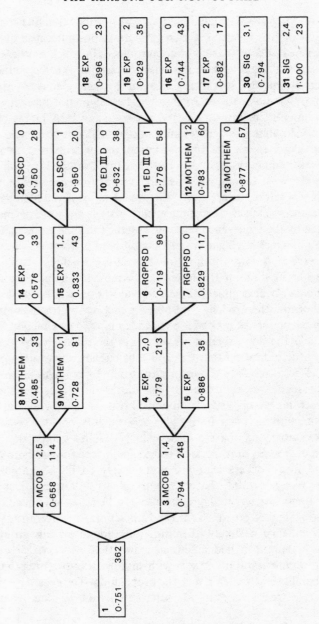

Diagram 5.9 Why eligible children do not take free meals
Taking free meals is charity (CHARD)
Agree = 1   Disagree = 0

NEGCOND scores are associated with low proportions thinking that the perception of free meals as a charity is an important cause of non-uptake. This is a combination of circumstances in which mothers may well have both negative contacts with the school and feel sufficient retreatist anomie not to feel it damaging to their identity to apply. They may well not be concerned with whether or not receiving free meals is an entitlement or a charity. NEGCOND is clearly highly correlated with MOTHEM in group 9, since NEGCOND is not correlated with MOTHEM in group 8. The interpretation of the apparent MOTHEM effect is also complicated by the fact that two-thirds of the full-time workers are West Indian, whereas three out of four group 9 mothers are Irish. Therefore the apparent MOTHEM effect may be due in part to the newcomers' unawareness of the meaning of the service. This may be reinforced by the higher income earned by the full-time workers, those with high incomes having a lower probability of learning the meaning of the service. A lower proportion had either recent or early EXP, whereas one in three of the foreign-born mothers in full-time work had eligible or near eligible incomes, and no less than three-fifths of all foreign-born mothers did so. This absence of a reason for learning the meaning of the service may well be reflected in the EXP effect of group 9, since it is the non-experienced who have the relatively low scores. There is little indication that this could be either an alienation or an anomie effect since only a minority of group 14 mothers are of low social class, all but a fifth have high scores on IRPSD, less than a third score highly on RGPPSD, and majorities score highly on EDID and EDIIID, although a majority also score highly on NEGCOND, and high NEGCOND scorers have a mean of only .476 (in comparison with the mean of .750 for the others). It is the experienced foreign-born part-time and non-workers that are more likely to be alienated and therefore likely to think that receiving a charity damages their self-respect, a majority having high IRPSD scores, being of low social class, and scoring highly on NEGCOND, and all scoring highly on RGPPSD. Further evidence of likely alienation or anomie among group 15 mothers is that LSCD had an impact, and that NEGCOND predicted variation almost as well as LSCD with high NEGCOND scorers having low probabilities of agreeing with the proposition. The degree to which the effects of these variables are separable is not obvious from the AID results.

One might have expected from some of the results for other forms of stigma that the recently EXP would have a lower probability of agreeing with the charity stigma proposition. Diagram 5.9 shows that the opposite is the case. Indeed, among British (and fifteen Asian) mothers, those with only recent EXP have a higher probability than either of the other EXP categories. This is unlikely to be a new feeling among the mothers with only recent EXP. Perhaps therefore they had withheld application until the strength (or influence over behaviour) of this feeling had been diminished by the Minister's Circular and its consequences. However this is certainly not so among those British mothers in group 5 who have low scores on IRPSD. None of those with recent experience, whose answers consistently reflected an attitude that the responsibility for poverty was individualized, accepted the proposition. It would seem that the link between a feeling that the service is a charity and IRSPD is pervasive since the analysis of residuals shows that the direction of impact is consistent in seven of the nine final groups, and that the effect is pronounced in four of them. Why therefore is the EXP 1 group more sensitive?

British (and Asian) mothers who feel poor relatively to other groups are less likely to accept the charity proposition, particularly if they score highly on EDIIID. A positive and participatory attitude towards schooling may increase the charity perception of the service among those who feel themselves to be poor, either the contact with the school having an effect on the perception of this service linked with the school, or the participatory attitude and non-acceptance of the charity perception being a reflection of a general attitude—possibly group 10 are relatively deprived, but not anomic, whereas group 11 both feel relatively deprived and anomic. The pattern of association with EXP in groups 10 and 11 are compatible with either argument. Although among group 10 mothers (with low EDIIID and high RGPPSD mothers), early EXP is associated with a low probability of agreement, EXP has an association in the opposite direction for high EDIIID scores in group 11, as in groups 12 and 30. However if all mothers, irrespective of their EDIIID scores, had had the same experience, one could conclude that experience of the school was not the important factor. Perhaps the negative association with EXP in group 8 is interesting here. Group 8 consists of Irish and West Indian mothers. The West Indian mothers are as likely as any to have been the victims of scapegoating and prejudice, and therefore to be sensitive to stigma; but early EXP did not increase the probability of agreeing with the proposition. Many of the children of the Irish mothers are likely to have gone to the same schools as others. For them, therefore, cultural factors are likely to be a more likely cause of variations in numbers agreeing to the proposition than variations in experience. For these reasons, experience may not have been a powerful cause, but an effect of attitudes. The anomie argument seems to provide a highly plausible explanation for groups 10 and 11. This is not compatible with the argument that early EXP never has a positive effect on the probabilities. Among those in group 7 (who do not in general have any such signs of alienation as high RGPPSD, low EDIIID or low IRPPSD),[27] early EXP clearly had an effect. Such mothers would seem to have learnt from some aspect of its provision its meaning as a charity.

In the last section, some evidence was found that suggested that the perception of the stigma-potential of the service among those most likely to be affected by the authority and its agents (the teachers) might have been more prevalent in the under-achieving authority, whereas the opposite might have been the case in the over-achieving authority. The charity perception of the service is likely to be affected by community perceptions as much as by school experience. If the Area argument were valid, one would expect the proportions to be higher in the over-achieving authority. Although Area does not split any group, the residual proportions vary in the direction compatible with the argument in all but one final group, and in this the difference is small. The effect is particularly large among the Irish and West Indians in full-time work, groups which may be highly sensitive to the stigma potential of a situation.

Whatever effects LSCD may have are not consistent. LSCD does not split any group; but the difference in residual proportions are large in groups 14 and 16. That the LSCD have higher proportions among Irish and West Indians is compatible with our expectations. The relationship between class and attitudes among these were discussed in the introductory argument. That the LSCD have lower proportions among the British mothers is clearly compatible with what would be predicted from the culture of poverty argument. The correlation between SIG and agreement with the proposition conceals a small negative effect of LSC on the proportion agreeing in group 13. This again is compatible with the culture of poverty argument. However the test is not conclusive if only because different variables are controlled in group 8 than in groups 16 and 13.

Although MOTHALD does not split any of the groups, it has substantial positive effects on groups 10 and 16, and would be expected if MOTHALD enhanced the probability of perceiving a context as potentially stigmatizing.

---

[27] Four out of five of the group 7 mothers had high IRPSD scores.

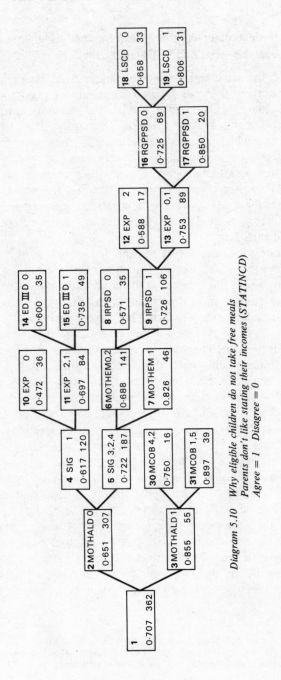

Diagram 5.10 Why eligible children do not take free meals
Parents don't like stating their incomes (STATINCD)
Agree = 1 Disagree = 0

(iv) 'Parents don't like stating their incomes' an important reason for not applying—(STATINCD)—Diagram 5.10

Much the same high proportions agree with this as with the charity proposition; it is not in itself surprising that MOTHALD is the best predictor of this, although it is relatively unimportant for other perceptions of stigma from the service. The same part of the procedure of applying which demands a declaration of income demands an admission of the marital status of the mother; and being widowed, separated, or unmarried may be as potentially stigmatizing as admitting that the sole source of income is social security. This to some extent exaggerates the true importance of MOTHALD, since MOTHALD is correlated with other potential causes. In particular, 48 of the 55 persons in group 3 had early EXP.

Stating incomes seems to worry the Irish mothers of fatherless families less than it worries British mothers.[28] This is compatible with the argument put forward in the last section about the role of culture in the perception of free meals as a 'charity'. Among British lone mothers, the area in which they live has a substantial effect. The effect is what would be predicted if the behaviour of the employees of public authorities generated more stigma awareness in the under-achieving than the over-achieving authority. It is possible that the teachers and the education welfare officers are not the only relevant public authorities in this case, since lone mothers are often referred to the Education Department by the local officer of the Ministry of Social Security. The levels of local employment and traditions of female employment may well be a major factor causing variations in this. Only eight of the 39 mothers in group 31 are in employment.

Among the non-MOTHAL families, those whose incomes are at the eligibility level or under would appear to mind stating their incomes less than others. This is not what would be predicted from the argument that low income is itself seen by potential recipients as a stigmatizing characteristic. That mothers of eligible children without experience of receiving free meals tend to have low scores does not suggest that the dislike of stating incomes is one of the most important reasons for not applying among those not receiving free meals by the

---

[28] There are only three Asian mothers in group 30 and four West Indian mothers in group 31. Unmarried mothers stating that someone played the role of father (as would be the case in co-habitation) are not classified as MOTHAL.

Easter of 1968.[29] However it may suggest that among the 52 persons who had had early experience, a number had suffered experience which caused them to dislike disclosing their incomes. But since the proportion agreeing was higher among those whose first experience was recent than those whose first experience was early, it is very likely that a number of mothers earlier deterred from applying by the dislike of declaring incomes had done so in response to the Ministerial circular and the resulting events of late 1967 and early 1968.[30] Part of the explanation attributed by the model to EDIIID is in fact due to the recentness of the first experience, since a higher proportion of group 15 than group 14 had their first experience recently. The remaining effect of EDIIID is entirely compatible with the argument that those relatively alienated from such cultural institutions as the school are likely to be alienated from society as a whole, and therefore feel their identities as members of society to be less threatened by stating their incomes.[31] Moreover, the analyses of the residuals for most of the groups yield differences in proportions that are in the direction predicted by the argument in all but one of the groups with a substantial difference in proportions.[32]

The split of group 5 by MOTHEM, and the subsequent split of group 6 by IRPSD is theoretically of interest, because the analysis of the residuals for group 7 shows that the gradient of proportions by IRPSD group is in the opposite direction to that in group 6. Some families may well have incomes above the eligibility level because mothers work part-time. One might also have expected that many mothers work part-time because they have an individualized perception of the causes of poverty. But in fact there is in general no correlation between IRPSD and working part-time among group 5 mothers,[33] and high IRPSD mothers working part-time are less (not more) likely to accept the proposition than low IRPSD mothers working part-time. The opposite is true among mothers not in employment: IRPSD is positively associated with acceptance of the proposition. Presumably among the non-employed, the 'alienation effect' associated with low IRPSD reduces the feeling that

[29] Some group 10 mothers could certainly have been deterred, the proportion accepting the proposition being 47 per cent.

[30] The proportion agreeing among the 32 mothers with only recent experience was 72 per cent, and that among the 52 mothers with early experience was 65 per cent.

[31] EDID seems to have a similar effect on the residuals for groups 8 and 18.

[32] The residuals imply that the Irish are more sensitive than the British.

[33] Of the 25 mothers with low IRPSD scores who work either full-time or who are not in employment, 9 are in part-time employment. The proportion is almost identical to that among the 99 high IRPSD mothers in the same MOTHEM group, 37 of whom work part-time.

identities are spoiled by stating incomes. Similarly, IRPSD is not positively associated with working full-time rather than part-time—indeed,
if anything, the association is negative. And, as among the non-
employed, IRPSD is positively associated with the proposition. Again
the alienation effect may operate.

The branches of the tree growing from group 9 distinguish exceptional sub-groups among the non-eligible. Perhaps the early EXP high
IRPSD mothers with low probabilities shown in group 12 distinguish
those who claimed their entitlement early partly because they felt no
stigma in declaring their incomes. The others (group 13) felt more
sensitive about this, particularly if they felt worse off than important
reference groups (and thus scored highly on RGPPSD as in group 17);
or had low incomes, as had the seven recent EXP mothers in group 18
who are presumably much the same group as the seven SIG 2 mothers
whose proportion is identical.[34] The recentness of the latter group's
experience is an indication of this sensitivity. The LSC characteristic
similarly may make the better off more sensitive. Thus high scores on
RGPPS and being of low class both have a similar positive effect in
this branch. It is an effect opposite in direction to that reported elsewhere. Presumably among mothers not eligible on income grounds, the
alienation arguments apply to only those with early EXP.

Among the non-MOTHALS, there is little prima facie evidence that Area
has strong effect. However the proportions for the under-achieving
area are greater in group 19. This difference is in the direction postulated by our argument.

(v) 'Don't like employer to know' an important reason for not applying (EMPLD) Diagram 5.11

The sources of stigma we have distinguished differ along several
dimensions: the source of the prejudice that is stigma-generating, the
degree to which they reflect subjective perceptions, the internalized
'meanings' of the service, and the object of the prejudice or stigmatization. Dislike of the employer's knowing is likely to be felt by the male
head of household to a greater degree than dislike of revealing
incomes.[35] That this is not reflected clearly in Diagram 5.11—MOTHALD

[34] The non-LSC group 19 contained only 2 persons in SIG 2. The class effect in the
diagram may well be due to the correlation with SIG.

[35] Indeed, if sensitivity about stating incomes was mainly felt by the male head of
household, MOTHALD could hardly have been a predictor of such power in the positive
direction shown in Diagram 5.11, though it might have had a negative effect.

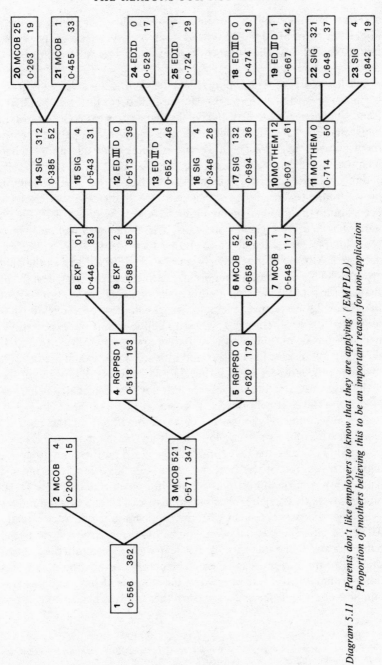

Diagram 5.11 'Parents don't like employers to know that they are applying' (EMPLD)
Proportion of mothers believing this to be an important reason for non-application

and MRSD are unimportant for instance—suggests that asking mothers about this form of stigma may lead to an underestimate of its importance. Nevertheless the proportion of mothers accepting the proposition is substantial.

The low scores of Asians may reflect their purdah unawareness of the prejudice operating in the work-place described, for instance, by Hilary Land.[36] In general, the British have the highest scores, as can be seen in Diagram 5.11. The effect of RGPPSD is in the direction expected from the argument that those with a sense of being relatively poor and so having a high incentive to obtain the meal, feel their identities to be less endangered by stigmatizing characteristics than others. The gradient in proportions between the RGPSD categories is slight; IRPSD would have been almost as good a predictor of variation in group 3, the high scorers having the higher proportion. Therefore Incentive and Alienation interact, the alienated also feeling their identities to be less endangered. Also IRPSD is negatively correlated with EMPLD in all the final groups.[37] This association is more likely to reflect differing degrees of shame or loss of face among mothers than differing expectations about the practical consequences of employers knowing that an application has been made, since there is no reason to suppose that the expectations would be less favourable among high than low IRPSD mothers. Indeed, if the expectations were to be associated with IRPSD, one would predict that the low IRPSD mothers' expectations would be worse than those of the high IRPSD mothers; and in that case IRPSD would be negatively associated with EMPLD. It is however possible that factors other than expectations affect the relationship. For instance, if one of the possible consequences of the small employer knowing was felt to be an increased probability of being made redundant, low IRPSD mothers might have a higher expectation of this outcome than high IRPSD mothers, and yet have a lower probability of accepting the proposition if low IRPSD mothers were to worry less about their husbands being made redundant —in other words, agreement with the proposition would vary directly with expectations of unwanted outcomes and the intensity of fear of the outcome, and if the intensity of that fear was less, a positive relationship between IRPSD and EMPLD would be observed even though expectations of undesirable outcomes were associated with IRPSD. This combination of circumstances is not altogether implausible, since it is not

[36] Hilary Land, *Large Families in London*, op. cit.
[37] The ratio of BSS/TSS of .0091 for IRPSD is to be compared with a ratio for RGPSD of .0107. The proportions for IRPSD categories were 49.4 and 60.0.

unlikely that low IRPSD scores are associated with participation in secondary labour markets where both workers and employers expect high rates of turnover.[38] Unfortunately however, we failed to make use of utility theory to collect data that would allow us to separate the effects of subjective expectations and subjective evaluations to these expectations.[39]

Group 4 is split by EXP, those with early EXP having the higher probability. EXP 2 mothers in group 5 also have a higher probability.[40] That those with early experience had higher scores suggested that some aspects of the early experience created a perception of the disadvantages of the employer knowing. It is certainly not compatible with the argument that persons did not apply because of this dislike, since the recently-experienced had low scores, and those among the non-experienced who were most likely to be eligible on income grounds, tended to have the lowest scores. Among those with early experience, the attitude to education and the school are good predictors. An analysis of residuals shows that EDIIID has a positive correlation with proportions for all but group 22; EDIIID also has a positive effect on group 10, and residual proportions are highest among high NEGCOND scorers. Again, close participatory contacts and a positive attitude to the school increases rather than diminishes the probability of agreeing with the proposition, but it is not clear whether this reflects a closer opportunity to observe stigmatization amongst those with close positive contacts with the school, or a greater sensitivity to the possibility of stigmatization among those who most wish their children to do well and to be well thought of in school, and who may tend to project positive attitudes to those who are involved in schooling. That group 4 and all the groups formed from it score highly on a variable (RGPPSD) which is likely to be an alienation correlate, that 17 of the mothers in group 12 are lone mothers, and that EDID—which reflects attitudes to education in general not the specific experience of particular schools—has a positive effect, lend support to the sensitivity argument, as does the direction of the

[38] The concepts of primary and secondary labour markets have been introduced into the British literature in N. Bosanquet and P. Doeringer, 'Is there a dual labour market in Great Britain?', *Economic Journal, 83*, 3, June 1973, pp. 421–35. One would expect alienation to be particularly rife in secondary labour markets.

[39] J. D. Hull *et al.*, 'Modern Utility Theory', *Journal of the Royal Statistical Society, A, 136*, 1, March 1973.

[40] The 46 mothers in group 6 with early EXP have a probability of .652, the others have a probability of .609. Thus the difference between EXP 2 and other mothers is much smaller than among mothers in group 5.

income effect on group 8 shown in Diagram 5.12.

Arguments related to incentives may play a large part in the explanation of the associations shown in the branches growing from group 4. One would expect incentive arguments to suggest themselves less pervasively in the explanations for mothers in group 5, all of whom have low scores on RGPPS. However, it is by no means clear that this is the case. The importance of MCOB could reflect a more prevalent feeling among the West Indians (probability .500) and Irish (probability .575) that they neither cared much what society in general thought of them, nor did they think that prospects would be much affected by their employers knowing about their application. The latter might depend upon whether they work in a secondary labour market. However a lower proportion are LSC than in group 7. It is also rather unlikely that one third of low RGPPS scorers should care little about their image in the wider society. It seems far more likely therefore that the West Indians are not fully socialized into the meanings of receiving the service and the possible adverse effects of employers receiving requests for the verification of earnings, and that the Irish are members of a sub-culture with reference groups rather different from the English. That it is the better off Irish and West Indians who have the lowest probability of agreeing with the proposition also strengthens the argument. Perhaps, however, the alienation argument is more relevant to the British mothers in group 7. Among these it is the better off, high IRPSD mothers, whose family incomes are not supplemented by the mothers' earnings, that have the highest probability of agreeing with the proposition. Perhaps the more nearly mothers conform to bourgeois ideology and life experience, the more likely they are to think that people would be reluctant to apply for meals because employers would thereby know about it.

The generally higher scores among residuals for the over-achieving area lends support to the argument that community-generated stigma is more powerful there, as has been argued in the preceding sections.

4. Complexity and lack of knowledge

A. Applying is Too Complicated (COMPD)—Diagram 5.12

That those without experience of applying are more likely to quote this reason cannot necessarily be interpreted as evidence that those put

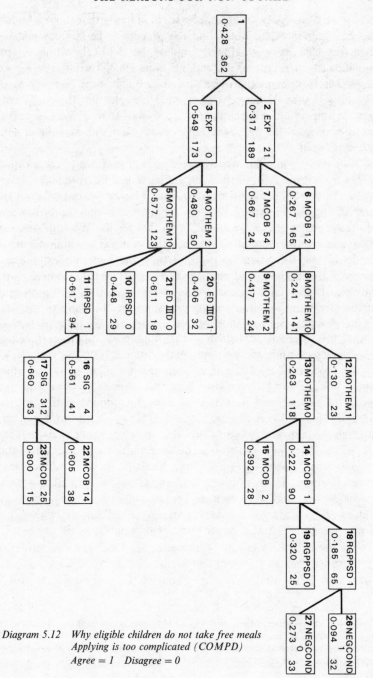

Diagram 5.12   Why eligible children do not take free meals
Applying is too complicated (COMPD)
Agree = 1   Disagree = 0

off by the complexity do not apply. It could imply that those who had gained experience had not found the process to be less complicated than they had expected. However out of the 167 in the whole sample classified as SIG 1, only 37 are without experience. The latter interpretation therefore seems the more probable. But it must be emphasized that no less than 32 per cent of group 2 thought that the complexity was an important reason for not applying—that is a third of the group confirmed the impression of external observers that the process is complicated.[41]

Of those who had had experience a high proportion of the mothers who were born in Asia or the West Indies claimed that the complexity was an important reason for not applying. However, this was not the case among the 23 West Indians in group 3, although the proportion of the Asians in group 3 was similar to that for the West Indians and Asians in group 7, and although the same cultural gap split occurs in group 17. All the Asians in group 3 thought that complexity was a reason. The language and cultural barriers between the Asians—and particularly the Asian mother—could well have made the complexity of the procedures an overwhelming obstacle in obtaining the service.

One possible interpretation of the importance of MOTHEM is that among the 'experienced' British and Irish mothers who do not work or who work part-time, and particularly the latter, it is not the complexity of the process of applying that is considered important, but other factors (like stigma). One might think that some of the 23 mothers in group 12 had worked part-time to avoid this stigma until after the circular, all but 3 being in SIG's 1 and 2. However all but 4 mothers in group 12 had received early EXP. It is therefore more likely that the fact of holding a part-time job made them think themselves more able to cope with the necessary form-filling. Similarly the Irish mothers may have a lower level of educational attainment than the British as well as less assistance, and so thought the process more complex. (The same factors are at work for the Asians and West Indians in group 7, but more strongly, and also among the poorer mothers of group 17.) Among the British in group 14, indicators of incentive and retreatist anomie are important, RGPPSD and NEGCOND. That these have negative effects may imply that RGPPSD and NEGCOND are sub-cultural rather

[41] No lower proportion of those applying since the circular stated the complexity as an important reason. 36 per cent of the 56 recent applicants opined this, compared with 30 per cent of those with earlier experience. Perhaps there is evidence that some, not applying before the circular, were influenced by the complexity.

than individual characteristics; they may imply membership of close-knit sub-cultures that provide some *savoir-faire* in handling the means-tested services of the wider society without damaging the identity of applicants. However the proportions LSC and with high IRPS scores are little different in groups 26, 27 and 14. Incentive, Anomie and Alienation indicators seem relatively unimportant.

Similarly, the mothers who had never applied but were in full-time work, particularly those scoring highly on EDIIID, may have thought other reasons to be the important ones. Perhaps the mothers with the closest positive contacts with the school knew of the help that the teachers often gave in handling the service. The analysis of residuals for group 20 shows that these high EDIIID mothers are particularly unlikely to think complexity an important reason in the over-achieving area—as would be predicted from our supply-demand argument. (The same effect is evident in groups 26 and 16.) We have elsewhere noted that the over-achieving authority had taken more steps to provide the service and make it accessible, and done so over a substantial period of time.

Perhaps the most interesting mothers in group 3 are those whose incomes make their families eligible for free meals, or nearly so. These mothers have never applied for the service. Is it likely that they have not done so because applying is too complex? It is certainly the case that 93 SIG 4 mothers have the same or a lower probability (.52) than the 26 SIG 3 mothers (.54), and that SIG 3 mothers have a lower probability than the 37 SIG 1 and 17 SIG 2 mothers (.59 and .65). SIG is correlated with MOTHEM, so that only 8 of the 50 mothers in group 4 are SIG 1 and 2. Although the SIG 1 proportion is similar to the SIG 4 proportion in group 5, SIG splits group 11 in such a way that the worse off have the higher probabilities. The case for the argument that some of the eligible and the near-eligible were deterred from applying because of the complexity of the service thus seems strong, though some factors may reduce the impact, like LSCD in group 22 and IRPSD in (the experienced) groups 27 and 20 where the inverse association is what might be expected if the IRPSD scorers were more likely to be sensitive to the stigma-potential of free meals and so less likely to think other reasons to be important.

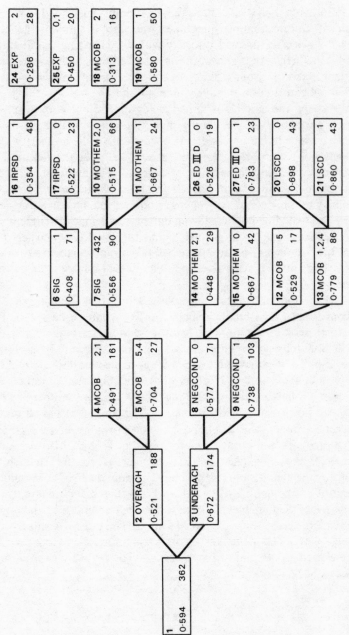

*Diagram 5.13   Why eligible children do not take free meals
The parents don't know about the service (PDKD)
Agree = 1   Disagree = 0*

B. Parents don't know about the service (PDKD)—Diagram 5.13

That Area is the best predictor, and that the proportion in the under-achieving area is 15 percentage points higher than in the over-achieving area is striking support for the major plank of the argument, that authorities to a considerable degree determine their own uptake rates. In the over-achieving area the proportion was lower among the mothers from groups settled in the country for a longer time than among the West Indians and Asians. This supports the argument that newcomers to the country do not understand the meaning of a means-tested service. Nevertheless, almost 50 per cent of the British and Irish mothers said that lack of knowledge was an important reason for non-application. In the under-achieving area the mothers in birth place groups associated with long stay are no less likely to think lack of knowledge important than the West Indians and Asians, the proportion in group 3 being not dissimilar to the newly-arrived mothers in group 2. Perhaps it is not unexpected for the length of the mother's residence in a country to have a greater positive effect on their knowledge of the service in an area whose authority (as in our over-achieving area) had taken pains to publicize its existence; the longer the residence the more likely it would be that the effects of the repeated attempts would cumulate to make a conscious impact on the awareness of the citizen. If the publicity was very recent, effectively directed at an interested group, and presented in the most appropriate way, the opposite could be the case since its effect would be immediate absorption and long-term retention of the knowledge; almost all persons (like mothers) would know about the service and would think that others for whom it was intended would know about it, and there would be almost no association between the probability of knowing about it and length of residence (except among recent arrivals). The form of the association between Area, MCOB, and PDKD therefore contributes to our understanding of the way in which the form of publicity used nationally and by the authority in which the over-achieving area has its effect. It confirms the impressions derived from some of the tabulations not reported here, and it explains why *national* publicity failed to destroy the effects of the longer-term propensity of the authority in the over-achieving area to promote the service to a greater degree.

Among British and Irish mothers in the over-achieving authority, those with incomes below the eligibility level are least likely to agree with the proposition. This reflects the high proportion of the mothers who had actually received the service. IRPSD is negatively correlated with scores among these mothers, as among mothers in groups 19, 20 and 21. The consistency of the IRPS effect is interesting because it makes it incompatible with the argument that those with high IRP scores attribute non-uptake to stigma variables rather than to lack of knowledge. Similarly that group 7 in the over-achieving area is split with non-employed mothers with low proportions, whereas group 8 is split with the non-employed having a high proportion, is of interest since it suggests that in the over-achieving area knowledge was particularly possessed by the crucial non-employed group. The residuals confirm the pattern in which the non-employed appear to expect people to be well-informed in the over-achieving area. Perhaps the lower proportion for Irish than British mothers reflects other features of the composition of the groups; but it may reflect a greater homogeneity in culture among the Irish-born mothers.

EDID, NEGCOND, and EDIIID like IRPSD are indicators of specific characteristics, but may indicate membership of sub-cultural groups—particularly characteristics associated with anomie and alienation from some of the cultural institutions of society, which the (mainly American) theory of lower class sub-cultures suggests would be correlated with LSCD. The division of the under-achieving area sample, the division of group 13 on LSCD, the residuals gradients for group 20 on EDID, group 21 on RGPPSD, and group 19 on LSCD, could therefore be interpreted as evidence implying that the existence of the service is least well known among those having the greatest probability of needing it at some time or other, and most likely not to know of it through the school. The importance of the relationship with the school being clear, the positive effect of EDIIID on group 13 is interpretable as a contribution of school-orientation to an understanding of the range of services available. However, not all the correlations would support such an interpretation. Nevertheless, the comparison of these results with those for the stigma indicators suggest that among those with low EDID, low EDIIID, high NEGCOND, or low IRPSD, LSCD mothers in the under-achieving area, stigma may be a less important reason for non-uptake than a lack of knowledge of the service. Some of these are low income mothers without EXP. That all 9 of the recent EXP mothers in group 21 accepted the proposition confirms that before publicity was given nationally, the absence of knowledge was clearly an important factor.

If our main focus had been the development of sociological theory, we would have used the analysis of this chapter to estimate the relationships important to our causal argument. However, as our principal interest lay in policy analysis, we gave priority to constructing models of a different kind. These are discussed in Chapter 6.[42]

[42] Some important participants in policy-making have clear criteria by which they evaluate policy research. The following dialogue between Sir William Pile, then Permanent Secretary of the Department of Education and Science, and Miss Janet Fooks is instructive.

Sir William Pile: ... the hope is that the researcher will turn out some ideas that are really relevant and that we shall be influenced accordingly and act accordingly. I have to say, of course, that the great thing about research is that a part of it is rubbish, and another part (I will not be specific about the proportions) leads nowhere, and is really rather indifferent; it is, I am afraid, exceptional to find a piece of research that really hits the nail on the head and tells you pretty clearly what is wrong, or what is happening, or what should be done ... But wherever we get the results of these projects coming to us, we have to evaluate them to see if they fall into the rubbish category, the indifferent category, or the rare category where we get real insight into what is to be done.

Miss Fooks: It is like searching for sultanas in a pudding, is it? There are very few?

—The word itself is so debased these days. People say they have done some research when they really mean they have stopped to think for three minutes.

By Sir William's criteria, further elaboration of our causal analysis would be less worth while than the modelling of Chapter 6. (See *Tenth Report from the Expenditure Committee. Session 1975/6. Policy Making in the Department of Education and Science, H.C. 621*, Questions 446 and 447.)

PART III: THE POLICY DISCUSSION

6 The Eligibility Criterion as a Policy Instrument

The principal conclusion of our causal analysis was the unsurprising one that the theory elaborated from the arguments of the universalist and selectivist writers does not explain variance sufficiently to be the basis for policy judgement. One wonders whether the same conclusion would hold for the many other issues of social policy for which much of the prescriptive argument is based on untested and often virtually unexplicated causal theory. It is a conclusion that forces us to a direct evaluation of the costs and consequences of the interventions themselves. The salience of the theory developed in Chapter 4, and tested and elaborated in the causal analysis of Chapter 5, is that it contributes to the development of indicators that between them cover the most important of the consequences of intervention.

The focus of the argument is again the testing of the universalists' assertions about the consequences of selectivist provision. This is inevitable, since our evidence is about the workings of a selectivist system. More fundamentally, the assymetry of our approach is the logical consequence of the simplicity of the kernel of the selectivist argument. In contexts like the school meals case, the most important of the selectivists' propositions is that the universalist solution costs more to public funds and to society as a whole without being greatly more effective. In contrast, the universalists' objection to the selectivists' policy prescription is that it has complex consequences for potential and actual recipients of services, and therefore for society as a whole. One can therefore quantify the selectivists' argument without great trouble. The cost to public funds of providing a free meal for every child is one of the questions most frequently asked about the school meals service in Parliament. It would be difficult to estimate what the cost of providing a free meals service would be to society as a whole since it would cause a large change, whose consequences our data could not be expected to predict. Both because of this unpredictability and because of the intrinsic importance of the consequences for individuals of the selectivist policy, the focus of our evaluation must be the selectivist system.

A selectivist system has two main mega-policies: a set of criteria which specify those to receive the services at a reduced price or free of charge, and a set of criteria for fixing charges. This chapter presents models predicting cost and welfare consequences of alternative eligibility criteria. Section (i) discusses the criteria of effectiveness implicit in the statement of Chapter 4. Sections (ii), (iii), and (iv) examine the cost effectiveness of different policy options. Section (v) puts the results into the broader perspective of the long-run development of our tax and social security systems. Chapter 7 discusses criteria for fixing prices.

(i) Criteria of Effectiveness

What mothers perceive to be the benefits obtained from the service varies greatly from person to person. Although for certain purposes it might be advantageous to use consumers' surplus techniques to estimate some unique value of the benefits from each of the alternative policies to compare with their costs, to present such a unique estimate would conflict with one of the principal findings of the study—that the factors that influence the effectiveness of a policy vary greatly in their incidence among population groups. A good policy for one group might therefore be inappropriate for others. Only by understanding the consequences of policies for a substantial number of groups can we design and choose policies that make the best use of our interventive capability. The more important implication of the results is not that the discussion of alternative policies has been inadequately based on evidence, so that the nature of causal processes has been misrepresented—an inference that would hardly have required an expensive survey to make—but that it has been at too high a level of generality. It would therefore be more illogical for this study than for most to conclude with an attempt to embody the complex balance of costs and benefits of a proposal in a single estimate, even if the data it was feasible for us to collect seemed to make that possible.

Two types of criteria are paramount in evaluating the consequences of adopting different eligibility levels. First, the acceptability of the policy would determine the uptake rate, and therefore the extent to which a programme, intended to benefit a particular group, in fact benefits all the members of that group. The degree to which this is so is defined by Burton Weisbrod as the 'horizontal' target efficiency of the programme; namely the proportion of those eligible who receive the subsidy.[1] Several of the factors that affect acceptability also affect the psychic welfare of those to whom the incentive to receive the service is great enough for them to claim it (because their income level is far below the eligibility level) although they dislike doing so intensely. One such factor is stigma. Another factor is their perception of the wisdom and rightness of the policy itself. One set of criteria of efficiency should therefore be the proportion of those made eligible who show signs that they are likely to find it acceptable.

Secondly, there is evidence to suggest that deprivation and the probability of malnutrition vary substantially between groups with similar assessed *per capita* incomes. It is legitimate to consider treating such groups as targets for the service—albeit targets of lesser importance than the children eligible by the income-based criterion. A child with such characteristics who is eligible by the standard criterion is likely to be needier than a child who does not possess the characteristic but is eligible. It is therefore legitimate to consider that the more efficiently allocated is the service, the greater the proportion of its recipients who are eligible and who also possess the characteristic. Further, it is important to know the consequences for the proportions of these secondary 'target' groups made eligible under alternative eligibility criteria, and to work out the consequences of embodying the definitions of the target groups in the eligibility criterion itself, by adopting different income levels for eligibility for different groups. The Finer Report has made out an impressive case for arguing that the ex-

---

[1] Burton A. Weisbrod, 'Collective action and the distribution of income', op. cit. The acceptability of a policy option contributes to its consequences for legitimacy and support in the politics of the policy process of that area of intervention. The obverse of the remission of charges is the subsidization of some recipients. Whether or not the incidence of subsidization implicit in the options is perceived as legitimate can be politically important. For instance, it seems to be legitimate to differentially subsidize households of similar incomes but cultures creating dissimilar risks of malnutrition. But would it seem legitimate to the general population if these variations in culture were to reflect differences in ethnicity associated with recent immigration? However, survey data and opinions about such matters are difficult to interpret if the opinions are sought before politicians attempt to lead public opinion—before, for instance, they publicize an inevitable divergence between social and private interests in the absence of differential subsidization; or before they can link the subsidy with such issues as child poverty in which the legitimacy of state intervention is well established.

Perhaps more important are the consequences of options for the diffuse support of the government. The assumptive worlds of policy makers tend to be most influenced by those pressure groups with a particular interest in that territory of policy. Since politicians are often insulated both from the general population and many of those most influenced by social policy, the assumptions they make tend to be generalizations of the opinions of their supporters. It is in this context that survey evidence about the acceptability of options can be most important.

penditure needs of the fatherless family are understated by assessed net income. For instance, the Report argued that their housing might tend to be more expensive,[2] that they would have to incur additional child-minding costs to achieve a similar quality of life,[3] and that because of the greater pressure on parental time, it was necessary to spend more on food.[4] The Report therefore considered that lone parents should receive a special addition to their Supplementary Benefit scale rate of 'at least £1.50' to compensate for such factors.[5] Professor George has shown much the same to be true for motherless families.[6] Again, the dangers of malnutrition among some ethnic groups are relatively high, and their needs for free meals therefore greater than others. Children of some nationality groups have disproportionate probabilities of suffering a range of forms of deprivation. Of course, the target groups thus defined include many whose needs are not great, so to the extent that these target groups are unconditionally embodied in the eligibility criterion, the programme is at risk of achieving diminished 'vertical efficiency' —a lower ratio of the benefit received by needy beneficiaries to total benefits distributed.[7]

The effectiveness indicators analysed below far from completely cover the main benefits and disbenefits. The cost indicator is perhaps even less adequate. In principle, unit costs would vary with the scale of output, and with the time period to which the policy relates. Moreover, the cost concept would be the cost of a marginal unit of output of a standard quality produced in the most efficient manner. No substantial research has been undertaken on the cost functions of the school meals service. Therefore this analysis treats unit costs as invariant with respect to output and equal to marginal costs. (The salient cost concepts are discussed in Chapter 7.)

Appendix 6.1 outlines the computations undertaken in the analysis. Most of the variables are based on those used earlier in this study and

---

[2] Department of Health and Social Security, *Report of the Committee on One Parent Families, Cmnd 5629*, H.M.S.O., London, 1973, para. 5.42.

[3] Op. cit., para. 5.47.

[4] Op. cit., para. 5.46.

[5] Op. cit. para. 5.254.

[6] Victor George and Paul Wilding, *Motherless Families*, Routledge, London, 1972. Although relatively ungenerous for all families with children, British family benefits for single-parent families seem particularly inadequate compared with what is provided in Germany, France, Italy, Belgium, and Luxembourg. See Edward James, 'Social policy and the one-parent family in Europe, *Concern*, Autumn 1976.

[7] The concept is explained in Weisbrod, 'Collective action and the distribution of income', op. cit.

listed in Table 5.A and Table 2.3; the exceptions being SUPERI and CUMPFMCOST. SUPERI is the difference between assessed net income and the eligibility level, the continuous variable on which SIG of Chapter 5 was based, and CUMPFMCOST is the potential cost of providing free meals to a group, assuming 100 per cent uptake. Sections (ii) and (iii) discuss the patterns of costs and effectiveness at varying eligibility levels for the two areas. Section (iv) discusses some target groups separately.

(ii) Effectiveness at Three Eligibility Levels

The first group of effectiveness indicators in Table 6.1 show the proportions made eligible in some important secondary target groups. The general conclusion is clear. The data imply that at the eligibility levels current at the time of the survey, the proportions of the members of these groups entitled to receive free meals were in general low. Only children from MOTHAL and Asian families had probabilities of being eligible twice or more than those of the general population of named children. This was so in both towns. The same would have been true had the eligibility level been £2 higher, save that the Asian children would not have had twice the probability of children in general in the over-achieving area. An eligibility level £2 below that current would have yielded a broadly similar picture. We may therefore conclude that there is only a weak association between income and those characteristics that enhance children's needs that are not specifically taken into account in the means test. Therefore, a means test is not an adequate substitute for a more sophisticated eligibility criterion that takes into account a broader range of handicapping characteristics. A means-tested scheme intended to countervail the effects of low incomes in conjunction with a high need for expenditure must either be much more complex or have an element of flexibility that will help match the extraordinary diversity of needs for expenditure.

The cost effectiveness of the level depends in part upon the acceptability of the means-tested scheme, since this influences the willingness to take up the entitlement. In the under-achieving area, a lower (but still high) proportion of those persons that would have been eligible by the then standard than of those who would have been eligible at a standard £2 lower felt stigma to be a pervasive factor influencing the uptake of others, but the proportion would have been similar among persons eligible at a level £2 higher. This was so in the over-achieving area also, save that at the then eligibility level, the proportion feeling

Table 6.1 Selected cost and effectiveness indicators at varying eligibility levels

	UNDER-ACHIEVING AREA				OVER-ACHIEVING AREA			
	Difference between level postulated and then current eligibility level—£ per week.[1]							
	−£2	0	+£2	+£4	−£2	0	+£2	+£4
Cost (£ million)[2]	0.89	1.30	1.80	2.15	0.55	0.86	1.17	1.37
(then eligibility level = 100)	(69)	(100)	(139)	(165)	(64)	(100)	(136)	(159)
Proportions of groups made eligible:[3]								
High RGPPS	7	13	26	37	14	23	35	42
MOTHAL	68	72	87	95	68	83	97	100
MCOB Irish	17	33	43	51	13	34	43	50
West Indian	30	41	54	70	35	42	63	67
Asian	40	76	88	88	48	58	72	86
LSC	23	33	42	55	26	40	52	65
High TRAVCOST	24	30	36	38	19	30	44	50
High TRAVTIM	16	24	32	36	19	31	44	53
Opining that the most important advantage of taking nutritional	30	39	43	55	24	33	46	52
Proportions of those eligible:[4]								
Declare own stigma (OSD)	29	21	18	17	16	13	10	11
Having High OSPS	23	29	29	34	44	48	45	42
Opining OCHLDD	77	71	71	66	56	52	55	58
TCHERSD	30	24	25	24	18	13	10	12
CHARD	68	68	71	67	71	70	74	76
STATINCD	75	68	70	71	66	64	64	66
EMPLD	64	58	62	61	45	49	53	54
COMPD	65	58	58	57	44	40	40	40
PDKD	87	81	81	78	49	45	47	49
Recommending that make more children eligible for free meals	65	65	61	61	56	56	54	56
Subsidize service as a whole	79	75	71	71	56	50	50	51
Opining most important advantage to be nutritional	50	46	36	37	41	36	35	34

Notes: [1] The 'eligibility level' is Net Income (estimated as in the free meals assessment) at which the 'named child' would be eligible for free meals applying the gradients of net income by number of children current at the time of the survey.

[2] Assuming 100 per cent uptake and attendance, and 1968 school meals costs. School meals costs are taken to be unit costs.

[3] The proportion of named children in the group specified by the effectiveness indicator who are made eligible at the postulated level; e.g. (High RGPPS named children eligible at postulated level)/(All high RGPPS named children)%.

[4] The proportion of mothers whose named child would be eligible who are in the group specified in the row; e.g. (Mothers declaring own stigma and would be eligible)/(All mothers who would be eligible)%.

the stigma potential of the service to be pervasively important was lower than at the levels £2 above and below. In the under-achieving area, the then eligibility standard also resulted in a proportion of eligible persons thinking that the parents' dislike of stating incomes was an important reason for non-uptake which was lower by 8 percentage points than it would have been at a level £2 lower, though it made little difference in the other area. The proportion thinking that applying was complicated or difficult was also lower by 7 percentage points than at a standard £2 lower in the under-achieving area. Again, a standard £2 higher would have made little difference in that area, and all three standards yielded similar proportions in the over-achieving town. The then standard resulted in a lower proportion ascribing non-uptake substantially to parents' absence of knowledge about the service than a standard £2 below in both areas, whereas a standard £2 higher would have made little difference. There is therefore some evidence that might support an argument that the standard then current would have been more acceptable than one £2 below, and that it was not obvious that a standard £2 higher would have made much difference to the acceptability of the service. Of course such conclusions as this must be hedged with caveats. First, although there are no indicators implying markedly greater acceptability at the higher level among those analysed here, the ones analysed are a small proportion of those which could be considered important. Secondly, a different eligibility level would have caused a pattern of responses which would certainly have been slightly (and might have been considerably) different, because more respondents would actually have experienced free meals—unless the higher standard had been introduced in one step at a point in time not long before the survey period.

(iii) The Population of L.E.A. Areas

The costs of varying the eligibility levels do not differ greatly between the two areas. Again, some of the benefit consequences of doing so by £2 are similar—those for the proportion of children from MOTHAL families, LSC families, Irish or Asian families, or high RGPPS families, for instance. However, others are very different. In particular, the proportion of West Indian high TRAVCOST, and high TRAVTIM named children made eligible would be much greater in the over-achieving area, as would be the proportion opining that the meal itself was the most important advantage of consuming the service. Therefore, although the cost of increasing the eligibility level by £2 was similar in both areas, this was not so of some of the effects.

Judging from the effectiveness indicators shown in Table 6.1, one would surmise that in a system in which the same rules for income assessment were used, but authorities financed the service from their general rate and grant-borne expenditure, and could choose the net income at which children became eligible, the over-achieving area might well choose the higher eligibility income. This is so because the returns on the expenditure, as indicated by most of the proportions of the target groups covered, were in general higher in that area. Some of these differences are large. The proportions of named children from MOTHAL and high RGPPS families attained in the under-achieving area at the then eligibility level would have been attained in the over-achieving area at a level of income £2 lower. There may therefore be grounds for questioning a policy in which large, efficient, democratically responsible, if subordinate, governments are actually required by central government departments to use their resources less effectively than they might. This is a subject to which we must return below.

(iv) The Effects of Varying Eligibility Criteria by Secondary Target Groups

One way in which account could be taken of the need-related characteristics would be by varying between target groups the level of SUPERI used as the criterion for eligibility. For instance, a standard level of SUPERI might set a ceiling level of SUPERI below which any child would be eligible, while some target groups might be made eligible at higher levels of SUPERI. The evidence of the effects of doing this for four secondary target groups is summarized in Diagrams 6.1 and 6.2, and Tables 6.2 and 6.3. From Diagram 6.1 can be deduced the cost and consequences for the proportion of children made eligible of operating any combination of a standard eligibility criterion based on income— or rather, SUPERI, as this has been defined above—and different eligibility criteria for individual target groups. For instance, taking as the basic eligibility level the one operating at the time of the survey, that is a SUPERI of zero, and an eligibility level for MOTHAL children £2 higher, that is, a SUPERI of +£2, the total cost would be the £2.16 m incurred from the population as a whole plus an amount equal to the difference between the cost for MOTHAL families at SUPERI of +£2 and that at a SUPERI of £0; namely, £0.09 m. The proportion of all children made eligible by the eligibility level of £0 SUPERI would be 34 per cent; that of children from MOTHAL families by the level £2 higher would

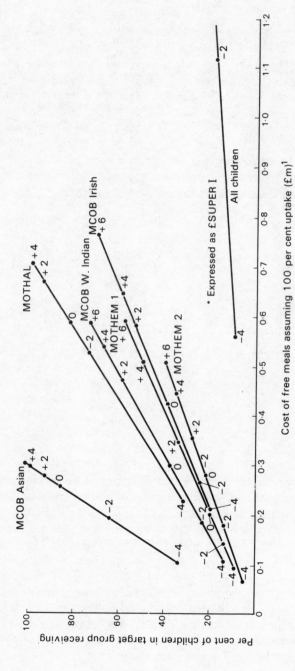

Diagram 6.1   Costs and proportions receiving at varying levels of eligibility by target group

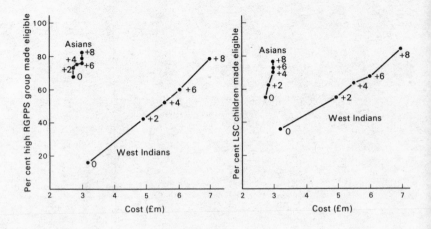

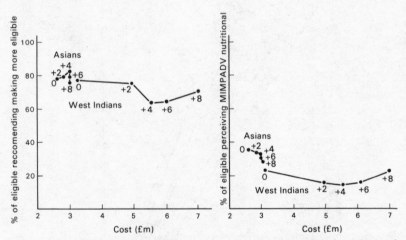

Diagram 6.2   *The cost-effectiveness of more generous eligibility incomes for 'Asian' and 'West Indian' children.*
Effectiveness with eligibility at various levels of £ SUPERI

be 92 per cent. The 'horizontal efficiency' criterion used in the diagram is only one measure of efficiency. The tables show the effectiveness of different eligibility levels as reflected in the other indicators discussed above.

Table 6.2 Selected cost and effectiveness indicators at varying eligibility standards for ethnic groups

| | | Difference between eligibility level postulated and the then current level | | | | |
		$-£2$	0	$+£2$	$+£4$	All
Cost						
Irish (£m.)		0.277	0.439	0.603	0.668	1.150
(then level = 100)		63	100	137	152	262
West Indian (£m)		0.191	0.314	0.486	0.556	0.835
(then level = 100)		61	100	155	177	266
Asian (£m)		0.200	0.267	0.287	0.296	0.313
(then level = 100)		75	100	108	111	117
Proportions of Target Groups made eligible						
High RGPPS	Irish	7	15	34	39	100
	West Indian	15	17	42	53	100
	Asian	30	65	76	76	100
MOTHAL	Irish	85	95	97	97	100
	West Indian	100	100	100	100	100
	Asian	100	100	100	100	100
LSC	Irish	26	36	42	53	100
	West Indian	35	38	56	64	100
	Asian	27	55	63	70	100
Proportions of the eligible with various characteristics						
High OSPS	Irish	32	38	32	32	36
	West Indian	57	54	50	53	53
	Asian	32	50	52	50	60
Recommending	Irish	75	75	52	52	58
that make more	West Indian	70	77	73	64	57
people eligible	Asian	93	79	80	81	70
Most important	Irish	69	55	37	41	35
advantage	West Indian	36	23	15	14	24
nutritional	Asian	49	34	32	30	26

(a) Mothers' country of Birth (MCOB)

Since high proportions of Asian children are from families whose incomes are below the 1968 poverty line, an eligibility criterion of as much as £4 higher than that prevailing would have cost the two authorities only £300 thousand. Whereas most Asian children were actually eligible, some 40 per cent of West Indian children were from families with a positive SUPERI of £4 or less, so that the cost of operating an eligibility level £4 higher than the standard would have been £0.24 m. Special treatment of Irish children is expensive both because of the numbers and the distribution of incomes of their families. Table 6.2 shows that an increase by £2 in the eligibility level would cause substantially higher proportions of the LSC and those with a pervasive feeling of relative poverty to be eligible—characteristics that would be difficult to make the basis of eligibility, but which would nevertheless be judged by many to be important to 'need'. The table also suggests that free meals would be acceptable since high proportions recommended that more children should be made eligible for free meals. The limited analysis whose results are discussed here suggests that it may be more effective to set a special eligibility level for the Asians than for the West Indians for both horizontal efficiency and acceptability reasons. The groups are similar with respect to MOTHAL and OSPS, but on the other counts assessed here, allowing the Asians a more generous limit would seem more effective. This is illustrated in Diagram 6.2. Although at very high eligibility levels the West Indian group has a similar (and in one case a higher) effectiveness score, and the service is noticeably less acceptable to Asians at these levels, at the more realistic level of +£2 and +£4, the Asian group has the higher scores.

Readers will require no reminding that this analysis is not based on recent or national data, and that the range of effectiveness indicators computed is small. More fundamentally, one should (and in practice one could) not use race to define an eligibility criterion, though it would sometimes be feasible to select whole schools in immigrant areas for the application of particularly generous eligibility criteria. The results are therefore of interest only because they pose issues for further investigation.

(b) Fatherless Families (MOTHALD)

The costs and the most important of the consequences of adopting various eligibility levels for MOTHALD families are outlined in Table 6.3. To provide compensation for the higher needs for expenditure by £2 to roughly the degree recommended by the Finer Committee, which recommended an increase in the scale rate of Supplementary Benefit for unmarried mothers of at least £1.50,[8] would increase costs by 15

---

[8] Department of Health and Social Security, *Report of the Committee on One Parent Families*, *Cmnd 5629*, H.M.S.O., London, 1973, para. 5.254.

Table 6.3 *Cost and effectiveness indicators at varying eligibility standards for*
MOTHAL group

| | Difference between eligibility level postulated and the then current level | | | | | |
	−£2	0	+£2	+£4	+£6	All
Cost £(m)	0.54	0.61	0.70	0.73	0.74	0.75
(then level = 100)	89	100	115	120	121	123
Proportions of Target Groups made eligible						
High RGPPS	28	47	76	97	100	100
MCOB Irish	85	95	.97	97	100	100
West Indian	100	100	100	100	100	100
Asian	100	100	100	100	100	100
LSC	68	77	91	99	100	100
Proportions of the eligible with various characteristics						
High OSPS	15	17	14	16	16	15
Recommend: make more eligible	70	69	68	68	68	66
MIMPADV Nutritional	69	69	59	62	62	60

per cent, but would result in a large increase in the coverage of persons
with high RGPP scores. An increase in the eligibility level to £4 SUPERI
would cost only another £30 thousand, and almost all the high RGPPS
mothers would then be eligible. However, universal eligibility would
cost little more. Redefining the eligibility levels thus would make little
difference to the proportions of the eligible group which were sensitive
to stigma, save that there was a group of MOTHALDS with high TCHERSD
who would have been made eligible if the level were raised by £2, and
they would have raised the mean level of TEACHERSD from 28 to 35 per
cent.

(v) *The broader perspective*

The models reinforce an impression that gains support from every
chapter of this book: that the extension of means-testing is not in itself
unacceptable to mothers. But it would be quite wrong to infer from this
that such an extension would be good policy. The reasons are well
known. Inferences drawn from evidence about perceptions and
behaviour in the late 1960s, the end of an era of growing prosperity,
widening life chances, and optimism about the capacity for society to

improve the lot of the members, cannot be assumed to hold in an age of disillusion, disappointed expectations, diminishing real incomes, higher unemployment, the strains created by the anomalies of inflation, and more overt conflict between groups nakedly pursuing their own interests.

Secondly, an extension of the policy may seem attractive when it is considered in isolation, but might be quite inappropriate when considered simultaneously with similar extensions in related areas. Without examining comparable evidence for other means-tested services for children, we cannot assert that the extension of this is more cost effective than the extension of others. We cannot extend the means-testing of more than one or two areas without making more acute the fundamental dilemmas of anti-poverty policy—deepening and extending the poverty trap by narrowing the gap in household incomes between those drawing higher and lower proportions of their real incomes from means-tested benefits, increasing the overlap between the payers of income tax and receivers of means-tested benefits, and generally increasing the degree to which the subsidy is financed by virtually horizontal rather than vertical redistribution; extending transaction costs of claiming to higher proportions of families; and increasing the proportion of social welfare resources devoted to these transaction costs. Some of these objections equally apply to the use of more generous income limits to groups in special need. Indeed, there could be a risk of replicating a system in each authority even more byzantine than the one that now exists—it would be ironic if authorities were encouraged to complicate their system at a time when the Chairman of the Supplementary Benefits Commission is arguing the merits of simplification of criteria for cash benefit.[9] Nevertheless, we should not neglect the potential of such measures as extending claw-backed family allowances for diminishing the holding power of the poverty trap.

Thirdly, the application to some groups of more generous criteria risks increasing the latent resentment felt towards them by those who do not receive the benefit, and makes necessary more encounters in which the claiming of a benefit can be a catalyst which allows the expression of this hostility. At any rate, it makes necessary encounters which generate conflict between individuals and groups. They similarly make the incidence of benefits even less easily predictable, and more dependent on factors that have little to do with poverty-related need,

[9] David Donnison, *Supplementary benefits: principles and priorities*, *The James Seth Memorial Lecture, 1976*, Department of Social Administration, University of Edinburgh, 1977. See also David Donnison's reply to 'Dear David Donnison', *Social Work Today*.

and whose importance for uptake we have shown. From the broader perspective, we must agree with David Donnison 'that major groups whose needs are in total a reasonably predictable public responsibility should not have to rely indefinitely on means tests for their support ... we must consider how these groups can be lifted off dependence on means-tests'.[10] The extension policies such as the Child Endowment scheme, or its Tory predecessor (the Tax Credit scheme) deserve support not mainly because they are 'the biggest, best, and most complicated simplification' of our systems of tax and social security;[11] but because they do less to damage the cohesion of society.

(vi) Conclusions

Although based on slender and fragile data, this limited cost-effectiveness analysis allows us to draw two general conclusions. First, the cost-effectiveness of more generous eligibility criteria may have been much greater in some areas than in others. Secondly, the cost-effectiveness of different eligibility levels varied substantially between target groups. These are conclusions of great importance when seen in a context, the most important features of which are that the school meals *subsidy*, though not necessarily the school catering service as a whole, is mainly intended as a weapon in the battle against child poverty, and as such is only one weapon to be deployed to the best advantage as this seems most appropriate, given the state of the armoury as a whole and the nature of the enemy.

Only in the medium term can we feel reasonably sure that the flexible use of income-related eligibility criteria in a free-meals scheme should be an important weapon in the war on child poverty. In the longer run, we may have to abandon most of the important means-tested services for families with low incomes. This is because in an economy in which transfers bulk ever larger in relation to personal incomes, and in which income differentials are becoming rapidly narrower, the incidence of the taxes and benefits will become increasingly complex but powerful determinants of individual and family behaviour as spenders (and probably also earners). In order to make out a case for the survival of a means-tested free meals scheme in the long run, it would be necessary to be able to demonstrate that its use was more cost-effective than the use of means-tested interventions in other areas. Our data is such that we cannot do this. However, these data (and a great

---

[10] David Donnison, op. cit.
[11] *The Economist*, 30 September 1972, p. 84.

deal of other evidence) suggest that this might well be so. Not only is it arguable that the free meals scheme is less objectionable than many other means-tested benefits, but also that it has a role in removing the principal distributional constraints on adopting a better basis for pricing policy in the school catering service as a whole. This we discuss in the next chapter.

Appendix 6.1 The Cost Effectiveness Analysis of Varying the Eligibility Levels of Income

Nature of the Model

1. This analysis was restricted to an examination of the consequences of varying the level of assessed income at which one child would become eligible, the difference between the eligibility level for one child and others in the family being the same as at the time of the survey.
2. Costs were the product of the unit cost of a school meal, the number of school children, and the number of feeding days. A value of a variable thus derived showing the potential free meals cost (PFM COST) was calculated for each family. Thus the uptake rate among those eligible was assumed to be 100 per cent.
3. Effectiveness indicators were of two kinds: (a) proportion of 'target groups' eligible for free meals at the specified eligibility level; and (b) proportions of those eligible at that level who had a specified characteristic. More precisely, of those cases which formed the basis of the analysis (set M); let J be the subset of M that possesses an attribute (e.g. MOTHALD); let K_s be the subset of set M with SUPERI less than or equal to the specified level s; and let L_s be that subset of cases common to subsets K_s and J. Then type (a) indicators are of the form L_s/J, and type (b) indicators are of the form L_s/K.
4. The cases were weighted by their probabilities of being chosen in the samples.

Method of computation

1. Most of the basic variables were defined for other purposes and explained in earlier chapters. However, Supersubsistence Income, SUPERI is defined as Assessed Net Income – Eligibility level; and cumulative potential free meals cost is defined as an aggregate of the potential free meals cost of a number of families.
2. SUPERI was derived, and cases arranged in ascending order of SUPERI. CUMPFMCOST of family i was calculated as CUMPFMCOST of family $(i-1)$ + PFM cost of family i.

7 Charging as a Policy Instrument

Social welfare is notorious for the imprecision of the intellectual basis of the assumptive worlds of its policy-makers, and for the scant basis in evidence for its assumptions about cause and effect and its beliefs about the costs and consequences of intervention. The normative theories on which interventions are based are usually both vague and scarcely tested against salient evidence. This is as much a symptom as a cause of the primitiveness of the area: as I have argued elsewhere, sophistication of the intellectual, organizational, and political aspects of a policy paradigm mutually complement and reinforce one another.[1] Because the beliefs about the costs and consequences of intervention are untested against evidence, their form is more determined by what is compatible with the higher order values of the political culture of those that dominate the intellectual development of the area than by evidence-based judgements about relative success in attaining goals: the latent function of intervention is more powerful than the instrumental manifest function. (Indeed, the causal assumptions themselves more directly reflect the high order preconceptions of these dominant cultures.) Policy decisions depend much less on evidence about effectiveness in relation to clear goals.

No aspect of social welfare policy has a less explicit intellectual basis than charging policies. Professor Roy Parker has recently analysed what appears to be the rationale of charging policies in a wide range of social services. His account makes it clear that the normative theory of pricing has had little impact on the perceptions of politicians and others, and the concept of 'allocative efficiency' appears to be almost completely absent from their discussions.[2] To a visiting social scientist from a parallel universe, this would seem surprising, since the theory of

[1] Bleddyn Davies, 'Needs and outputs', in H. Heisler ed., *Fundamentals of Social Administration*, Macmillan, London, 1977, pp. 129–62 and pp. 237–40.
[2] R. A. Parker, 'Charging for the social services', *Journal of Social Policy*, 5, 4, October 1976, pp. 359–74.

price is a main focus of the oldest and most populous branch of social science, and since the normative theory of pricing has had such a clear impact on other policy areas. In particular, it has had a large (and during the 1960s an increasing) impact on the pricing policy for public enterprises. The central tenets of the theory and its salience to the policies of the nationalized industries now seem to be unquestioned by political opinion, as this is reflected in the pages of Hansard.

The reason for the political success of the normative theory of optimal pricing is simple: there exists no alternative normative theory that is both widely understood by Western economists, and also offers an intellectual basis for a pricing policy that leads to an efficient allocation of resources. Because the theory has a salience that transcends welfare capitalism, it is acceptable to those whose attitudes to the market are ambivalent. A socialist historian of the early economic literature that laid the foundations for what is now called the theory of optimal pricing argued that it would be more useful under Socialism than under Capitalism.[3] Applied economists have accepted it for much the same reason: their theoretical colleagues have shown that its proper application requires precise specifications of values and knowledge about the context that is hardly likely to be available, but have presented no simple but superior alternative to rules of thumb based upon this theory.[4] Neither the politician nor the applied economist in the public service can avoid making a recommendation for action. To them it is inappropriate to reject policy rules even if these rules do not perfectly satisfy the theoretical test that they must give optimal results with logical certainty whatever the context. What seems relevant to them is whether they are better than alternative policy rules. To fail to select a policy rule is to leave the policy to be settled by default, or by decisions that are arbitrary in the sense that they are unrelated to theories about efficiency in the allocation of resources.

Since the social policy analyst is without an alternative normative theory of optimal pricing, it is for him to demonstrate the irrelevance of the economist's approach. In particular, it is for him to demonstrate that the subject of his enquiry is sufficiently different from areas where the normative theory of price has been applied with apparent success if he is to justify a decision to ignore it.

[3] B. P. Beckwith, *Marginal cost prices—output control*, Columbia University Press, New York, 1955, p. 9.
[4] See, for instance, the Department of the Environment, *Transport Policy*, H.M.S.O., London, 1976.

(i) The School Meals and Public Enterprise Contexts Compared

Resource Allocation and Marginal Cost Pricing

The pattern of variation in consumers' marginal valuations varies too much and (for individuals) it can change too quickly for an administered system of rationing to be more likely to yield an efficient allocation than the price system. The determination of consumers' marginal valuations of the products of the public enterprise is complex, reflecting levels of income, the prices of close substitutes and complements (many of which are produced by the private sector), and many other factors. This was implicit in the argument of the socialist economists, and gains some recognition for the growing importance of markets in communist countries. Most of the commodities concerned are what the economists would call 'private' goods—in particular the consumption of a unit of one of them by a person excludes the consumption of that unit by someone else. Moreover, the main substitutes and complements are provided by independent commercial suppliers. For instance, oil is a close substitute for coal, gas, or electricity in the market for space heating; privately provided road haulage is a substitute for rail in the market for freight transport; the motor car is a substitute both for rail and bus in commuter transport. The pattern of consumption is sensitive to the relative prices of the alternatives.

The more this is so—the greater the cross-elasticity of demand—the more important is it that (in the words of the Select Committee on Nationalized Industries):

> prices should reflect costs so that a transfer of resources from one activity to another can raise consumer welfare. If consumers are willing to pay more for some extra output than it costs to produce, welfare will *prima facie* rise if that expansion of output and sales takes place. In the reverse case, if consumers are unwilling to pay a price that covers the costs of producing marginal output, welfare will rise if a contraction of output and sales takes place. This is the rationale behind a policy of marginal cost pricing. It means that if any industry can use certain resources to produce output of greater value than another industry, those resources should be transferred from the latter to the former.[5]

The real cost of consuming any commodity is the alternative forgone

---

[5] *1967/8, H.C. 371–I*, paragraph 194. See also *Nationalised Industries: a review of Economic and Financial Objectives, Cmnd 3437*, H.M.S.O., London, 1967.

as a result of the decision to consume it. Therefore the individual will get most satisfaction from his income only if he values each unit of consumption more highly than cost; that is, more highly than the alternatives forgone. Assuming that the consumer has some appreciation of the money prices of other goods, the money price of any particular commodity is an indication of the real alternatives that the consumer will forgo by purchasing it. Thus, by producing a service for which consumers are not willing to pay the full costs, society is failing to get the best out of the resources so used.

The importance of implementing a policy that would ensure a system of prices that achieves economic efficiency seems all the greater in the assumptive world of policy-making for public enterprises because they handle large resources, because their outputs are important inputs to a wide range of other productive activities, and because although their cross-elasticities of demand with other commodities are substantial, they often exercise considerable monopoly power and so are not controlled by the 'polygon of forces' ensured by competition.[6]

The White Paper of 1967, *Nationalised Industries: a Review of Financial and Economic Objectives (Cmnd 3437)* marked a climacteric in the development of the policy paradigm—a confluence of the perceptions of economists, civil servants, and politicians. Not only did it separate resource allocative and financial considerations, but it gave pre-eminence to the former. Three months later the Select Committee on Nationalised Industries were told:

We used to say that financial objectives gave us the necessary basis for finding the right policies on investment and other things. We now say that the objectives are economically justifiable only to the extent that they reflect sound investment and pricing policies ... The starting point on the road to finding a suitable pricing policy is marginal costing ... what we are doing in circumstances in which we are talking about the extremely diverse circumstances of a very varied range of industries, is to establish the validity of certain general economic considerations and then to ensure that an informed and rational decision is taken related to the particular circumstances of each industry.[7]

The prices that in a context secure the incentives to the pattern of consumption that uses resources most efficiently may not be equal to the 'marginal costs' of the commodities. However, they are generally not less than marginal cost. (Indeed, some have argued that in not

---

[6] See *The Report of the Committee of Inquiry into the Electricity Supply Industry*, Cmnd 9672, 1956, paragraphs 22–7.

[7] 1967/8, H.C. 371–II, Q. 2091.

untypical circumstances prices should exceed marginal costs. For instance, both Feldstein[8] and Acharya[9] appeared to postulate likely circumstances that appeared salient both to British State industries and the school meals case. However Forsyth[10] argues that the circumstances in which their arguments are valid are less plausible than either author postulated.)

Optimal pricing requires (*ceteris paribus*) that the optimal ratio of prices to marginal cost for a commodity is a weighted sum of the ratios of prices to marginal costs of substitutes and complements.[11] As long as the positive weights of substitutes outweigh the negative weights of complements, the optimal 'second best' price will lie between the smallest and largest ratios for other commodities. There can be few privately-produced substitutes or complements of the products produced by public enterprises that are priced at below marginal cost. Therefore taxes or monopolistic conditions are likely to produce an optimal price less than marginal cost only when they are heavily concentrated on goods complementary to the public utility. The optimal price is likely to be lower than marginal cost only where there are commodities that are both so closely related to the commodity in question that they weigh heavily, and also where they are sold at prices less than marginal cost (possibly because they are produced by other State enterprises).

The school meals case is one social service where the substitutes are either unsubsidized private producers in the market (like local café proprietors) or are unsubsidized producers of services for themselves (and so evaluate market opportunities in a manner analogous to notionally selling services to themselves at the marginal cost price). No doubt there are circumstances in which the commercial providers of substitutes enjoy some monopoly power due to special factors, and may therefore charge in excess of marginal cost. The pricing policies of the school meals service are hardly controlled by the polygon of competitive forces discussed by the inquiry into the electricity supply industry. Unlike personal social and health services, there are neither complements nor substitutes provided by other statutory or voluntary

[8] M. S. Feldstein, *Financing on the evaluation of public expenditure*, Harvard Institute of Fiscal Research, August 1970.

[9] S. H. Acharya, 'Public enterprise pricing and social cost–benefit analysis', *Oxford Economic Papers, N.S., 24*, 1, March 1972, pp. 3–53.

[10] P. J. Forsyth, 'The pricing of public enterprise outputs', *Oxford Economic Papers N.S., 26*, 3, November 1974.

[11] H. A. J. Green, 'The social optimum in the presence of monopoly and taxation', *Review of Economic Studies, 29*, 1, October 1961.

agencies offered at zero price or at a price much less than marginal cost; and unlike some social services they satisfy the 'excludability' criterion for being 'private goods'. The component commodities in the chains of substitutes and complements do not enjoy markedly different taxes or subsidies, save that the commercial organizations pay VAT on their value added. Like the assumptive world of policy-making for the public enterprises in the early 1960s, the use of pricing to secure the best use of society's resources is not the centre of attention. By these criteria the school meals case has more in common with public enterprises than their policy-makers would suggest, living as they do in very different assumptive worlds.

'Social service' obligations

The second feature of this assumptive world of policy-making in the public enterprises is the importance of what the politicians often call their 'social service' obligations. An analysis of the argument suggests that these are of two kinds: what the economists call 'externalities', costs that are not borne by the enterprise or benefits that do not accrue to it, but which must be taken into account if efficient allocation of resources is to be attained, and the distributional consequences of the resource allocation decisions, particularly the effect of these decisions on the welfare of vulnerable groups. Externalities abound. Decisions about rural transport have consequences for the economic development of geographically large areas. The closures of coal mines or tin-plate works have passed death sentences on small communities heavily dependent on them. Similarly, decision-makers in urban transport generate congestion costs that they do not fully bear.

Such externalities are less important in the school meals case. It is true that if only a minority of pupils remain in school during the lunch break, numbers are insufficient to organize the cultural and recreational activities which would otherwise be possible. These school activities may confer more than the purely private benefit that is taken into account in this consumption decision. Many activities clearly contribute to attaining educational objectives. Quite apart from the effect of numbers on the quality of the activities, there is therefore an externality to be taken into account, albeit one that is both difficult to quantify and enormously variable between schools. It is therefore reasonable to argue that a lower charge than marginal cost should be levied. However, the important substitutes for the school meal are home-produced sandwiches for consumption on the school premises, snack meals bought from the school catering service, and food purchased in a local café. None of these is necessarily more likely to make it difficult for a child to participate in lunch-time activities than the consumption of the school meal. Perhaps more important may be the effect on the probability of lunch-time consumption of alcohol; though one may doubt whether a subsidy to the price of the meal would affect it greatly. In short, it is unlikely that a subsidy at the existing level would be justified by such externalities. Making the conservative assumption that the long run marginal cost of a meal is on average equal to the gross running cost, the subsidy of over 60 per cent of the cost in late 1975 would have required an external benefit of perhaps £50 per pupil a year for that price to be optimal. The expenditures on books and related materials in primary schools then averaged £7.63 per child. There is also a 'merit good' argument which is not identical with the externalities argument; that the consumers consistently underestimate the benefits of taking the school meal. Our survey evidence does not suggest this to be so.

The second main 'social service' preoccupation of politicians in discussing public enterprises is the distributional effects of policies. One example is the argument about the underpricing of rail transport when used more by higher than lower income groups—an argument used, for instance, in the influential paper on transport policy in *Socialist Commentary*.[12] A second example is the keen concern shown by Members of Parliament in the consequences of rises in fuel prices for low income households. Here again the similarities with the school meals case is evident. However, in the school meals case, at any rate in the medium term, the free meals scheme can handle the worst of the distributional consequences of marginal cost pricing of school meals.

Technical efficiency

The third concern of the assumptive world of policy-making in public enterprise is the technical efficiency of the organizations. Indeed, there is now a group of economists who argue that allocative inefficiency is unimportant relative to technical efficiency and the capacity of the organizations to take advantage of technical progress through innovation. For instance, Richard Pryke has written that 'economists seem unprepared to face up to the fact that one of the most important

---

[12] 'Report of the Transport Policy Study Group', *Socialist Commentary*, April 1975.

discoveries of economic science is the unimportance of allocative efficiency'.[13]

The argument does not support such a sweeping generalization. To understand why, it is necessary to glance briefly at the development of the economic literature on the subject. The argument about allocative inefficiency in public enterprise depends on judgements about the welfare losses due to sub-optimal pricing. It was argued by Harberger[14] that economists had used inappropriate indices of the concentration of production as their indicator of monopoly. It would have been more appropriate to measure the welfare losses directly. Harberger attempted to do this for the whole of the American economy and concluded that the sum of welfare losses due to monopoly in the 1920s would have been trivial in relation to the national income. This was tantamount to arguing that the consequences of allocative inefficiency due to a failure to price at marginal cost was trivial. Leibenstein[15] accepted the arguments put forward by Harberger[16] and writers who improved his method of estimation, and drew the same conclusions. Additionally, he noted that although the losses due to allocative inefficiency seemed to be trivial, the rate of return of the investment in innovation and improved efficiency were high. He concluded that 'neither individuals nor firms work as hard, nor do they search for information as effectively, as they could'[17] and that '... where the motivation is weak, firm managements with a considerable degree of slack in their operations do not seek cost-improving methods'.[18] He argued that innovations yielding high returns were the outcome of progressive cost-reducing forces overcoming constitutional inertia against change.

A major objective in nationalizing several industries was to modernize them and make them technically innovative after a long period of under-investment and demoralization, both of management and workers. The inheritance of attitudes and skills was such that both workers and management may have been more resistant to innovation

---

[13] Richard Pryke, *Public Enterprise in Practice*, McGibbon and Kee, London, 1971.

[14] A. Harberger, 'Monopoly and resource allocation', *American Economic Review, 44*, 2, May 1954, pp. 77–87.

[15] H. Leibenstein, 'Allocative Efficiency versus X-efficiency', *American Economic Review, 56*, 3, June 1966, pp. 392–415.

[16] A. Harberger, 'Monopoly and resource allocation', *American Economic Review, 44*, 2, May 1954, pp. 77–87.

[17] H. Leibenstein, 'Allocative Efficiency versus X-efficiency', *American Economic Review, 56*, 3, June 1966, pp. 392–415.

[18] Leibenstein, op. cit.

in the search for greater economic and technical efficiency than industry generally. Thus it is very likely that Pryke is correct to argue that over the post-war period as a whole, the reduction of the degree of inefficiency due to overcoming 'inert areas' within the enterprises has been a major source of improvement. However, this is a gain that once made cannot be replicated. More important, over the longer run, the main constraint may be the capacity of the organization to innovate without increasing the resistance of its inert areas—it may be that it is the interaction between X-efficiency and the ability to absorb or create innovations that is important, rather than X-efficiency itself. But to accept the potential importance of X-efficiency and technical innovation is not to demonstrate the unimportance of allocative inefficiency. The calculations made by Harberger and others who developed his approach have been criticized by economists like Stigler[19] and Bergson,[20] Bergson's hypothetical calculations restored the possibility that departures from optimal pricing could result in important losses due to allocative inefficiency. Indeed Bergson estimated that the loss through allocative inefficiency might be between $1\frac{1}{2}$ and more than 15 per cent of the national income.

There is no doubt reason to question the existence of considerable variations in X-efficiency, and capacity to innovate without causing X-inefficiency, in the school meals service. No doubt it has increased its efficiency through time. For instance, Edward Short claimed that a considerable increase in the efficiency of the school meals service occurred during the 1960s, arguing that this was the reason why costs of the school meals rose less than the retail price index.[21]

Nevertheless, the Hudson Report described large variations in average costs per meal that it claimed were only weakly correlated with scale, the quality of the meal, or the choice of dishes offered. Research (like that by Bender) showed that plate waste varied greatly between schools, and that such plate waste was considerable in quantity. Of his forty-eight schools, only four attained the calorific target suggested by the Department of Education and Science. Such work also showed variations in the deleterious effects of cooking on the nutritional quality of meals.[22] The Webbs argued for the supply of

[19] G. J. Stigler, 'The statistics of monopoly and merger', *Journal of Political Economy*, *64*, 1, February 1956, pp. 33–40.

[20] A. Bergson, 'On monopoly welfare losses', *American Economic Review*, *53*, 4, December 1973, pp. 853–70.

[21] See *H.C. DEB.*, *1969/70*, *791*, Col. 864.

[22] A. Bender, 'Feeding the school child', *Poverty*, 23, Summer 1972, p. 3.

data by public enterprises sufficient for experts who are not involved with employees, management, or politics to criticize and to appraise their efficiency.[23] Professor W. A. Robson suggested an audit commission to hold periodic efficiency audits on each public enterprise.[24] The Select Committee on Nationalized Industries recommended that there should be one Ministry for the nationalized industries which among other things would make the efficiency and productivity comparisons that Professor Robson's audit commission would have undertaken.[25] However the recommendation was rejected by the Labour government. A similar case might be made out for a body to stimulate improvements in the local efficiency of the school catering service, though a more appropriate model would be the Health Advisory Service publishing independent reports than either an audit commission or a branch of the Department of Education and Science. The subject has recently been discussed and recommendations made by the Report of the Layfield Committee on Local Government Finance.[26]

(ii) Charging as a Local Policy Instrument

It is difficult not to conclude that the normative theory of the pricing of public enterprise activities is as salient to the discussion of charging for school meals as it is to the pricing of the products of public enterprise. For this reason, it can be used to 'lay down criteria which [can] have a regulatory effect' on local authorities in the same way that it does for nationalized industries.[27] Providing the intellectual framework for regulation and the collection of data for monitoring local provision, it allows the flexible local use of charging as a weapon to enhance allocative efficiency, and the more effective waging of the war against child poverty—so far, its use thus has not been discussed by academics, politicians, or the Hudson Report, though a Parliamentary question suggesting that authorities should fix their own charges shows that the issue is not considered unreal by all practising politicians.[28]

We have no wish to suggest that it provides policy formulae for automatic application. Indeed, where this and other theory has been

[23] Sidney and Beatrice Webb, *A constitution for the socialist commonwealth of Great Britain*, Longmans, London, 1920.

[24] W. A. Robson, *Public Enterprise*, Allen and Unwin, London, 1937.

[25] *1967/8, H.C. 371–I*, paragraphs 777–89 and 892–99.

[26] *Report of the Committee of Enquiry on Local Government Finance, Cmnd 6453.*

[27] See *1967/8, H.C. 371–II*, 1–7.

[28] *H.C. DEB., 1975/6, 867*, Col. 272.

misused thus, the areas of policy have rightly fallen into disrepute. It would certainly be inconsistent for a study that argued that the application of simple *nostra* like the principles of universality and selectivity provide a poor basis for policy-making, to suggest that the unthinking application of other simple *nostra* based on optimal pricing would be any more satisfactory. What is claimed for it is that it contributes to the intellectual basis for the discussion of the consequences of alternative options, and hence for the handling of evidence for each of its contexts.

Its significance can be illustrated with examples of some of the relevant arguments in contrasting contexts.

Falling marginal cost curves in low growth and income areas

It is clear from the data collected for the Hudson Report that there are considerable economies of a scale at the plant (school) level in the provision of school meals.[29] Small (particularly primary) schools serving catchment areas whose populations (and therefore school populations) are falling and can be expected to decrease indefinitely, are frequently found serving communities whose average incomes are low and diminishing in relation to the national average. Such cases may frequently be found in rural areas. Of the ninety junior schools in Carmarthenshire on 20 May 1968, seventeen served twenty but less than thirty meals, and ten served less than twenty.[30]

As average incomes fall, so the paid meals uptake rate falls in

[29] *Catering in Schools*, op. cit., Appendix 3, para. 19. No doubt variations in scale as well as in efficiency help to account for the variations in the energy and protein content between schools in what was actually consumed, observed by Bender *et al.* The following table illustrates the variation found by Bender.

Schools		Energy consumed (kcal)		Protein consumed (g)	
Type	Number	Median	Range	Median	Range
Infant	8	420	360–600	13	10–16
Infant/junior	18	480	330–790	15	11–30
Junior	12	475	280–660	16	8–26
Senior	10	650	420–1340	20	11–31

Bender's data for each school are averages for twenty meals. They do not control for fluctuations in appetite and the popularity of menus. (See A. E. Bender, 'Survey of School Meals', *The British Medical Journal*, 2, 13 May 1972, pp. 383–5.)

[30] Personal communication from the Chief Education Officer.

relation to the national average, given a standard national price. The combination of low uptake rates and falling school populations causes a considerable under-utilization of capacity at levels of output at which the marginal cost curve is falling fast. As can be shown in response to the price rise of 1971, the elasticity of demand for school meals is substantial; taking the country as a whole, the elasticity of uptake with respect to price in 1971 being of the order of −0.62. There is some evidence that the elasticities may be large in areas with low household incomes and falling populations. The elasticity of the uptake rate in relation to the price in the early 1950s tended to be greater in areas of low social class among both counties and county boroughs, the correlation being significantly greater than zero at the one per cent level in administrative counties and at the 5 per cent level among county boroughs. In 1971 the elasticities appeared high in some of the poorer counties. For instance, the elasticity for Monmouthshire was −0.96 and that for Glamorganshire −0.76. At that time it was alleged by Fred Evans that the fall in uptake rates was highest in areas of high unemployment within these counties.[31] Eric Heffer argued that the same was true of Liverpool.[32] Unfortunately, no data is available for school catchment areas. But even for such small areas, many of whose households have incomes just above eligibility levels, elasticities of uptake rates with respect to price will be lower than those of individual

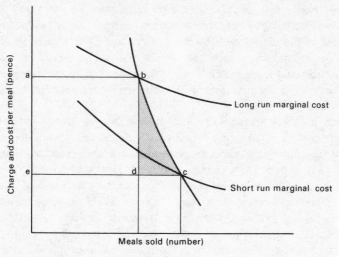

Diagram 7.1

[31] *H.C. DEB., 1971/2, 820*, Cols 16–17.
[32] *H.C. DEB., 1971/2, 820*, Col. 1497.

families on the margins of eligibility. It is clear that for these, the elasticities must be large.

Diagram 7.1 illustrates the position. Both long and short run marginal costs are falling rapidly over the relevant levels of output. Demand is substantially responsive to price. The marginal cost concept that is relevant is the opportunity cost. Costs that are inescapable in the short or long run by closing down the plant or by varying its level of output—for instance, capital equipment of negligible scrap value and not easily usable elsewhere in the event of closure—have virtually no opportunity cost. (Neither do canteen staff who would otherwise be unemployed. Dennis Skinner argued that some of those made unemployed as a result of the 1971 increase remained so for some time.[33]) The cost curves are falling fast because indivisibilities are important at that level of output.

In this context to set the charge at the long-run marginal cost rather than the relevant short-run marginal cost would result in a loss to consumers indicated by the size of the triangle, bcd, and to charge the long-run marginal cost would result in a transfer from consumers to the local authority equal to ade. The welfare gain from charging at the short-run marginal cost rather than the long-run marginal cost would occur partly because the short-run marginal cost curve is in this case lower than the long-run marginal cost curve at each level of output shown, partly because the short-run marginal cost curve is falling steeply as better use is made of labor and capital capacity, and partly because of the substantial elasticity of demand. The greater the elasticity of demand, the greater the welfare that can be gained by pricing at the short-run marginal cost rather than the long-run marginal cost. Similarly the greater the slope of the short-run marginal cost curve, the greater the welfare gain.

There are circumstances in which, if the school meal were offered at a lower cost, children might actually be attracted to a school operating at less than its optimal capacity. (Examples are schools serving housing estates whose populations have an unbalanced structure.) It is true that in such schools the service is typically operating at levels of output where the cost curves are less steep. However, a school whose canteen is working at less than its optimal capacity is also likely to be working at less than its optimal capacity in other ways. The mutual benefit to children and the local education authority of securing equalization by voluntary allocation rather than by compulsion (for instance, by a change in zoning) could in some circumstances be considerable. A

[33] *H.C. DEB., 1971/2, 820*, Col. 1495.

casual inspection of the components of school meals expenditure over recent years suggests that on average over the country as a whole, the short-run average variable cost might be of the order of 90 per cent of the gross-running cost. The accounts do not permit a precise estimate, since some of the detailed heads would include both fixed and variable cost elements.

There would of course be a deficit to be covered by some means. The deficit might be financed by a Rate Fund subsidy. However, a subsidy for some families selected on other than income grounds might not be politically acceptable. An alternative is to finance deficits from the surpluses which accrue from marginal cost pricing in schools in which there was a greater pressure on the service than could be met within the facilities without increased costs; that is, school catering services which were producing levels of output in which the short-run marginal cost was rising fast at the levels of outputs being achieved. This is one of the solutions suggested in the original Hotelling paper.[34]

Increasingly Strained Capacity in an Affluent Area

More typical is the case of the school kitchens and canteens working near their capacity and producing an output large enough to reap the economies of scale available at the school level, but where the area has an expanding and increasingly affluent population, and a rising school population. Such schools are frequently working near their short-term capacity output, additional meals being produced in the short run only by incurring greater costs per meal. Since the uptake rate depends on family incomes, demand is expected to rise. At the current level of output, the short-run marginal cost will typically be below the long-run marginal cost; and also below the accountants' gross cost per meal. Since the plant is already of a scale where no further economies are likely to be reaped, the long-run marginal cost curve is flat. The situation is described in Diagram 7.2, case a.

An assessment of pricing policy in such a case should take into account a number of arguments.

1. In the immediate future, fixing the price at the long run marginal cost would mean a loss of consumer welfare equal to the triangle bcd.

2. The cost not only of the maintenance of the existing plant, but also of the expansion to meet rising demand, are real costs to society— they would not be incurred if the decision to increase output conse-

[34] H. Hotelling, 'The general welfare in relation to problems of taxation and of railway and utility rates', *Econometrica*, 6, 3, July 1938, pp. 242–69.

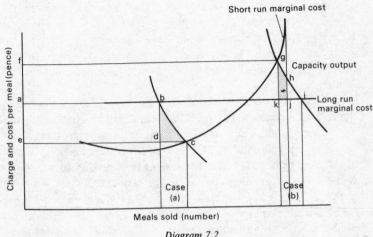

Diagram 7.2

quent upon the further demand were not implemented. These escapable costs would not include the loan charges on past investment, which are merely transfer payments, and which do not correspond to the flows of real resources usable elsewhere, but would include a replacement cost depreciation and an allowance for a rate of return on the marginal investment which would be equal to the social rate of time preference. (This minimum rate of return would be necessary because the investment in this use would only be more profitable than investment in alternative uses if such a rate of return were yielded.)

3. The quantities of substitutes for school meals, demanded as a result of the price charged, act as signals to the producers of those substitutes. For instance, the demand for his output is the best guide the café proprietor has to the rate of return on investment on increasing his capacity. In order to make a good decision about this, the café proprietor needs a stable long-run pricing policy for school meals in his area, and so a stable demand. Similarly, the L.E.A. itself needs evidence to guide its investment plans for catering capacity in the school. The nature of this investment will depend upon the mix of demand for eating snacks, full meals, and home-produced sandwiches. The L.E.A. has also to consider whether the output it expects to be demanded will be such that the long-run marginal cost of meals produced using newer techniques (like cook-freeze) are lower than the long-run marginal costs of more conventional techniques. The price is also a direct signal to the consumer who must consider in the longer run whether or not

the utilization of a motor car will be sufficient to make its maintenance worth while; and so, since the mileage devoted to running children back and forth from school in families with children of school age is not inconsiderable, whether such journeys will be undertaken.

4. In some schools the level of output might almost have reached its short-term maximum (Diagram 7.2, case (b)). There was evidence in 1975, as in 1967, that a considerable number of schools were unable to discharge their statutory obligation to offer those children who wished to take up meals the facility of doing so.[35] In such circumstances there would be a strong argument for pricing meals at the short-run marginal cost in order to ration the capacity in a way that does not involve arbitrary judgement on the part of the head teacher, or further means testing. The use of pricing to ration meals in such a context would allow those consumers who value it most to take up the service. Our survey results illustrate how many contextual factors influence consumers' evaluation of the meals.

5. That it would generate profits in the short run is not a substantial objection, since these could be used to cover the deficits that would arise in the contexts discussed in the first example, and could also finance other forms of related expenditure, either educational spending or spending on other interventions that form part of the broader strategy to prevent or alleviate the consequences of child poverty.

Conclusion

This discussion has sought only to draw attention to the potential

---

[35] The most significant findings of *Leicester's Hungry Children* (Leicestershire Child Poverty Action Group, Leicester, 1975) were (i) that although it might have been the increasing numbers eligible for free meals due to unemployment that caused the increase in demand, it seemed that priority was not universally given to free meals recipients; and (ii) that at least one headmistress would not allow children to take packed lunches to school ('because of the mess created by the crumbs'), would not allow children who were not having school meals to remain at school, and had refused parents' requests to extend the lunch-hour to permit two sittings. One would have thought that such apparent inflexibility would be difficult to justify when teachers consume meals free of charge of a total value of £23m a year.

It was less surprising that there were schools in which not all children who would like to have taken up meals could be provided with them. The replies to a questionnaire we circulated to the Chief Education Officers of county boroughs in February 1967 showed that there were some authorities with an acute supply problem at that time. (See Bleddyn Davies and Valerie Williamson, 'School meals—short fall and poverty', *Social and Economic Administration*, 2, 1, January 1968, p. 9.) However our analysis showed that in general scarcity of capacity did not influence the dining rate to a detectable degree (ibid., pp. 10–11).

for varying the charges between schools at the discretion of the L.E.A. so as to create strategies of intervention that fit well the variability of local circumstances. What makes it possible to conceive of charging in this way is the existence of a normative theory of pricing. This normative theory enables the central government to define criteria, to collect data, to monitor their applications, and so to stimulate, to guide, and constrain local policy-making. The school meals context is such that the efficient allocation of public and private resources is too important to be neglected, and it can only be achieved by the conscious use of pricing policy. It is not only the large use of current resources that are involved, but the more effective deployment of the one pound in ten spent on capital account on maintained primary and secondary schools and devoted to canteens. By adopting the criteria suggested by the normative theory of pricing, a reasoned appraisal of canteen investment would become possible for the first time.

The adoption of the criteria could result in central government supervision of local investment decisions which was both effective and efficient. Here again, the public enterprises are an interesting model. For instance, the Department of Environment's role in the investment appraisal of transport is to set out ground rules like the pricing criteria, and the techniques of evaluation to be used to estimate externalities, to provide standard values for certain externalities, a test rate of discount, the size of the investment budget, a lower limit on the size of an investment decision, and to monitor the authorities' analyses in detail. The detailed work of evaluation is done by implementing bodies, but the Department of the Environment reviews the analyses on which the decisions are based.[36] The Financial Secretary to the Treasury (Robert Sheldon) recently argued that nobody dealing with a nationalized industry would want to revert to the situation in which the rate of return of these assets is not in accord with the best principles of their efficient use.[37]

It has not been our purpose (and it would be inappropriate in a book such as this) to further elaborate a discussion of the theory. Unfortunately, our policy analysis has been weakened because we failed to collect data for the estimation of cost and demand functions for school meals in various circumstances—a particularly serious omission in a study that argues the indispensability of quantitative evidence for specific contexts deployed with the help of an appropriate logic of resource allocation. However, there is nothing intrinsically difficult in applying

---

[36] Department of the Environment, *Transport Policy*, op. cit.
[37] *H.C. DEB., 1974/5, 892*, Col. 1829,

the orthodox techniques to estimate such functions. They have already been estimated for health and education services.[38] And there is nothing intrinsically difficult in filing these economic boxes in the school meals context.

Effectiveness, efficiency, adaptation to local variations in the costs, and benefits of alternative strategies demands above all local initiative and responsibility. Unless the central government generate the criteria, but allow the local education authorities to exercise initiative within the constraints imposed by them, it is impossible to create conditions in which efficiency, effectiveness, and adaptability can flourish. That basing criteria on the normative theory of prices has analogous effects on the nationalized industries is at the heart of the assumptive world of policy-making for the public enterprises. The Chief Secretary to the Treasury of the Labour government (John Diamond) giving evidence to the Select Committee on Nationalized Industries claimed that the most effective way of using instruments of overall economic policy in the control of nationalized industries was:

> To rely in this sphere ... on human endeavour and on encouraging human endeavour. If one usurps the enterprising energy of individuals, and takes it on one's shoulders, one must not expect those individuals to exert themselves to the same extent as otherwise would be the case. If, therefore, you want to get the best out of nationalised industries, ... having secured the best people there, you must encourage them as much as possible to use their individual capacity and to stretch it to the full within certain broad parameters or guidelines.
>
> I am quite sure that the more one can remove those restraints and the more one can allow freedom of management to those concerned in the management of nationalised industries, the more one will be encouraging their fruitfulness.[39]

The quotation is equally pertinent to the school meals case.

[38] See for instance Donald Verry and Bleddyn Davies, *University Costs and Outputs*, Elsevier, North Holland, 1975.

[39] *1967/8, H.C. 371–II*, Questions 2351A and 2439.

8 Effectiveness, Local Responsibility, and Territorial Justice

The weight that it is appropriate to give to criteria for judging the aims and effectiveness of school meals policy have changed out of all recognition in the last thirty years. At the end of the war, the school meals service as a whole was seen as a social welfare service in an educational setting. Discussions about its objectives reflected both the food situation of a siege economy and the vivid memories of pre-war, when large numbers of school children were malnourished. At that time, it was inevitable that the service should have been seen as a weapon in the fight against malnutrition. By the later 1960s, living standards had improved well beyond the expectations (and probably beyond the imaginings) of the politicians of 1945, who had expected that the cessation of the military hostilities would restore conditions not unlike those of pre-war times, save that the State would adopt novel weapons and a new vigour in its longer-term fight against Beveridge's five giants. The new framework of social benefits introduced in the 1940s was administered in an increasingly generous spirit, and had changed the nature and scale of child poverty. By 1965, fewer children were under-nourished than were obese. Adolescents had acquired the power to exercise their tastes in a wide range of markets, and it was not to be expected that they would forbear from asserting them through their demand for school meals. Further, parents and teachers increasingly recognized the rights of all persons of school age to exercise individual preferences in the multeity of contexts of daily living.

Thus by the late 1960s, the Hudson Report was right to state as the

¹ Department of Education and Science, *Catering in Schools*, H.M.S.O., London, 1975, para. 19. Estimates of the proportion of children aged between 7 and 15 that are obese have been made for one London borough. The proportions for each social class group were: 4.9 per cent (Social Classes I and II), 5.1 per cent (Social Class III), and 8.5 per cent (Social Classes IV and V). (See A. G. J. Whitelaw, 'The association of social class and sibling number with skinfold thickness in London schoolboys', *Human Biology, 43,* 1971, pp. 414–420.)

appropriate general aim for the service the provision of mid-day meals and other refreshment 'which are not only attractive to the pupils, but also make good sense in terms of their nutritional needs'.[1] Not that the Hudson Report denied an important role for the partial or total remission of charges. It argued that the social welfare aim should remain important, if not paramount, in some areas of social deprivation (paragraph 14), and in areas containing groups—sometimes large groups —of children who, because of their religious or cultural background, had special catering needs, and who were at risk of being nutritionally deprived (paragraph 20). More generally, it recognized a serious danger of malnutrition among children of low income families. However one cannot but agree that the prevention of malnutrition among children of school age is not now appropriate as the primary objective for the service.

The rationale of providing the service must be distinguished from that of subsidizing it. The case for providing free (or heavily subsidized) meals for children who are at risk of malnutrition because of poverty would be clear if it were not for the universalist objections which have been the subject of our research; and the research has suggested that the impact of these objections may be less pervasively powerful than has at times been implied. The case for subsidizing the catering service as a whole progressively diminishes as it becomes more feasible to define (and deliver services to) the target groups for social welfare interventions with greater precision, including the remission of school meals charges. The size of the subsidy remains of great symbolic importance. For instance, Labour members taunted Margaret Thatcher with 'taking the bread out of the mouths of innocent children': and during the 1970s the charge for school meals has occasionally loomed large in negotiations between the government and the Trades Union Congress about the constituents of the 'social wage'. (An example was the T.U.C. response to Mr Healey's budget of May 1976.) Symbols of ideological commitment are often inexpensive. This is not so of the school meals subsidy, as we showed in the opening chapter. Although any subsidy to families with children of school age is on the whole progressive, it is difficult to justify the paid meals subsidy on the grounds of the progressive-

---

In answer to a question about the prevalence of malnutrition, Baroness Philips stated that less than 0.39 per cent of all children were considered to be of unsatisfactory physical condition. The proportion of these whose unsatisfactory physical condition was due to malnutrition had not been estimated. (See *H.L. DEB., 1967/8, 279,* Col. 1239.)

ness of its incidence among families with children of school age. The subsidy was shown to be inefficient in the later 1960s. For instance, among smaller families (those with one or two children) the probability of receiving a school meal and paying for it was higher, the larger the income of the household. Therefore the higher the household income, the greater the school meals subsidy enjoyed.[2] Again the paid meals up-take rates tended to be higher in the areas having most prosperous popu-lations. Had the price remained unchanged in 1967 and subsequently, the incidence of the subsidy would have been regressive in 1972, and probably even in 1978.[4] That the subsidy was 60 per cent rather than 30 per cent or zero seemed as much the arbitrary consequence of broad economic and political forces in early 1976 as it was in the spring of 1968. It would be difficult to argue that it was the beneficial outcome of a process of partisan mutual adjustment that reflected mainly relevant considerations and interests.

We have argued that the main foci for policy discussion of the school catering service as a whole should be the development of a pricing policy that would secure greater effectiveness in the use of resources, and the improvement of technical efficiency and market responsiveness of the service, the subjects discussed in Chapter 7. We have also argued that the main focus of policy debate about the free meals scheme should be its medium-term role in area strategies designed to combat the consequences of family poverty, the subject introduced in Chapter 6. If the principles of optimal pricing were applied, it is almost certain that a great deal more of the subsidy would be available to deploy in the campaign against the consequences of child poverty and the broader war against poverty itself.[4]

There is little doubt that the greater part of what rationale the school meals subsidy possesses is its contribution to this war. Un-doubtedly, this is the perception of the context that would prevail in the Treasury or in Parliamentary debate, if Parliament found time to discuss the matter in depth. It seems also to be the dominant perception among those higher civil servants at the Department of Education and Science who are most concerned with policy. That this is so can be seen from the Hudson Report[5] which reviewed the traditional aims of

[2] Bleddyn Davies, 'The cost effectiveness of education spending' in Peter Townend et al., Social Services for All, Fabian Society, London, 1968.

[3] Bleddyn Davies and Valerie Williamson, 'School meals: short-fall and poverty', op. cit., and Bleddyn Davies et al., 'Some constraints on school meals policy', op. cit.

[4] Thus facilitating desirable redistribution to social service from other purposes without necessarily transfering services between departments. Compare the use of ILEA employees for social service purposes.

[5] Department of Education and Science, Catering in Schools, op. cit.

the service in the light of changing needs. Although a few of the arguments rested on confident assertions whose validity is incompatible with the evidence analysed in this study, this Report was sufficiently non-incrementalist to contribute greatly to the ability of the central government to discharge one of its principal responsibilities, that of contributing to more relevant and sophisticated policy appreciations among those who run the service and affect its success. But because it lacked depth, a depth which only a careful collection and analysis of evidence about causes of demand and the consequences of alternative interventions could contribute, the Hudson Report is an insufficient basis for a new 'meta-policy', a new policy paradigm for school catering. It insufficiently discussed the values and assumptions which are the essential basis for developing criteria by which to judge the success of the service in achieving its aims. It is too vague to provide a framework of policy appreciations in which authorities could intelligently develop policies within the terms of which their employees could exercise their discretion to reduce or remit charges for children in need, using criteria other than the nationally-prescribed means test. To grant such discretion without policy guidance to those making the decisions, or even policy discussion with them, is to invite gross inequity—indeed, it invites capricious allocations.

The logic of encouraging local initiative in extending the criteria of eligibility is not undermined by the superficiality of some of the arguments in the Hudson Report. The case for such initiatives rests on four arguments. First, the pattern of local needs differs. Family incomes may be low for a variety of reasons and salient characteristics of the circumstances of families may likewise vary. What such differences imply for the severity of child poverty is imperfectly understood. But it is clear that the differences are likely to be important enough to make extremely questionable the application of an inflexible and uniform eligibility standard. Secondly, unless we can handle the most important problem of distributing benefits to the needy in a way that takes account of the variety of such needs, there is little hope of developing a more efficient pricing policy.

Thirdly, the costs and feasibility of alternative programmes vary between areas. The marginal cost of a school meal itself must vary substantially between areas, at least in the short run. The relevant area with respect to costs is that served by the single plant (school canteen or dining room) rather than by the firm (the entire local education authority). The interviews yielded abundant evidence to confirm that physical constraints on the supply of meals, or space for eating them, resulted in the over-utilization of capacity and rationing. In areas with rationing, the short term marginal cost of the meal was clearly much higher than the unit cost. Despite eventually falling school populations over the country as a whole, there is reason to believe that the marginal cost would be high in at least some areas over a decade or more, as long as the cost of meals continues to outstrip charges, since limitations of space that make it difficult to provide canteen facilities will continue to exist for many of the schools now approaching (or already at) capacity utilization; and the service it would be possible to provide in such schools at the unit cost would be inferior in quality. This has not been a study of the supply of school meals designed to yield evidence about cost functions, but there are good *a priori* reasons for suspecting that similar unit costs disguise large differences in marginal costs, particularly when account is taken of variations in quality. Bender has produced evidence of considerable variations between schools both in the quantity and quality of the meals consumed.[6] The school meals service has long conceded that uniform meals are inappropriate, and the Hudson Report makes valuable suggestions for encouraging greater variety and flexibility in the system. However, the relative costs of meals and other weapons in the battle against child poverty also vary greatly between areas. For instance, there are variations in the costs to Social Service Departments of mounting effective strategies against poverty, the capacities of councils to influence the labour markets (and so the incidence of poverty in their area), the possibilities for providing assistance with transport for school children, or for providing more competitive local markets for food.[7] The whole constellation of circumstances relevant to choosing the best packages of interventions varies between areas.

The fourth argument is that it is wrong to neglect the opportunity of developing the potential of the large new local authorities created in 1974 for adopting new responses to the problems of their communities. The consequences of most forms of local interventions to alleviate the

[6] A. Bender, 'Feeding the school child', *Poverty*, 23, Summer 1972, p. 3.
 [7] Authorities should not be forced to apply the same strategy over their entire area. Target groups can be highly concentrated within the areas covered by school (particularly primary school) catchment areas. Catchment areas are also the areas between which the costs of providing additional school meals vary. It is therefore possible that the most cost-effective strategy for many authorities would be to vary the eligibility rules between catchment areas within authorities, particularly those authorities consisting of a number of separate and very different ecological areas. This would have political costs political costs which it is easy to enumerate qualitatively, but whose quantitative significance must vary between areas.

effects of child poverty are geographically localized.[8] Local authorities should be given increased responsibility (and freedom) to develop corporate and inter-corporate strategies of intervention that exploit local opportunities and circumstances—indeed it is a stated objective of public policy to develop the capacities of the authorities to act with vigour and in new ways. Local authorities should bear the responsibility for developing the strategies not only because they already provide many of the services that would be the instruments of the strategies. Also they are politically accountable at the local level, and political accountability is as necessary a safeguard as is the control of some key policies by the central government. Indeed, a specific local responsibility for developing and monitoring inter-corporate local strategies could simultaneously contribute to the solution of two of the major political problems of our times: the weakness of the political control over the activities of the central government executive, and the inadequacies of the local political processes. This is not incompatible with the pursuit of territorial justice so long as the central government is not deprived of the power to monitor local performance, and to safeguard the welfare of citizens by having the capacity to intervene to control policy and provision in those rare cases where it might prove necessary.

Of the four arguments, the last is the weakest. The next section of the chapter develops it, and discusses how area strategies co-ordinated by local authorities might be administered.

Towards Local Strategies

Before the machinery of government can be discussed, we must first clarify the nature of the task. In particular, we must distinguish between the prevention of child poverty and the mitigation of its effects.

I The prevention of child poverty

The distribution of incomes of households with children within an area reflects above all the local labour market. Can authorities influence this more effectively than they have hitherto done? Authors of Community Development Project (C.D.P.) Reports are pessimistic: authorities

---

[8] The first devolution white paper recognizes this to be a general characteristic of social intervention. See *Democracy and Devolution: Proposals for Scotland and Wales, Cmnd 5732.*

would seem to have little influence over the decisions of national and supra-national firms, and to have little effect on the success of regional policies. The C.D.P. analysts suggest that 'to rectify this situation requires fundamental changes in the distribution of wealth and power[9] and that such approaches as the Department of the Environment's Inner Area scheme or the Home Office's Comprehensive Community Programmes are doomed to failure because they are 'founded on the belief that technical solutions in terms of minor adjustments to local and national government systems will provide a basis for the solution of the problems of the poor.'[10] They also show that local authorities' own policies often reinforce the problems of their areas: the need for a more thorough understanding of the unintended consequences of policies is at least as great at the local as at the national level, as is a willingness by decision-makers to give more weight to those consequences. They argue that it is necessary 'to work with local people in generating a political awareness of these processes, and support action which works towards change'.[11]

The C.D.P. analysis has much in common with that of similar contexts by French urbanists. Such authors as Biarez,[12] developing the arguments of Poulantsaz,[13] argue that in seeking to counteract basic economic forces, authorities are unable to do more than make symbolic gestures. The importance of the French studies is not that they are theoretically self-conscious but that they are of a local government system to which the aim of securing local economic growth is more central. However, the C.D.P. writers draw other conclusions similar to those of Biarez. For instance, they argue that the central government desires little more of the local authorities in the declining areas than the management of the local political reaction by means of symbolic gestures, since the State is used by the hegemonic class, at least to the

[9] National Community Development Project *Forward Plan, 1975–6*, Community Development Project Information and Intelligence Unit, London, 1975, p. 2.

[10] Ibid.

[11] Ibid. The comprehensive redevelopment policies of metropolitan authorities have been focused on housing, and have ignored employment. In some cases, they have deliberately caused the expulsion or closure of 'bad neighbour' industries. For instance, Lambeth's housing programme is reported to have resulted in the closure of three hundred firms. The result has been political pressure to subsidize transport for workers whose journeys were in part made necessary by the diminution of local employment opportunities caused by planning policy.

[12] S. Biarez *et al.*, *Institution communale et pouvoir politique*, Mouton, Paris, 1973.

[13] M. Poulantzas, *Political Power and Social Classes*, New Left Books, London, 1968; and *Classes in Contemporary Capitalism*, New Left Books, London, 1975.

degree that the balance of forces in the class struggle allows.[14] Although this may be so of Gaullist France, we cannot assume it to be the case for Labour Britain without further analysis. However, the C.D.P. writers argue that in practice central government policy-making in such issues as the Rate Support Grant has so far shown little sign that the problems of declining areas receive high priority.[15] However the reason for this may be the insulation of the R.S.G. from political debate.

The French studies are of interest for another reason: they have also examined the role of local government in areas of economic growth. Castells shows that when an area satisfies some of the preconditions for growth, authorities which are committed to securing it can be successful. They achieve this partly by carefully providing the infrastructure needed by the investors of national and international capital, including training institutions and the local transport systems that increase the effective size of labour markets.[16] The Report of the Expenditure Committee *Public Money in the Private Sector* gave weight to the opinion of industrialists that the creation of infra-structure was a more effective inducement to settle in declining areas than cash aid from the central government.[17] However, such infra-structure may be crucially important in some contexts, but unimportant in others. Moreover, Castells' Monopolville and Biarez's Roanne are polar cases. Of greater interest are those with less extreme growth potential. Clearly much depends on the general level of investment, what proportion of authorities compete hard to attract capital, and with what success they comprehend the needs of investors.

[14] Such French urbanists as Lojkine, Poulantzas, and Castells are Marxists. Differences of emphasis among them are analysed in C. B. Pickvance, *Marxist approaches to the study of urban politics*, Urban and Regional Studies Unit, University of Kent at Canterbury, England, 1976.

[15] C. Tyrrell, *Rates of Decline*, C.D.P. Information and Intelligence Unit, London, 1975.

[16] M. Castells and F. Godard, *Monopolville*, Mouton, Paris, 1974. Some British authorities have moved in the French direction. An example is Bradford. The Bradford Area Development Association undertook studies which led to the assessment of the most viable directions for growth. As a consequence, the local authority appointed an Industrial Officer, a regional merchant bank was founded, and a determined series of political lobbies were undertaken in order to get the city's growth problems aired within the larger planning region and at the headquarters of central government departments. (See M. G. Christopher and G. S. C. Wills, 'Market analysis in regional economic development', *Socio-economic Planning Sciences*, April 1975, pp. 61–6.)

[17] *Sixth Report of the Expenditure Committee, 1971/2, Public Money in the Private Sector, H.C. 347*, H.M.S.O., London, 1975. See also the answer to question 1497 in *H.C. 347–I*, op. cit.

The prevention of poverty does not entirely depend upon authorities' direct influence on private sector investment decisions. Public expenditure is particularly influential: indeed there are examples of local economies whose growth owes more to increasing public consumption than to private investment (or public investment in industry or public utilities). Probably authorities behave in a way that reflects the balance of forces between economic classes with different material interests as much in Britain as in Lojkine's France.[18] Dan Smith's Newcastle is certainly more dependent on State provision than Chamberlain's Birmingham. This can be illustrated by comparing the data for the Northern and East Midland regions. The proportion of household income derived from social security benefits in the Northern region was 12.1 per cent, in the East Midlands 8.7; the proportions of households renting from a local authority or new town were 40 and 28 per cent respectively; the *per capita* value of regional development grants were £18.5 and £0.9; and of Rate Support Grant were £156 and £130.[19] There is little doubt that it is the North-Eastern councillors, Members

[18] J. Lojkine, 'Strategies des grandes entreprises politiques urbaines, et mouvements sociaux urbains', *Sociologie du Travail*, 1975, pp. 18–40.

[19] Central Statistical Office, *Digest of Regional Statistics, 1975*, H.M.S.O., London, 1975, Tables 52 and 91, and 'June 1975 Census of Employment', *Department of Employment Gazette*, *84*, 8, August 1976. However the following Department of Environment, Rates and Rateable Values 1974/5 table implies that the Northern Region does not depend more on local government employment than the East Midlands. In this respect, Lord Heycock's South Wales may be a better contrast with the East Midlands than the North.

Expenditures	Northern	Wales	S. East	E. Midland
Rate support grant 1974/5 *per capita* 1973 (£)	156.0	152.2	156.0	130.5
Social security benefits				
average per household per week (£)	4.92	4.87	3.69	3.89
per cent of household income (%)	12.1	11.5	7.0	8.7
Regional development grants *per capita* (£)	18.5	11.7	—	0.9
Employment				
Per cent employed in local government	4.4	5.3	4.5	4.6
Per cent employed in education	7.6	8.7	8.1	7.9
Housing tenure				
Per cent rented from local authority or new town	40	28	26	28

of Parliament, and others who represent local views in the *réseaux* between the regional and national bodies[20] who have the greater normative commitment to State corporatism.

Unfortunately, it must have seemed easier to some during a period of depressed industrial development to affect local prosperity by canvassing public sector *réseaux* for local and regional support than by providing the preconditions for private sector investment. However, it seems likely that in the future, the level of prosperity will depend upon satisfactory growth in the economy as a whole, particularly in the private sector; and that this will be as true at the local as at the national level.

II   The mitigation of child poverty

The mitigation of the consequences of poverty raises different organizational and political issues from its prevention. The prevention of local poverty above all requires a commitment to attracting private investment and so understanding better what are the main factors which make the areas unattractive for private investment,[21] mobilizing resources in an explicit inter-corporate strategy to modify these factors, communicating well in a variety of ways with those who control private investment, creating and exploiting political and bureaucratic *réseaux* with national authorities so that local interests are taken into account. The inter-corporate strategy for mitigating the effects of low incomes must be compatible with that for economic growth. For instance, the latter must influence the location of public sector housing. But many of the instruments are sufficiently separate from those of the growth strategy for it to merit an independent existence.

Local authority responsibility

It is not feasible here to attempt to do more than to raise some of the issues which would need to be faced if local strategies were to be developed. First, there must be a clear statement about what body is responsible for developing, co-ordinating, monitoring, and securing the

[20] Continental political scientists have explored more fully the way linkages between national, regional, and local bodies influence policy outcomes than have the British. I argue that the British have understated their influence in 'Values, needs, and the outputs of local services', in Richard Rose and Jerzy Wiatr, *Comparing Public Policies*, Polska Akademia Nauk, Warsaw, 1975.

[21] The Expenditure Committee's report *Public Money in the Private Sector*, op. cit. lamented the inadequacies of such understanding.

adaptation of the strategy. We have already asserted that this should be a local authority responsibility. There are several reasons why this should be so. First, local authorities provide most of the services, and the major authorities have some co-ordinative functions with respect to services provided by minor authorities. Organizational development will be most effective where it can exploit the existing personal links on which inter-organizational co-operation depends. Secondly, an argument that is not unimportant because it is more speculative, a major local authority responsibility could contribute to facing the two pervasive problems of government to which we alluded in the first section of the chapter. One is the weakness of the national political processes on which depends the quick and co-ordinated adjustment of policy and executive action to changing social needs. It is the weakness discussed in *A Joint Framework for Social Policy*.[22] The school meals case is one example. A better example is the survival, indeed continuing development, of what must surely be a false consensus on which is based the allocation to authorities of the Rate Support Grant—the allocative decision which most influences the territorial distribution of the social wage and, if multiplier effects are taken into account, the area variations in economic activity (particularly employment).[23] The other pervasive problem of government is the unresponsive nature of local authority decision-making to citizen preferences. This is not just due to creeping political centralization and a system of local government finance which has substantially relieved local authorities of the political responsibility for expenditure decisions, as the Layfield Committee argued. It is also because local politics has not defined a few issues that seem overwhelmingly important to citizens.[24] To make the co-ordination of inter-corporate strategies of local economic development and the mitigation of poverty two of the main responsibilities of local authorities would be to help create some of the

[22] Central Policy Review Staff, *A Joint Framework for Social Policy*, H.M.S.O., London, 1975.

[23] I discuss this in three papers written for the Layfield Committee on Local Government Finance. Bleddyn Davies, *Determinants of spending and the measurement of 'need'*, *Report of the Committee on Local Government Finance*, H.M.S.O., London, 1976, Appendix 10; and also 'Territorial Injustice', *New Society*, 36, 710, 13 May 1976, pp. 352–4.

[24] Support for this argument is provided by research using subjective social indicators. Such research suggests that citizens perceive their quality of life to reflect mainly personal efficacy, family life, adequacy of means and housing. (See F. M. Andrews and S. B. Withey, 'Developing measures of life quality: results from several national surveys', *Social Indicators Research, 1*, 1974. See also J. Hall and J. Ring, 'Indicators of Environmental Quality and Life Satisfaction: A Subjective Approach', SSRC Survey Unit, London, August 1974.)

preconditions for a more effective local political system in many areas.

The third reason why local authorities should now bear a responsibility is closely related. It is that the perspectives of senior politicians and managers are becoming less dominated by the department to which they belong and the provision of the services which have been the departments' *raisons d'être*. The model of the local authority as a 'federation of spending departments'—some education committees for instance, virtually making precepts on the Council—is rapidly becoming out-dated, as the objective of corporate planning with elements of P.P.B. systems is being developed to become one of community planning. The lessons of corporate planning are beginning to bear fruit in some areas in the clearer analysis of values, objectives, and the criteria of decision-making; the identification of new alternatives means drawing on the resources of a range of departments; the improvement of the making and implementation of policy through attempts to collect evidence on the consequences of activity; and a more conscious and theoretically based attempt to structure organizations and develop management skills. Increasingly, the better authorities are adding to corporate management a broader perception of the role of the authority, one based on an overall strategy for the government of their territory, and a concern for the overall impact on the distribution of welfare of the policies and actions of public authorities and private enterprises.[25] As authorities become better organized to face the complex choices about ends and the integration of means which such a conception of their role entails, it becomes less justifiable to subject individual services to the control of central government departments who cannot understand the role of each service in the overall strategy. Variations in local provisions will become far more legitimate as authorities can justify their claim to autonomy on the grounds of an ability to govern an area rather than an ability to manage separate services. As John Stewart has written, 'local government has yet to govern';[26] but it may increasingly do so in the future and so gain a legitimacy for

[25] One aspect of this is that authorities are beginning to attempt to monitor territorial justice within the city in a systematic way. See for instance Newcastle and Coventry. On the latter, see Barbara Webster and John Stewart: 'The area analysis of resources', *Policy and Politics*, 3, 1, September 1974, pp. 5–16. No doubt the move to the perception of the local authority's role as community planner reflects the recent development of territorial justice studies in the city that go far beyond the earlier work of the Chicago school, and which draw directly from a number of other approaches including the social administrators' theory of territorial justice.

[26] J. D. Stewart, *Management–Local–Environment–Government: a few words considered*, Institute of Local Government Studies, Birmingham, 1973, p. 7.

territorial variation that is quite different from the variations demanded for Pareteian optimality in a system with a single national objective function, and where service levels take a long time to adjust, and the marginal costs of services and the relative prices of collective and private resources vary considerably.

Those who argue that local authorities should have more power to govern must also suggest how they can be enabled to govern better. Good local government requires a responsive political system as well as an able, efficient, and well-informed executive. British local government has the reputation of being a closed political system insensitive to the needs of its area and the demands made upon it. Writers like Edward Banfield have contrasted it with the American system, with its greater flow of information to the outside world, the higher status of the press in local politics, the greater importance of pressure groups, and the greater political visibility of the executive.[27] John Dearlove's is the most recent study in a long line which emphasized the insularity of local politicians, stressing that it is the way in which environmental pressures are perceived by local politicians that determine their impact, and therefore the significance to the understanding of local authority performance of theories of selective perception and cognitive dissonance.[28] The importance of these characteristics is undeniable, though none of the British studies that put such emphasis on this finding have been so designed as to assess the degree to which differences in the imports of local politicians are themselves a reflection of long standing differences in the characteristics of their areas.[29] More important is the evidence that local issue and pressure groups are having an increasing effect on the decisions made by local authorities.[30] This is clearest in conceptions of what constitutes good planning, where what Hart calls the 'cohesive' policy mode typified by the Abercrombie Plan, which focussed on end-states, and tended to be regarded as irrevocable, infallible, and inviolable, has been combined with, if not replaced by, other modes which take better account of political conflict,

[27] Edward Banfield and James Q. Wilson, *City Politics*, Harvard University Press, Cambridge, Massachussetts, 1963.

[28] John Dearlove, *The Politics of Policy in Local Government*, Oxford University Press, London, 1972.

[29] I have developed this argument most specifically in 'Causal processes and techniques in the modelling of policy outcomes' in K. Young ed., *Essays in the Study of Urban Politics*, Macmillan, London, 1975, and more generally in *Variations in Services for the Aged*, Bell, London, 1971.

[30] See, for instance, F. J. C. Amos, 'Competing priorities for land use' in B. Benjamin *et al.*, *Resources and Population*, Academic Press, London, 1972.

uncertainty, and change.[31] Some of the changes already mentioned will help to make the local political process more open. Management reform has in many places resulted in fewer committees, the rationalization of the formal organization to make the partisan basis of local (particularly urban) politics yield better decisions, and the delegation of detail to officers, freeing members to think more about policies and the cases which raise important value issues. These changes also promise to curb what Jim Sharpe has described as the 'obsessive professionalism' of British local government,[32] and the high degree of dependence on the professionals for innovation described (for instance) by the analyses of the power of planning officers and for other services by Donnison.[33] The larger size of the major authorities is itself important. How many lack the range of committed experts to form the basis of forceful Child Poverty Action Group and Claimants' Union? The conventional wisdom of British political science describes characteristics that may soon have altered substantially.

Indeed, it has not been obvious why those who have campaigned most energetically for devoting more resources to fighting child poverty have implicitly assumed that a system that concentrates power and responsibility at the centre will achieve more than one which has two foci with more equal power. One with two foci certainly has the greater potential for inducing experiment and publicity, as well as the changes that occur because of conflict between central and local governments of different political persuasion. It is too often forgotten that power has frequently been concentrated at the centre partly in order to keep down spending and to silence the publicity that is generated by conflict between local and central governments.[34] A system which

[31] D. A. Hart, 'Ordering change and changing orders', *Policy and Politics*, *2*, 1, September 1973, pp. 27–41. The cohesive mode is caricatured in Jon Gower Davies, *The Evangelistic Bureaucrat*, Tavistock, London, 1972, and analysed in R. Batley, 'An explanation of over-participation in planning', *Policy and Politics*, *1*, 2, December 1973, pp. 95–114, and Edward Banfield, 'Urban Renewal and the Planners', *Policy and Politics*, *1*, 2, December 1973, pp. 163–9.

[32] L. J. Sharpe, 'American Democracy Reconsidered', *British Journal of Political Science*, *3*, 1, January 1973, pp. 1–28.

[33] D. V. Donnison *et al.*, *Social Policy and Administration*, Allen and Unwin, London, 1969, pp. 2–3.

[34] Eric Briggs and Alan Deacon describe the factors involved in one case in 'The creation of the Unemployment Assistance Board', *Policy and Politics*, *2*, 1, September 1973, pp. 43–62. The ambivalence of the central government politician's attitude to local politics is wittily described by the same authors in 'Local Democracy and Central Policy', *Policy and Politics*, *2*, 4, June 1974, pp. 347–64. Conversely, the existence of local responsibility forces consideration of issues requiring fundamental assessment of the role of policy interventions. See, for instance, Brenda Swann, 'Local initiative and central control: the insulin decision', *Policy and Politics*, *1*, 1, September 1972, pp. 55–64.

placed more responsibility on elected representatives would make it far more open to pressures from and on behalf of those it is intended to serve. No one would suggest that discretionary social security payments should become a local responsibility. Yet can one be happy with a system which makes it practically impossible to develop explicit and substantial local variations in their role in inter-corporate strategies to mitigate the consequences of family poverty? Indeed, before David Donnison became Chairman of the Supplementary Benefits Commission, it seemed clear that the distance (deliberately) created between the political controllers of the Commission and the client interface had caused the politicians not to appreciate and face even the most general of long-term policy problems. Responsible government must necessarily be responsive government. It was surely a mistake to have created a system whose capacity for securing responsiveness seems to depend on the presence of a head, whose ability and integrity is universally recognized as exceptional. Moreover it is often not the high policy that weakens the contribution of the service to the overall system of social support and development for the disadvantaged: it might well have been a mistake to create a structure that in principle virtually limits the political responsibility of elected representatives to matters of high policy. Now that authorities are large, there is everything to be gained by making the system open to local as well as national pressures.

This is not to suggest that local authorities should be granted immediate and absolute autonomy in the design of programmes to combat child poverty; merely that we should attempt in the long run to move towards systems which acknowledge the changing balance of advantage between centrally imposed uniformity and local initiative. In particular, one would foresee the need for the central government to find effective ways of controlling meta-policy; and since the central government has policies that are about means as well as ends, effective ways of fixing overall minimum standards and minimum standards in some key forms of intervention (like school meals). One might, for instance, have the central government experiment with what I have elsewhere called an output-defined standard[35] applied to the entire package of interventions. This would be measured as a discounted present value of a flow of benefits from interventions. The central government would issue a set of valuations which they would consider appropriate for

---

[35] See United Nations Division of Social Affairs, *Report of the Expert Group on Standard-Setting in Social Welfare*, UN/ESDP/1974/2, United Nations, Geneva, 1974, Chapter 6.

low income children in various circumstances, and these values would
be the basis for the estimation of the output. The standard for each
authority would be variable, depending on the number of children with
each of the need-related characteristics, as estimated for each major
authority by sample survey. (The surveys would surely be needed for
other purposes also.[36]) This output-defined standard might be supplemented by minimum standards of eligibility for service items (like free
meals or education maintenance allowances). Total output and performance more generous than the minima would be at the discretion of
the authority, but monitored and made public (to stimulate national,
regional, and local political processes) by the central government
through its annual survey and the reports based thereon.

The Social Services Department and the Strategy

Those responsibilities that are most effectively borne by local authorities are the ones which are central to the functions of a major department. One would not advocate the creation of a single department
whose sole purpose was to develop the strategy for mitigating family
poverty, if that were technically feasible. But at least an attempt should
be made to place the responsibility on one that is already conscious of
the interdependence between the demand for some of the most impor-

---

[36] The expense and difficulty of obtaining adequate data for the minorities who constitute the target groups for social welfare interventions should not be understated. It is
difficult both to estimate the numbers eligible, and to estimate the numbers receiving
from official data. For instance, the author of *Two-Parent Families* (J. R. Howe,
H.M.S.O., London, 1971), wrote about two-parent families whose heads were in full-
time work, but whose net resources were below the SIG level:

> ... assuming only normal sampling errors, the number of such families is esti-
> mated (from FES data) to be probably in the range of forty-five thousand and
> 105 thousand, in the sense that there is a 1 in 20 chance that the actual number will
> be outside that range ... However the assumption that the estimate is affected only by
> normal sampling errors may be incorrect and the range within which the actual
> number will probably be found may be wider ...

Not only are the sample numbers small, but FES respondents tend to understate their
incomes, thus causing a bias towards overstating the numbers eligible. The estimates of
the numbers eligible for FIS were also subject to very broad confidence intervals. (See
J. Stacpoole, 'Running FIS', *New Society*, 13 January 1972, pp. 64–6.) Problems arise in
comparing the numbers receiving benefits with the numbers eligible, since once established, eligibility continues for a period of time, and since the income concepts of the
FES and eligibility criteria sometimes differ. Also the history of FIS estimates during 1971
and 1972, when take-up was a main focus of political argument shows how unreliable
can be estimates of numbers of recipients. (Compare the estimates printed in *H.C. DEB.*,
1974, 870, Q. 211–12; *H.C. DEB., 1972/3, 850*, Q. 300.)

tant services it already provides, and the provision of other interventions that would be important components of a co-ordinated strategy; it should be so positioned as to have a personalized understanding of the interacting needs of primary social groups that are most frequently the victims of poverty, including small communities, racial minorities, families, and individuals. Planning departments may be the departments on which it is logical to place the responsibility for co-ordinating policies for local economic growth; but there seems to be some validity in Harrison's suggestion that British planners have not been sufficiently preoccupied with the welfare consequences for primary social groups of the processes they have controlled to have acquired the type of understanding and orientation required for strategies to mitigate poverty.[37] That the Ralphs Report described education welfare as a 'sadly neglected service',[38] and that school meals policies have been allowed to develop the expensive contradictions described in this book suggests that education departments could not seriously contend for the responsibility. The analysis of policies for the means-tested services of housing departments would have yielded similar conclusions. Only the claims of the social services department could even be seriously discussed.

The Location of the Education Welfare Service

The formulation of a new general responsibility for the strategies should not require radical changes in the machinery of government, but some minor transfers are long overdue. The case for transferring the education welfare service to the social services department has been gradually strengthening since the Seebohm Committee first made its recommendation. In particular, neither the Department of Education and Science nor most local education departments have faced the problems of developing the service. The Ralphs Report found that the duties

[37] M. L. Harrison, 'British Town Planning Ideology and the Welfare State', *Journal of Social Policy, 43*, July 1975, pp. 259–74. One would imagine that Harrison would also be sceptical about the way in which planning departments would influence the development of the strategy for securing a pattern of growth which would prevent poverty.

[38] Local Government Training Board, *The Role and Training of Education Welfare Officers: Report of the Working Party*, Local Government Training Board, Luton, 1975, para. 30. The working party was appointed by the Local Government Training Board, and consisted of persons with special interest in the field, including chief education officers, a chief inspector of the Department of Education and Science, the secretary of the National Association of Chief Education Welfare Officers and the Education Welfare Officers National Association and others.

of what it called this 'undervalued and underdeveloped' service[39] varied greatly between authorities, and created roles for officers that were inconsistent: they found that 'no two authorities were alike',[40] in the tasks they allocated to the service, and that the jobs demanded 'vastly different kinds of skill and a variety of levels of responsibility'.[41] The Ralphs Report attributed the neglect to the absence of legislative specification of function, or even of central government guidance. 'Despite many approaches by the education welfare officers' associations, no direct legislation has ever ensued outlining the specific responsibilities of the service, and no general guidance to authorities on its functions and development has ever issued from successive Ministries or Departments of Education'.[42] The Report also commented that education administrators had failed to give the service consistent thought: 'There is little recognition of its future potential in the new field of socio-educational need. Education administrators, with notable exceptions, have not seen the service as having any relevance to those needs, and therefore have not accorded its development any priority.'[43]

Unsurprisingly, the Ralphs Report concluded that 'a re-structured and re-orientated service' was a necessary prerequisite for effectiveness. Of which department education welfare officers should form part was outside the terms of reference of the working party: but the preface to its report reminded authorities that both associations of welfare officers wished to remain with the education service, and expressed the view that close liaison with the education service would continue to be essential. However the argument of the Report left no doubt about the need for training in common skills. Indeed, the social work skills required were far more common to the service of different authorities than the functions officers performed,[44] and perhaps 70 per cent of the time of education welfare officers was spent 'on duties of a social work character'.[45]

The development and standardization of the service can best take place if ultimate responsibility for it lies with the social services department. The accumulating evidence suggests that the Seebohm arguments

[39] *The Role and Training of Education Welfare Officers*, op. cit., para. 172.
[40] Ibid., para. 30.
[41] Ibid., para. 30.
[42] Ibid., para. 31.
[43] Ibid., para. 172. The Report confirms what we had suspected; that our overachieving authority was exceptional.
[44] Ibid., Chapter 5.
[45] Ibid., para. 44.

are more powerful today than they were in the late 1960s.[46] The attempts to cope with socio-educational needs in new ways by appointing school social workers and others whose relationships to the education welfare service are unclear, have in some cases held back the development required.[47] There is a real danger of attempting to duplicate the social work service, but achieving only a backward enclave of officers with little prestige and slight self-esteem. Evidence is accumulating from the training courses that the stunted career prospects for officers noted by the Ralphs Report[48] cause high proportions of those seconded for training to leave the service to take jobs in social services departments as soon as possible after they qualify—a rate of loss that can be expected to accelerate as the numbers qualifying increase. There is evidence not just that the seriousness of the problems with which the education welfare service deals are increasingly recognized, thus generating pressure towards a more effective service, but also that officers do not understand the problems of the children sufficiently well either to deal adequately with them or to refer a high enough proportion. They have contact not only with many children handicapped by poverty, but also with a large number of highly disturbed children needing referral for skilled attention and treatment.[49] The education welfare service could therefore contribute greatly to reaching target populations. No doubt, the problems of status for the untrained education welfare officers in the social services department would in themselves be great—great enough for them to wish to remain employees of the education authority. But there can be little doubt where the interests of the client lie. The service would develop far more effectively if education welfare officers formed part of the social services department, albeit specialists on secondment to the education service. This has been recognized by some authorities.[50]

Means-tested Material Benefits and Social Services Departments

There is a strong case for transferring responsibility for the budget that

[46] Report of the Committee on Local Authority and Allied Personal Social Services, Cmnd 3703, paras 222–38.

[47] The Role and Training of Education Welfare Officers, op. cit., para. 36.

[48] Ibid., para. 41.

[49] See for instance, Colin Pritchard, 'The Education Welfare Officer, truancy, and school phobia', Social Work Today, 5, 5, 30 May 1974, pp. 130–3.

[50] The following authorities transferred responsibility to Social Services Departments before 1974: Cheshire, Derbyshire, Devon, Holland (Lincolnshire), and Somerset county councils, and Burnley, Bury, Coventry, and Newcastle county borough councils. (See R. G. Colman, Social Work Service to Schools, unpublished M.A. Thesis, University of Bradford, 1974.)

pays for those other means-tested education benefits intended for the poor. An essential part of the work of the department having responsibility for the local strategy for mitigating the effects of poverty should be to co-ordinate policies on means-testing, and the more the services concerned are within its control, the easier this would be. The social services department should handle the local development of the national prototype instruments for combined assessment of the kind now being developed by the Department of Health and Social Security, the Department of the Environment and others. Peter Taylor-Goobey argues that with criteria as standardized as possible, the application of these can make the procedures very simple to handle, and have a substantial impact on uptake rates.[51] The costs of computerization are spread over more benefits under combined assessment. Computerization considerably improves the accuracy of assessments. Both the Supplementary Benefits Commission and Adler and du Feu have shown to be general a result yielded by our studies of school meal assessments in a selection of authorities: that a high proportion are substantially inaccurate, and in at least some services (including free meals) the error tends to be biased towards depriving claimants of their entitlement.[52] Computerization also makes it possible for the social services department to offer a free accounting service for choosing that combination of entitlements that minimizes the family's liability to poverty surtax.[53]

The attitudes of social services departments are ambivalent towards their provisions of material (particularly cash) benefits.[54] This is particularly so of social workers, whose perceptions partly reflect the American literature, but are also a response to the failure to develop

[51] Peter Taylor-Goobey, 'More welfare for less cost: The logic of Combined Assessment', *Poverty*, *34*, Summer 1976. Mr Taylor-Goobey's argument is based on the evidence yielded by the introduction of combined assessment in Manchester. The multiple purpose claim form in Liverpool increased uptake rates substantially; for instance the uptake of rate rebates was increased by one fifth. The use of the same form for both rent and rate rebates increased take-up by $2\frac{1}{2}$ times. The Liverpool system also provided better administrative statistics for the estimation of numbers eligible, uptake rates, and the costs of subsidies given high uptake rates. (See Gavin Weightman, 'Claim Forms', *New Society, 39*, 752, 3 March 1977, p. 446.)

[52] *Annual Report of the Supplementary Benefits Commission for 1975*, op. cit.; Michael Adler and David du Feu, 'Using the computer to estimate entitlement', *Policy and Politics*, *3*, 1, September 1974, pp. 61–8; and *Welfare Benefits Project: Final Report*, Department of Social Administration, University of Edinburgh, 1974.

[53] The work described in Adler and du Feu, op. cit., demonstrates the potential. Given that the structure of benefits is the conscious outcome of a democratic political process, there seem to be no greater ethical problems in a social services department providing such a service, than in an accountant advising his surtax paying clients.

[54] See the analysis in Chapter 1 of Olive Stevenson, *Claimant or Client?*, Allen and Unwin, London, 1973, especially Chapters 3.1 and 2.

clear and well argued policies to guide the use of section 1 payments. It is clear that there are large variations in section 1 payments between authorities. Research by Frances Williams on the London boroughs using data for 1971/2,[55] using an approach similar to that used in some of our papers on the school meals subsidies,[56] obtained a similar result; that the greater part of the variation in spending cannot be accounted for by variations in need. More important, research described by Ruth Lister and Tony Emmett[57] has shown that quite different criteria have influenced section 1 payments and that the role of these payments has been influenced by the policies and practices of the Supplementary Benefits Commission (S.B.C.) and its local offices in a way that requires justification not yet provided. The policies have so developed (often at a local not national level) as to make section 1 payments a virtual alternative to discretionary grants under the Supplementary Benefits Scheme, particularly to S.B.C. emergency grants and exceptional needs payments. The S.B.C. has operated its criteria increasingly strictly, and has come to interpret the need for such help as a symptom of an inability to manage, and so a sign that social work assistance from the social services department is necessary. That social workers themselves vary in the criteria they use is not surprising. In part, these are variations in the theory-based assumptions of workers and teams about the consequence of giving cash aid. In part also, they reflect differences in the degree to which workers and teams think clients to be deserving or undeserving. The same factors influence all social worker allocation judgements;[58] but it would be quite plausible to argue that applications for cash aid are more influenced than others by judgements about moral worth, because (as Michael Adler[59] has argued) social workers lack a 'shared professional knowledge' about it: their paradigm provides a less coherent basis for their judgements about financial assistance than for their judgements about more conventional interventions. Certainly, although social workers believe in the indivisi-

[55] Frances Williams, *Cash Assistance for Families* (unpublished). Quoted in Ruth Lister and Tony Emmett, *Under the Safety Net*, Child Poverty Action Group, London, 1976, p. 6.

[56] For instance, Bleddyn Davies and Valerie Williamson, 'School meals: short-fall and poverty', op. cit.

[57] *Under the Safety Net*, op. cit.

[58] See for instance, Gilbert Smith and Robert Harris, 'Ideologies of need and the organisation of social work departments', *The British Journal of Social Work*, 2, 1, Spring 1972, pp. 27–46.

[59] Michael Adler, 'Financial assistance and the social workers exercise of discretion' in N. Newman ed., *In Cash or Kind*, University of Edinburgh, Edinburgh, 1975.

bility of material, social, and psychological needs, many have been shown to be ignorant of welfare rights and the material needs of their clients. It will not be otherwise until the training divisions of social services departments take this seriously, and until those whose training is based on the new unitary approaches to social work are numerous in social services departments; and then some individuals and (in the absence of management control) teams will prefer to limit their interventions, and ration their time and other resources accordingly.

It is reasonable to argue that the labelling of clients referred to the social services department by the S.B.C., and the dependence of social work decisions on criteria of moral worth enhance the danger that problems of poverty will be seen in a way that will make families appear 'suitable material for social work intervention', when that is not the case. Bill Jordan postulates an 'inexorable process of casework deviance amplification', and so an erosion of civil liberties.[60] However, to be among those able to recommend the allocation of a discretionary benefit in kind, or even bear a primary responsibility for the allocation decision, creates less danger than the power to recommend the payment of cash, except where the benefit in kind is very highly valued by the recipient. Moreover, acknowledging that this danger of eroding the civil liberties of the poor is a real factor to take into account, should not cause us to ignore other considerations. One is the uncontroversial reality that the problems of many social work clients are exacerbated by financial poverty, that material needs interact with other needs that are more related to social work intervention. A second is that if we were ever able to attain the goal[61] of a system of social security so effective as to leave the Supplementary Benefits Commission the small role intended for it, many more of those receiving discretionary cash

[60] Bill Jordan: 'Emergency payments', *Social Work Today*, Vol. 3, No. 23, 15–16. See also Bill Jordan, *Paupers: The making of the new claiming class*, Routledge, London, 1973.

Joel F. Handler and Ellen Jane Hollingsworth argued for the United States that 'there is a danger that expanded improved state and local governments service programmes will increase client dependency and coercion. If social service administration does what the clients really want—which is increasing delivery of specific tangible items, possibly including special money grants—then dependency as shown in this study will increase'. (See Joel F. Handler and Ellen Jane Hollingsworth, *The 'Deserving Poor'*, Markham Publishing Co, Chicago, 1971, p. 131.) Handler and Hollingsworth conclude that 'much of the hoped-for benefits of separating social services from income maintenance may not in fact reduce government discretionary power over welfare recipients' (p. 133).

[61] David Donnison, *Supplementary Benefits: principles and priorities*; and *Annual Report of the Supplementary Benefits Commission 1975*, Cmnd 6615, H.M.S.O., London, 1976.

benefits would also be social work clients. The proportion of those receiving section 1 payments also in contact with the S.B.C. is already high.[62] A third is that even in the long run that is now assumed, local authority social workers may be the only numerous professional group with a type of training close enough to what would be needed for them to be trusted to exercise a professional discretion within a politically accountable bureaucracy; it must be recognized that to place responsibility on them may be the only route available towards a system that allows real creative justice in cash benefits;[63] the only escape from a system in which the discretionary component of what are euphemistically called discretionary benefits seems to consist mainly in tolerating deviations from a complex set of rules which few really understand, deviations that probably as much reflect varying degrees of insight (even prejudice), or sheer ignorance of the code, as the matching of resources to needs.

This is a controversial and complex issue about which feelings run high—a minefield for the unwary. It would be a mistake to treat a variety of separable issues as a single issue. First, the inappropriate labelling by social workers of clients, and the wrongful application of criteria of moral worthiness to their decisions by social workers, and the transformation of the role of section 1 payments into that of support for the basic essentials of life, are all the direct outcome of the failure to recognize that it is necessary for one agency to have the responsibility to

[62] See *Under the Safety Net*, op. cit., Chapter 3. The low proportion of the budget devoted to financial aid does not adequately measure the proportion of the social services departments devoted to it. Michael Jackson *et al.* writes that in Glasgow it has been established that about 80 per cent of all initial enquiries by clients relate to financial assistance. As a result, many Scottish departments feel that they are unable to devote time to more important social work functions. In Glasgow, routine financial aid was separated from social work by the establishment of the Financial Assistance Group of trained clerical staff. However, this legitimated the practice by which the social services department regularly supplemented inadequate incomes. Therefore the scheme was modified after the reorganization of local government.

More than a half of the clients receiving financial aid through social work were also receiving assistance from the S.B.C. in a number of Scottish local authorities: 84 per cent in one area of Glasgow, 75 per cent in Edinburgh, 55 per cent in Clackmananshire. This is not peculiar to Scotland, it being so of one half of the clients in one London borough. (See Michael Jackson *et al.*, 'Social Work Donors', *New Society, 39*, 752, 3 March, pp. 444–5.)

[63] Even those American commentators who have been most sensitive to the coercion arguments recognize the importance of this point. Perhaps with the British case in mind, Handler and Hollingsworth argue that it is one thing to specify the objective criteria on which can be based the sophisticated allocations of social security that take into account variations in individual need, but that it is another to communicate these complex rights to clients. (*The 'Deserving' Poor*, op. cit.)

negotiate, develop, and monitor a strategic plan for the mitigation of poverty at the local level. No centrally-negotiated policy can by itself solve the problems thrown up by the variety of local circumstances, however complex that policy may be. Indeed, policies of labyrinthine complexity are much less effective than the central control of a few key mega- and meta-policies. The admirable intention of the Home Office in drawing Section 1 'in sufficiently wide terms to give scope for initiative and experiment by local authorities'[64] was defeated because it seems likely that 'few social services departments have coherently thought out policies, and that any rules or guidelines tend to be confined to specifying those items which should not be met by Section 1 payments'.[65] Authorities' policies must be formulated in the context of a broader local strategy.

Secondly, we should consider the preconditions for successfully handling discretionary allocations of a range of material benefits to families receiving social work assistance. Powers to make discretionary judgements about individuals should be vested in trained professionals and/or those to whom they are managerially accountable. Field workers from social services departments would be obvious candidates. It would be appropriate for the cost of such allocations to be borne by the budget of the agency exercising this discretion, if the recipients would not otherwise be eligible. Secondly, the power to make discretionary and other allocations quite separate from (other) social work intervention might be vested in the social service departments. Again, where the recipients would not otherwise be eligible, the cost should be borne by the departmental budget. There is a strong case for developing a role and profession of welfare rights officers to deal with such cases. Some authorities conceive of the task of welfare rights officers as involving little more than the application of rules prescribed in some detail to a context where little discretion is exercised about objectives; a job specification which requires little more than what the Brunel team call 'prescribed output'.[66] No doubt, the volume of work of this type justifies the creation of jobs with such limited terms of reference. However, discretionary allocations would inevitably be linked to the advocacy roles which many such cases would require, and would need workers capable of making what the Brunel team

[64] Home Office, *Circular 204/1963*.
[65] *Under the Safety Net*, op. cit., pp. 10–11.
[66] See for instance, R. Rowbottom and D. Billis, *The stratification of work and organizational design*, Brunel Institute of Organizational Studies, Brunel University, England; unpublished, undated, p. 7.

call 'a situational response': a judgement about the precise objectives that varies according to the needs of the situation. The latter requires a trained professional with experience. Such workers could greatly reduce the loss of self-esteem caused by becoming a claimant.[67]

Not only is it in the interests of clients to appoint welfare rights officers with the broader job specifications at least in the short run, and for individuals rather than 'the poor' as a group, it would also seem to be to the political advantage of the authority itself. Welfare rights workers who are not part of the social service department can easily subordinate the immediate interests of individual clients to other goals that reflect their own value systems more than those of their clients. The history of the welfare rights programme initiated by the Batley C.D.P. is relevant.[68] With welfare rights workers antipathetic to means-tested benefits, the original goal of improving take-up became unimportant. Other aims took their place—redefining the status of the poor, stigmatizing the society that condoned poverty rather than the poor themselves, developing educative situations in which the poor themselves confronted authorities which the workers conceived to be repressive, modifying and extending rights. The professional role must always involve tension between making the policy work, and promoting the interest of the clients and potential clients in a way that is not fully compatible with current policy. It is more likely that from an established power base within the social services departments the welfare rights workers will achieve the uneasy compromises that will get the best for their clients from the existing provisions in the current social order.

The organizational implications of placing on social services departments a responsibility for co-ordinating the development of local inter-corporate strategies for mitigating the effects of family poverty are too many and complex to discuss properly here. But they are issues which must be faced if our results and the interpretations we have put on them are valid.

This has been an essay in the analysis of policy issues of an arche-

[67] J. Bradshaw, 'Welfare rights: an experimental approach'. In R. Lees and G. Smith *Action Research in Community Development*, Routledge, London, 1975, pp. 106–18; and P. Taylor-Goobey, 'More welfare for less cost', op. cit.

[68] Horan and Austin suggest that A. F. D. C. recipients, who have contact with their local welfare rights organization, are less likely than others to feel stigmatized. (See P. M. Horan and P. L. Austin, 'The social bases of welfare stigma', *Social Problems, 21*, 4, Spring 1974, p. 655.)

typal social service. School meals policy would undoubtedly be classi-fied as social rather than economic policy. Yet in our analysis, we have not only been forced to seek inspiration from economic as well as socio-logical theory, and to use the ways of handling evidence developed for these subjects, but found the academic and political discussion of several areas of economic policy to be fruitful as a source of per-spectives from which to view neglected issues of school meals policy—indeed, for some issues they have been the only source of such perspec-tives that we have been able to discover. Conversely, we have found to be an increasingly important *leitmotif* of policy debates about national-ized industries and regional policies those features which Boulding,[69] Wilensky, and Lebeaux,[70] and others have treated as the hallmark of social policy; the concern with integration and the distributional con-sequences of the working of socio-economic systems. Indeed, such con-siderations now pervade all policy debate. It was the economics editor of *The Times* who described 'the political imperative of social cohesion' as one of the two principal criteria for evaluating the mini-budget of December 1976.[71] It is hardly surprising that the boundary between social and economic policy has all but ceased to exist in the Great Britain of the social contract—or that it is, at any rate, much less clear than it was in the United States of the late 1950s.[72] This is inherently desirable: it brings much nearer the goal of welfare society. Those institutionalists who argue otherwise are guilty of advocating a form of residualism, albeit a defensive residualism, which seems not to be congruent with their concept of a good society. It would be a mistake to try to create a special territory for social policy, an enclave within which con-

[69] Kenneth E. Boulding, 'The grants economy', in *Collected Papers*, II, op. cit.

[70] H. L. Wilensky and C. N. Lebeaux, *Industrial Society and Social Welfare*, op. cit., Russell Sage Foundation, New York, 1964.

[71] 'What the Chancellor risks', *The Times*, 59,887, 15 December 1976, p. 15.

[72] That there now seems hardly a boundary between economy and integry is the outcome of an era in which the omnicompetence of governments at controlling markets to achieve broad political purposes is alike assumed by many politicians and citizens. However, some question whether this is a permanent feature of our society. For instance,Andrew Shonfield perceives a trend away from belief in the doctrine that governments should have an economic omni-competence in West European social demo-cratic parties. (See A. Shonfield, 'Can capitalism survive until 1999?', *Encounter*, *48*, 1, January 1977, pp. 10–18.) Secondly, welfare backlash has implications for other than social service spending. Wilensky's argument would suggest that radical changes in structure would be necessary to reduce it. The most important of such changes would include a shift towards invisible indirect taxes. He would also argue that a shift away from the divisive means-tested benefits which deepen the poverty trap would also reduce the extent of welfare backlash. (See H. L. Wilensky, *The 'New Corporatism', Central-ization, and the Welfare State*, Sage, London, 1977.)

siderations of social integration and redistribution alone should dominate policy debate for fear that all policy might become in the end economic policy, and that the only values that might in time count would be those that can be measured in terms of money and pursued in the dialectic of hedonism. This research has suggested how we can define in such areas as school meals that 'comprehensive set of criteria' that could integrate economic and social considerations called for in a United Nations document just over a decade ago.[73] Far more real than the domination of the social policy imagination by alien values are the dangers of intellectual isolation within the enclave. Debate within it might be too much based on untested assumptions about the relationship between means and the ends of social cohesion and redistribution. The excessive preoccupation with these global objectives might make it impossible to achieve legitimate but narrower goals of social interventions; goals whose importance are sufficient for it to be immensely costly to society for them not to be achieved. Part of the cost could be a general disillusionment with the effectiveness of welfare spending. A second disadvantage is that the excessive symbolic meaning in the political process of social policy may deny to it the freedom to choose its instruments eclectically. Would it be as easy for a social service minister to offer a 25 per cent remission of charges to recipients of Supplementary Benefits or Family Income Supplement as it was for Mr Benn (as Secretary of State for Energy) to do so for electricity; and while admitting that non-claimers and those whose incomes were just above the margin of eligibility would not receive the benefit, to justify the method of allocation by arguing that 'whatever sum you took, you would be faced with the question of how to apply it where it can be of greatest assistance'.[74]

[73] U.N. Economic and Social Council Social Commission, *Methods of Determining Social Allocations*, United Nations, New York, 1965, p. 10.
[74] *The Times*, 59,772, 3 August 1976, p. 1.

Appendix A

Glossary of Variables used in Principal Exploratory Tabulations

Variable and description	No. of categories	Acronym
Dependable variables		
Analysed in Chapter 2		
Whether or not any of the children stopped having school meals when the price went up to $7\frac{1}{2}$p	2	
Whether or not there were times when the child could not have school meals when the price was 5p	2	
The alternative arrangement to taking school dinners a cooked meal	2	
The alternative arrangement to taking school dinners a packed lunch	2	
Mothers' policy preference that the government should make more children eligible for free meals	2	
Mothers' policy preference that the government should spend more on subsidizing the service as a whole	2	
Analysed in Chapter 5		
Others' Stigma Dummy[1]	2	OSD
Others' Stigma Pervasiveness Score. Scored 1 (low) to 5 (high)[2]	5	OSPS
Others' Stigma Pervasiveness Score Dummy[3]	2	OSPSD
Found difficulty or Received Help Dummy[2]	2	DIFFHLPD
Other children make Receivers feel Small Dummy[2]	2	OCHLDD
Picked on more by Teachers Dummy[2]	2	TCHERSD
Parents think Free Meals Charity Dummy[2]	2	CHARD
Applying too Complicated Dummy[2]	2	COMPD
Don't like Stating Incomes Dummy[2]	2	STATINCD
Don't like Employers to Know Dummy[2]	2	EMPLD
Parents Don't know about Free Meals Dummy[2]	2	PDKD

Explanatory variables

Used in the argument of Chapter 2

Area Over-achieving	2	OVERACH
Under-achieving		UNDERACH
Standardized income group	4	SIG

  1. Eligible on income grounds
  2. Not eligible on income grounds but less than £2 per week above that level
  3. £2 and less than £4 a week above that level
  4. £4 or more a week above the eligibility level

Mothers' employment	3	MOTHEM

  0. Not in employment
  1. In employment not more than 24 hours per week
  2. In employment more than 24 hours per week

Young child at home	2	DEPCHLD

  1. A dependent child of less than school age at home
  0. No such child at home

Food inadequate	2	FDINAD

  1. Food thought insufficient in quantity
  0. Food thought sufficient in quantity

Enough food	2	ENFD

  1. Food thought sufficient in quantity
  0. Food not thought sufficient in quantity

Accommodation inadequate	2	ACCOMINAD

  1. Accommodation thought inadequate
  0. Accommodation not thought inadequate

Supervision inadequate	2	SUPERVISINAD

  1. Meals supervision thought inadequate
  0. Meals supervision not thought inadequate

Particular advantages to named child	5	ADVCHLD

  0. Nutritional
  1. Child-minding
  2. Child socialization or recreation
  3. Financial
  4. None in particular

Particular advantage to Mother	5	ADVMOTH

  0. Nutritional
  1. Child-minding
  2. Child socialization or recreation
  3. Financial
  4. None in particular

Most important advantage	5	MIMPADV

  0. Nutritional
  1. Child-minding
  2. Child socialization or recreation
  3. Financial
  4. None in particular

Experience of applying for free meals for the first time only	3	EXP

  0. No experience
  1. Within last year
  2. More than a year ago

Individual Responsibility for Poverty Score Dummy[4]	2	IRPSD
Others' Stigma Pervasiveness Score Dummy[3]	2	OSPSD

Used in the argument of Chapter 5

(a) Alienation

Individualized Responsibility for Poverty Score Dummy[4]	2	IRPSD

(b) Anomie

Indicator of Positive attitudes towards and interest in Education[5]	2	EDID
Negative personal contacts with the schools (Retreatist anomie)[5]	2	NEGCOND
Positive opinion of Teachers, and attitudes to the particular school[5]	2	EDIIID

(c) Incentive

Reference Group Poverty Pervasiveness Score Dummy[6]	2	RGPPSD
Family Reference Group Poverty Dummy—Worse off than 'rest of the family'[6]	2	FAMRGPD
Locality Reference Group Poverty Dummy—Worse off than 'other people round here of similar age'[6]	2	LOCRGPD
Country Reference Group Poverty Dummy—Worse off than 'the average in the country'[6]	2	COUNRGPD
Self Reference Group Poverty Dummy—'Worse off than Ever'[6]	2	SELFRGPD
Standardized Income group.[7] The difference between assessed income and eligibility level	4	SIG

   1. Less than eligibility level
   2. The eligibility level and less than £2 per week above
      category 1 maximum
   3. The eligibility level + £2 p.w. and less than £3 per
      week above category 2 maximum
   4. Above the category 3 maximum

SIG is based on SUPERI, super-subsistence income, a continuous variable used in chapter 6

(d) Contextual factors and other causes

Occupation of Husband classified as RG Class V	2	LSCD
Marital Role Segregation Dummy	2	MRSD
Mother in paid Employment	3	MOTHEM

   0. Not in employment
   1. In part-time paid employment (not exceeding 5 hours
      a day)
   2. In full-time paid employment (exceeding 5 hours a
      day)

Area Over-achieving		OVERACH
Under-achieving		UNDERACH
Fatherless Family	2	MOTHALD[7]
Mother's country of birth	4	MCOB

   1. Great Britain
   2. Ireland
   3. West Indies
   4. India or Pakistan

Experience of applying for free meals for the first or only time	3	EXP

   0. No experience
   1. Within last year
   2. More than a year ago

(e) Used first in Chapter 6
Potential cost of providing free school meals to a group,   CUMPFMCOST
Assuming 100 per cent uptake. Continuous
variables[8]

Notes

[*] The diagrams code 1 the possession of a characteristic or high scores on a dummy variable.

[1] Others' Stigma Dummy was coded 1 if there was a reply implying stigma to *any one* of six questions. One of these was open-ended. The remainder are the stigma propositions discussed in note 2 (below).

[2] The questions on whose answers these variables are based have the following form:

'The Ministry of Education has found that there are some children eligible for free meals but who do not take them. Some people have suggested several reasons for this. Do you think that one or more of these reasons are *important*—in explaining why these children do not receive free meals:—

		Yes	No
(i)	Most of the eligible children do not in fact need them	1	3
(ii)	That other children know who gets them free and makes these children feel small	1	3
(iii)	That the children who take Free Meals are picked on more by the teachers	1	3
(iv)	That the parents of the children don't apply because they think that taking them is receiving charity	1	3
(v)	That the parents do not apply because applying is too complicated	1	3
(vi)	That the parents don't apply because they don't like stating their incomes	1	3
(vii)	The parents don't apply because they don't like their employer to know that they are applying	1	3
(viii)	The parents don't apply because they don't know about the service.'	1	3

The OSPS was derived by summarizing the number of affirmative responses to these questions.

[3] Other dummy variables were based on the responses to the individual questions, an affirmative response being coded 1.

[4] Individualized Responsibility for Poverty Score Dummy was based on two open-ended questions so coded as to record expressions that poverty was the fault of the poor themselves in the answers to question 122, to reflect a diagnosis of personal inadequacy in question 121, and to reflect an answer to question 120 that the main thing that the poor could do would be to help themselves.

Questions 120, 121, and 122 were as follows:

'120. If there is Poverty what do you think can be done about it?'
'121. What would you describe as Poverty?'
'122. Would you say that if people are in Poverty it's mainly—
    Their own fault
    The Government's fault
    The fault of their education
    The fault of industry not paying decent wages
    A combination of some of these
    None of these
    Anything else
    Don't know.'

The scores on each question were found to be substantially correlated. IRPSD was computed by scoring answers of the types distinguished, summing the three scores, and dichotomizing the cases around the median score.

[5] The three education variables were based on variables which were highly loaded on factors in the factor analysis of the survey analysed in Appendix 3 of the Plowden Report. (See Central Advisory Council on Education (England), *Children and their Primary Schools*, vol. II, H.M.S.O. London, 1967.) The 32 questions were intercorrelated and factor analysed. The analysis yielded factors indicated by the three variables eventually used. The three variables themselves are not factor scores but were based on the summation of responses to the questions most heavily loaded on the factors, and the subsequent dichotomization at the median to create a dummy variable. EDID was based on 12 variables; NEGCOND on 3; and EDIIID on 3.

[6] Reference Group Poverty Pervasiveness Score Dummy was based on four variables. These indicated a feeling of being worse off with respect to four reference groups. The pervasiveness score is the unweighed sum of the number of reference groups in respect to which the respondent felt worse off. The score was dichotomized at the median to create the dummy variable. The answers to the four were substantially intercorrelated and a factor analysis confirmed the feasibility of using a uni-dimensional measure.

The question on which the score was based had the following form:

123. (a) How well off do you feel these days on your income? For example: compared with the rest of your family (I mean the relatives who don't live here), would you say you are:

Better off
About the same
Worse off
Don't know

(b) Compared with other people round here of your age, would you say you are:

Better off
About the same
Worse off
Don't know

(c) Compared with the average in the country, would you say you are:

Better off
About the same
Worse off
Don't know

(d) On the whole is your situation getting better or worse. Are you:

Better off than ever
Worse off than ever
Have known better or worse times
About the same as ever
Don't know.'

[7] Mothers described in the text and tables as MOTHALS, or (adjectivally) MOTHAL, are those coded 1 on this variable.

[8] The questionnaire collected the income and expenditure data necessary to undertake the free meals income test. The difference between income and the eligibility level was described as SUPERI. Cases were allocated to SIGS 1 to 4 on the basis of SUPERI.

Author Index

Subject Index